BUILDING FOR A CHANGING CLIMATE

BUILDING FOR A CHANGING CLIMATE

THE CHALLENGE FOR CONSTRUCTION, PLANNING AND ENERGY

Peter F. Smith

publishing for a sustainable future
London • Sterling, VA

First published by Earthscan in the UK and USA in 2010

ISBN: 978-1-84407-735-9

Typeset by Domex e-Data Pvt. Ltd.
Cover design by Rob Watts

For a full list of publications please contact:

Earthscan
Dunstan House
14a St Cross St
London, EC1N 8XA, UK
Tel: +44 (0)20 7841 1930
Fax: +44 (0)20 7242 1474
Email: earthinfo@earthscan.co.uk
Web: **www.earthscan.co.uk**

22883 Quicksilver Drive, Sterling, VA 20166-2012, USA

Earthscan publishes in association with the International Institute for Environment and Development

A catalogue record for this book is available from the British Library

Library of Congress Cataloging-in-Publication Data

Smith, Peter F. (Peter Frederick), 1930-
  Building for a changing climate: the challenge for construction, planning and energy / Peter F. Smith. –
1st ed.
      p. cm.
  Includes bibliographical references and index.
  ISBN 978-1-84407-735-9 (hardback)
  1. City planning–Environmental aspects. 2. Housing–Environmental aspects. 3. Climatic changes.
4. Sustainable urban development. I. Title.
  HT166.S588 2009
  720'.47–dc22

                                                                                                2009021376

At Earthscan we strive to minimize our environmental impacts and carbon footprint through reducing
waste, recycling and offsetting our CO_2 emissions, including those created through publication of this
book. For more details of our environmental policy, see www.earthscan.co.uk.

This book was printed in the UK by TJ International, an
ISO 14001 accredited company. The paper used is FSC
certified and the inks are vegetable based.

FSC
Mixed Sources
Product group from well-managed
forests and other controlled sources
Cert no. SGS-COC-2482
www.fsc.org
© 1996 Forest Stewardship Council

Contents

List of Figures and Tables

Figures

Tables

Introduction

This book is about a scenario for the future that we hope will not happen, namely a rise in average global temperature of 4°C, within the century, with all which that implies. However, the book is not based on the premise that such a temperature rise is inevitable, although there is increasing concern among climate scientists that it is more than possible. Here the argument is that while we should hope for the best, we should prepare for the worst.

There is growing scientific agreement that the impacts of climate change predicted in the Intergovernmental Panel on Climate Change (IPCC) report of 2007 were seriously underestimated. In February 2009 Dr Chris Field, co-chair of the IPCC made this assertion: 'We now have data showing that, from 2000 to 2007, greenhouse gases increased far more rapidly that we expected, primarily because developing countries, like China and India, saw a huge upsurge in electricity power generation, almost all of it based on coal' (quoted by Ian Sample in the *Guardian* 16 February 2009 'The tropics on fire: scientists' grim vision of global warming').

The purpose of the book is to explore the implications for buildings and cities based on the assumption that the world will continue on the path of the 'high emissions scenario (HES)', what used to be called 'Business as Usual (BaU)'. Coupled with climate change is the fact that the ratio between the production of oil and the rate of demand has reached its peak, soon to be followed by gas. So security of energy is also a matter of great importance, not least because the built environment is the sector responsible for the highest emissions of carbon dioxide.

The UK government in particular is constantly asserting that changes in personal behaviour will be necessary if national CO_2 emissions targets are going to be achieved. An assumption behind the book is that voluntary actions will not be nearly enough to halt the advance of climate change. Societal changes are desirable but unenforceable. Governments may rely on market forces to bring about change, but these are unpredictable and driven by the profit motive. It is the unrestrained appetite for profit that has largely created the current economic predicament; it is unwise to assume it will get us out of it.

Only governments can bring about the fundamental changes that the times require, through a combination of incentives and regulations. Planning laws (not guidance notes), stiff and enforceable building regulations and direct taxes on carbon, independent of market forces, are the only way to make radical change happen. Governments may eventually come round to this view, but it will probably be too late to prevent catastrophic climate impacts.

The underlying theme of the book is that, given the cluster of uncertainties that darken the future, the precautionary principle dictates that we should be preparing now for a more hostile environment and change building practices accordingly. Also, ultimately carbon-free energy will not just be an option but a necessity. As Nicholas Stern stated in his forceful review, *The Economics of Climate Change* (2006) investing now in adapting to future climate impacts will be considerably more cost-effective than taking emergency measures after the event. Buildings are a long-term investment, especially housing, and so his warning is especially relevant to this sector.

The book is aimed at an international readership. Where UK examples are cited, it is because they have implications for many developed and developing nations. The text falls into three sections. The first three chapters consider the reasons why there should be concern about the future effects of climate change since the world shows little inclination to deviate from the path of BaU. In the 2007 report of the IPCC BaU has been superseded by the less blame-loaded HES. First there is a brief survey of the scientific evidence of global warming across a spectrum of indicators. From this evidence it follows that there will be impacts, the severity of which will depend on the level and pace at which CO_2 emissions are stabilized in the atmosphere.

The second part, which constitutes the main body of the book, considers the implications of the HES scenario for buildings ranging from existing and new-build housing to non-domestic buildings. Since the top rating under the UK Code for Sustainable Homes assumes the inclusion of integrated or onsite renewable energy, this also receives consideration. The outlook for non-domestic buildings rounds off this section.

In the third section the focus is on energy, starting with the outlook for conventional fuels and the speculations about the levels of reserves of oil and gas. Whilst small-scale renewable technologies are featured earlier, this part considers the potential for utility or grid-scale renewable energy within the energy mix.

To finish, there is a discussion about the prospects for stemming the progress of global warming by means of geo-engineering: mirrors or 'pies' in the sky?

Peter F. Smith
October, 2009

Acknowledgements

I would like to thank the following: Feilden Clegg Bradley for providing images and data for the Heelis Building; CABE for images of St Francis of Assisi School, Liverpool; Zedfactory for images of the Jubilee Wharf complex, Penryn, Cornwall; Norman Foster Architects for images of Masdar; Professor David Mackay for permission to reproduce wind speed diagram for the UK; Dr Robin Curtis of EarthEnergy Ltd for permission to use heat pump data for the Churchill Hospital; and Xiaochun Xing for images and data from China.

List of Acronyms and Abbreviations

ABC	Algae Biofuels Challenge (Carbon Trust)
ABI	Association of British Insurers
AC	alternating current
ACH	air changes per house
AHU	air handling unit
ASHP	air source heat pump
ASPO	Association for the Study of Peak Oil
BAS	British Antarctic Survey
BaU	Business as Usual
BIPV	building integrated photovoltaics
BMS	building management system
BRE	(trading name of the) Building Research Establishment
BREEAM	BRE Environmental Assessment Method
BSF	Building Schools for the Future
CABE	Commission for Architecture and the Built Environment
CBI	Commercial Buildings Initiative
CCS	carbon capture and storage
CDM	Clean Development Mechanism
CdTe	cadmium telluride (solar cell technology)
CEO	chief executive officer
CER	certified emissions reduction
CERT	Carbon Emissions Reduction Target
CHP	combined heat and power
CIBSE	Chartered Institution of Building Services Engineers
CIGS	copper, indium, gallium and selenium (solar cell technology)
CO_2e	CO_2 equivalent
Comare	Committee on Medical Aspects of Radiation in the Environment
COP	co-efficient of performance
CSH	Code for Sustainable Homes
CSHPSS	central solar heating plants for seasonal storage
cSi	crystalline silicon
CSP	concentrated solar power
CTL	coal to liquids
DC	direct current
DCLG	Department for Communities and Local Government
DCSF	Department for Children Schools and Families
DECC	Department of Energy and Climate Change
Defra	Department for Environment, Food and Rural Affairs
DoE	Department of Energy (US)
DSY	Design Summer Year

DfT	Department for Transport
EESoP	Energy Efficiency Standards of Performance
ENSO	El Niño Southern Oscillation
EPC	Energy Performance Certificate
EPR	Evolutionary Power Reactor
EPSRC	Engineering and Physical Sciences Research Council
E-REV	extended range electric vehicle
ESCO	energy service company
EST	Energy Saving Trust
ETS	Emissions Trading Scheme (Europe)
EU	European Union
FIT	feed-in tariff
GDP	gross domestic product
GIS	Greenland ice sheet
GM	General Motors
GNEP	Global Nuclear Energy Partnership
GSHP	ground source heat pump
Gtoe	gigatonne of oil equivalent
HES	high emissions scenario
HHP	Hockerton Housing Project (Nottinghamshire)
HiPER	High Power Laser Energy Research
HTT	hard to treat
HVDC	high voltage direct current
ICE	internal combustion engine
IEA	International Energy Agency
IGCC	integrated gasification combined cycle
IHT	interseasonal heat transfer
IIIG+	third generation
IPCC	Intergovernmental Panel on Climate Change
ISE	Institute for Solar Energy Systems (Fraunhofer, Germany)
IT	information technology
LA	local authority
LZC	low or zero carbon
MOD	Ministry of Defence
mpg	miles per gallon
Mtoe	million tonnes of oil equivalent
NAS	National Academy of Science (US)
NGO	non-governmental organization
NHS	National Health Service
NIA	Nuclear Industry Association
NREL	National Renewable Energy Laboratory (US)
OECD	Organisation for Economic Co-operation and Development
OPEC	Organization of Oil Exporting Countries
OTEC	ocean thermal energy conversion
PCMs	phase change materials
PEM	Proton Exchange Membrane (or Polymer Electrolyte Membrane)
PG&EC	Pacific Gas and Electric Company (US)
PIV	Pujiang Intelligence Valley
POE	post occupancy evaluation

ppm	parts per million
ppmv	parts per million by volume
PPS	Planning Policy Statement
PRT	personal rapid transit
PV	photovoltaic (cell)
PVT	PV/thermal
PWR	pressurized water reactor
RIBA	Royal Institute of British Architects
RSPB	Royal Society for the Protection of Birds (UK)
SAP	Standard Assessment Procedure
SIPS	structural insulated panels
SME	small to medium-sized enterprises
SMR	small to medium sized reactor
SOFC	solid oxide fuel cell
SRES	Special Report on Emissions Scenarios (IPCC)
SSTAR	small, sealed transportable, autonomous reactor
TCPA	Town and Country Planning Association
TIM	transparent insulation material
TREC	Trans-Mediterranean Renewable Energy Cooperation
UEA	University of East Anglia
UGC	underground gasification of coal
UHI	urban heat island
UKCIP	UK Climate Impacts Programme
UK-GBC	United Kingdom Green Building Council
VHC	volumetric heat capacity
VIVACE	vortex induced vibrations for aquatic clean energy
VLS-PV	very large-scale photovoltaic systems
VOC	volatile organic compound
WAM	West African monsoon
WEC	World Energy Council
WWF	World Wide Fund for Nature
ZEH	'zero-energy' homes

1

Prepare for Four Degrees

The UK government issued a report in summer 2008 entitled: *Adapting to Climate Change in England: A Framework for Action* (Defra). This is a clear statement of the perceived scope of government responsibility in this matter. In his Introduction the Secretary of State for the Environment, Hilary Benn, conceded that:

> *Even with concerted international action now, we are committed to continued global warming for decades to come. To avoid dangerous climate change we must work, internationally and at home, to reduce greenhouse gas emissions. Even so, we will have to adapt to a warmer climate in the UK with more extreme events including heat waves, storms and floods and more gradual changes, such as the pattern of the seasons.*
>
> (Defra, 2008a, pp4–5)

The report later explains the role of government which is:

> *Raising awareness of changing climate … will encourage people to adapt their behaviour to reduce the potential costs as well take advantage of the opportunities.*
>
> (Defra, 2008a, p20)

Finally the report concedes that 'Governments have a role to play in making adaptation happen, starting now and providing both policy guidance and economic and institutional support to the private sector and civil society' (Defra, 2008a, p8). In other words, 'over to you'.

Getting down to the detail, the report's action plan is divided into two phases. The objectives of phase 1 are:

- develop a more robust and comprehensive evidence base about the impacts and consequences of climate change in the UK;
- raise awareness of the need to take action now and help others to take action;
- measure success and take steps to ensure effective delivery;
- work across government at a national, regional and local level to embed adaptation into Government policies, programmes and systems.

In terms of the first objective, there is already enough evidence to gauge the impacts that will affect society, in particular urban society. The Fourth Assessment Report of the Intergovernmental Panel on Climate Change (IPCC) published between February and April 2007 contains data that should provide incentives to all concerned with the built environment to raise their sights to meet the extraordinary challenges that lie in wait as climate changes. However, since its publication, the IPCC report has come under some criticism.

The Defra document used the IPCC report as the framework for its adaptive strategies. The problem with the IPCC report is that the cut-off date for its evidence base was the end of 2004. Since then, there has been a considerable accumulation of scientific evidence that global warming and climate change have entered a new and more vigorous phase since 2004. This has caused scientists to dispute some of the key findings of the report. To understand why this is important to all concerned with adaptation strategies for buildings, it is worth summarizing the various divergences from the IPCC.

First, the IPCC Report has been criticized for understating projections of climate impacts, not least by Dr Chris Field co-chair of the IPCC and director of global ecology at the US Carnegie Institute. In an address to the American Association for the Advancement of Science he asserted that the IPCC report of 2007 substantially underestimated the severity of global warming over the rest of the century. 'We now have data showing that, from 2000 to 2007, greenhouse gases increased far more rapidly than we expected, primarily because developing countries, like China and India, saw a huge upsurge in electric power generation, almost all of it based on coal' (reported in the *Guardian*, 16 February 2009).

This has been endorsed by James Hansen (Hansen et al, 2007), director of the NASA Goddard Space Institute, who believes that the IPCC prediction of a maximum sea level rise by 2100 of 0.59m to 'be dangerously conservative'. Reasons include the fact that ice loss from

Greenland has tripled since 2004, making the prospect of catastrophic collapse of the ice sheet within the century a real possibility. The IPCC assumed only melting by direct solar radiation, whereas melt water is almost certainly plunging to the base of the ice through massive holes or moulins which have opened up across the ice sheet. This would help lubricate and speed up the passage of the ice sheet to the sea.

According to Dr Timothy Lenton (2007) the tipping point element with the least uncertainty regarding its irreversible melting is the Greenland ice sheet (GIS). Above a local temperature increase of 3°C, the GIS goes into mass melt and possible disappearance. As the Arctic is warming at about three times the global average, the corresponding global average is 1–2°C.

This rate of warming has resulted in the Arctic sea ice contracting more extensively in 2008 than in any previous year. A satellite image recorded on 26 August 2008 shows the extent of

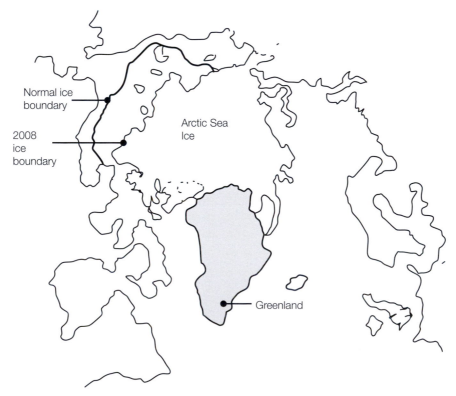

Source: Image: Derived from the US National Snow and Ice Data Center

Figure 1.1 Extent of Arctic sea ice on 26 August 2008 compared with the average extent 1979–2000

summer melt compared with the average melt between 1979 and 2000 (Figure 1.1).

As further evidence of impacts, 2007 has revealed the largest reduction in the thickness of winter ice since records began in the early 1990s.

Whilst the 2007 IPCC report considered that late summer Arctic ice would not completely disappear until the end of the century, the latest scientific opinion is that it could disappear in late summer as soon as three to five years hence (*Guardian*, 25 November 2008, p27). One consequence of this melt rate is that an increasing area of water is becoming exposed and absorbing solar radiation. According to recent research, the extra warming due to sea ice melt could extend for 1000 miles inland. This would account for most of the area subject to permafrost. The Arctic permafrost contains twice as much carbon as the entire global atmosphere (ref *Geophysical Research Letters, Guardian*, 25 November 2008, p27). The most alarming aspect of this finding is that the effect of melting permafrost is not considered within global climate models, so is likely to be the elephant in the room.

The latest evidence of climate change from Antarctica has come from the British Antarctic Survey (BAS). It reported in 2008 that the massive Wilkins ice shelf is breaking off from the Antarctic Peninsular. The 6180 square miles of the shelf is 'hanging by a thread' according to Jim Elliott of the BAS. The importance of ice shelves is that they act as buttresses supporting

Source: Photo Jim Elliott, BAS

Figure 1.2 Wilkins ice shelf undergoing calving

the land-based ice. This part of the Antarctic ice sheet has the least support from ice shelves. When it breaks away completely, this will be the seventh major ice shelf in this region to collapse. In January 2009 Dr David Vaughan of the BAS visited the ice shelf 'to see its final death throes'. He reported that 'the ice sheet holding the shelf in place is now at its thinnest point 500m wide. This could snap off at any moment' (Figure 1.2).

These are amongst the reasons why the Tyndall Centre for Climate Change Research has taken issue with the IPCC over its prediction that global warming will produce change on an incremental basis or straight line graph. Tyndall has produced an alternative graph linking temperature change to sharp and severe impacts as ice sheets melt; Figure 1.3 illustrates both

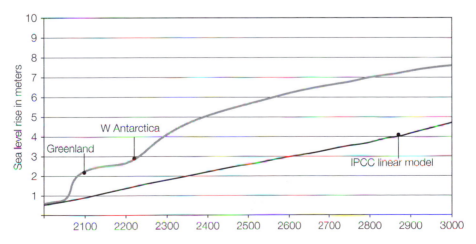

Source: Lenton et al, 2006

Figure 1.3 Potential for abrupt changes compared with linear IPCC forecast

scenarioa. The IPCC has since come to accept the validity of Tyndall's scenario.

The Tyndall Centre has produced a timetable of suggested tipping points for various climate change impacts such as the melting of Greenland ice sheet which, it indicates, is underway already (Figure 1.4).

The idea that climate changes could be abrupt has also received endorsement from proxy evidence from the Arctic. This relates to the Younger Dryas cold period, which lasted ~1300 years and ended abruptly about 11,500 years ago. Samples from insects and plants of the period indicate that the end of this cold episode was dramatic. This has been reinforced by ice cores that show that there was an abrupt change when the temperature rose around 5°C in ~3 years. This is just one example of many sharp changes revealed in the ice core evidence and offers little room for confidence that such a change will not happen in the near future for the reasons outlined by James Hansen above.

Inevitable warming

Hansen and colleagues (Hansen et al, 2007) suggested that the Earth climate system is about twice as sensitive to CO_2 pollution than suggested in the IPCC century-long projection. A conclusion that followed is that there are already enough greenhouse gases in the atmosphere to cause 2°C of warming. If true, this means the world is committed to a level of warming that would produce 'dangerous climate impacts'. The team has concluded that 'if humanity wishes to preserve a planet similar to the one in which civilisation developed and to which life on Earth is adapted ... CO_2 will need to be reduced from its current 385ppm to, at most, 350ppm'. They suggest that this can only be achieved by terminating the burning of coal by 2030 and 'aggressively' cutting atmospheric CO_2 by the planting of tropical forests and via agricultural soils.

John Holdren, president of the American Association for the Advancement of Science

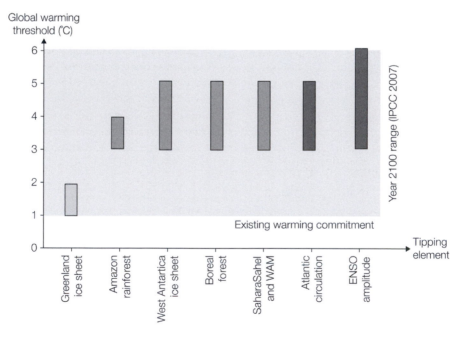

Source: Lenton, 2007

Figure 1.4 Tyndall tipping points

and appointed to a key post in the Obama Administration, has added weight to the argument: 'if the current pace of change continued, a catastrophic sea level rise of 4m (13ft) this century was within the realm of possibility' (BBC interview, August 2006).

Optimism over gains in energy efficiency

A further problem with the IPCC report has been explained by the UK Climate Impacts Programme (UKCIP) in a 2008 paper in *Nature* by Pielke, Wigley and Green. This paper claims that the technological challenge required to stabilize atmospheric CO_2 concentrations has been underestimated by the IPCC. In particular the IPCC Special Report on Emissions Scenarios (SRES) makes its calculations on the assumption that there will be much greater energy efficiency gains than is realistic, thereby understating the necessary emissions reduction target.

Pielke et al argue that the IPCC SRES scenarios are already inconsistent in the short-term (2000–2010) with the recent evolution of global energy intensity and carbon intensity. Dramatic changes in the global economy (China and India) are in stark contrast to the near-future IPCC SRES. This leads Pielke et al (2008) 'to conclude that enormous advances in energy technology will be needed to stabilise atmospheric CO_2 concentrations'.

The amended Stern Report

A further blow to the IPCC was administered by Nicholas Stern. His UK government sponsored report, known as the *Stern Review on the Economics of Climate Change* was based on IPCC data. Since its publication in 2006, Stern has admitted that he underestimated the threat posed by climate change as posited by the IPCC. He said:

emissions are growing much faster than we thought; the absorptive capacity of the Earth is less than we'd thought; the risks of greenhouse gases are potentially much bigger

than more cautious estimates; the speed of climate change seems to be faster.

(Stern, 2009, p26)

Stern concludes: 'Last October [2007] scientists warned that global warming will be "stronger than expected and sooner than expected" after new analysis showed carbon dioxide is accumulating in the atmosphere much more quickly than expected' (2006, p26). The Stern Review recommended that greenhouse gases should be stabilized at between 450 and 550ppm of CO_2e (equivalent). In January 2009 Stern amended the limit to 500ppm.

Scientists tend to refer solely to carbon dioxide since it is the gas that is the dominant driver of global warming and is the one that is most readily associated with human activity. It comprises around two-thirds of all greenhouse gases. On the other hand, politicians and economists often lump together all greenhouse gases and then refer to their CO_2 equivalent (CO_2e).

This means that the call to stabilize at 500ppm CO_2e equates to 333ppm CO_2, which, coincidentally, is close to the limit set by James Hansen (above) if the world is to achieve climate stability at a tolerable level. The latest concentration is 387ppm!

This view was reinforced by the Royal Society. On the 1 September 2008 it published a series of scientific papers in *Philosophical Transactions A* on the topic of geo-engineering as a way of countering global warming. This will feature in the closing chapter. At this point it is worth citing its authors on the reasons for embarking on this study, which are: 'There is increasingly the sense that governments are failing to come to grips with the urgency of setting in place measures that will assuredly lead to our planet reaching a safe equilibrium.' In a paper by Alice Bows and Kevin Anderson (Anderson and Bows, 2008), they state: 'politicians have significantly underestimated the scale of the climate challenge'. For example, 'this year's G8 pledge to cut global emissions by 50% by 2050 in an effort to limit global warming to 2°C, has no scientific basis and could lead to "dangerously misguided" policies'.

Furthermore, the authors cast doubt on the realistic chances of stabilizing carbon emissions at 450ppm. They assert that emissions are rising at such a rate that they would have to peak by 2015 and then decrease by 6.5 per cent per year for CO_2 to stabilize at 450ppm. This *might* limit the temperature rise to 2°C.

From cause to effect

A further cause for concern is implicit in Hansen's claim that the Earth is already committed to an average 2°C temperature rise (Hansen et al, 2007). This is due to the time lag factor. In a massive geophysical system like the Earth and its atmosphere, which is subject to change like global warming, there is an inevitable time lag between causes and effects. A distinction has to be made between global heating and global warming. The former is the energy input from solar radiation. Global warming is the result of the solar radiation being reflected back into space and heating the atmosphere in the process, thanks mainly to the 'insulation' effect of greenhouse gases.

According to David Wasdell, director of the Meridian Programme, there is a time delay between of perhaps 50 years before the full effects are experienced (Wadsell, 2006). According to James Hansen, about 30 per cent of the effect may be experienced in the first few years.

The implication of this is that we are currently experiencing the effects of greenhouse concentrations from the 1960s–1970s. Wasdell conjectures that if greenhouse gases were to be stabilized now, the world would still face a quadrupling of temperature change against the present. He speculates: 'If storm energy doubled between 1997 and 2000 on an increase in temperature of only 0.7°C, then what will the storm energy become when we quadruple that temperature rise? The cause of such a rise is already in the system. Dangerous climate change is now unavoidable.'

World CO_2 emissions record

Despite international undertakings by the developed countries, CO_2 emissions show little sign of reducing. In fact carbon emissions from fossil fuels have grown by 22 per cent since 2000. During this decade the US contributed ~4 per cent growth and the EU ~3 per cent. India's emissions grew by 8 per cent and China's by 57 per cent. Fossil fuels accounted for 74 per cent of all CO_2 and ~57 per cent of all greenhouse gases. China's emissions from fossil fuels exceeded those of the US in 2008. It is extremely unlikely that the West would have either the practical or moral authority to persuade China to cut back significantly on its 6–10 per cent annual economic growth rate. So, on this count alone, CO_2 atmospheric concentration is set to rise.

Things are not improved by a report in January 2009 by Professor Kitack Lee of the Pohang University of Science and Technology, which confirmed the prediction that warmer oceans would be less able to absorb CO_2 (Lee, 2009). Measurements of the gas content of the Sea of Japan have shown a sudden and dramatic collapse in its rate of absorption by sea water. The research revealed that the CO_2 dissolved in the sea between 1999 and 2007 was only half that recorded between 1992 and 1999.

The ultimate scenario

According to Professor Bob Watson, chief scientist at Defra, the UK should be planning now for the effects of a global average temperature rise of 4°C above the pre-industrial level (Watson, 2008). In this he was supported by Sir David King, former government chief scientist, on the basis that, even with a comprehensive world deal to keep CO_2 levels in the atmosphere below 450ppmv (parts per million by volume) there was a 50 per cent chance that temperatures would exceed 2°C, the figure linked to the level of 450ppm. There was even a 20 per cent chance that it would exceed 3.5°C. King advises that 'even if we get the best possible global agreement to reduce greenhouse gases, on any rational basis you should be preparing for a 20% risk, so I think Bob Watson is right to put the figure at 4 degrees'.

The *Stern Report* goes even further. It states:

> *The latest science suggests that the Earth's average temperature will rise by even more than 5 or 6 degrees C if emissions continue to grow and positive feedbacks amplify the warming effect of greenhouse gases (for example, the release of CO_2 from soils and methane from permafrost). This level of global temperature would be equivalent to the amount of warming that occurred between the last ice age and today. [The] effects could be catastrophic*
>
> (Stern, 2006)

and, if such predictions are correct, these effects would be well beyond the capabilities of current climate models.

The 4°C scenario

The possibility of a 4°C warmer world is not only determined by the amount of CO_2 that human action delivers to the atmosphere, but also the sensitivity of the world's climate to greenhouse gases. It also depends on the impact and timescale of tipping points. As mentioned, the Greenland ice sheet could collapse between a 1° and 2° increase according to the Tyndall Centre. Some models predict the 4° level by 2100; others show it could happen by 2050.

There is a view that an average warming of the planet by 4°C 'would render the planet unrecognisable from anything humans have ever experienced' and 'A 4°C rise could easily occur' (Vince, 2009).

Such a rise in temperature last occurred in the Palaeocene–Eocene Thermal Maximum era 55 million years ago. The average global temperature rose 5–6°C, which caused a rapid release of methane hydrates or clathates, previously ice-bound on the ocean bed. The rapid release of CO_2 lead to the polar regions becoming tropical forests; the oceans becoming virtually dead, having absorbed so much CO_2 that they became acidic. This resulted in a catastrophic collapse of marine life. And the sea level rose 100m above today's level. That is the prognosis for the planet if all land-based ice melts.

Recent predictions of impacts of a 4° rise

Most vulnerable to serious impacts are the tropics between the latitudes 30° north and south – about half the world's surface. Much of this area is set to become desert. This would embrace most of Africa and Asia, according to the above *New Scientist* article (Vince, 2009) much of central and southern US would become uninhabitable desert as would southern China, which is already experiencing desertification (Figure 1.5). South America would also become barely habitable.

On the positive side, Siberia, northern Russia, Scandinavia and Canada would have an acceptable climate with favourable conditions for most of the world's subsistence crops. Even west Antarctica and western Greenland would be habitable.

From the energy point of view, vast areas of desert would be available for solar energy, especially northern Africa and the Middle East, the central US and Australia. It has been calculated that 110,000km^2 across Jordan, Libya and Morocco could accommodate photovoltaic cells and/or power towers to provide sufficient output to meet 50–70 per cent of world electricity demand. If such a project were to begin in 2010, by 2020 it could deliver 55 terawatt hours per year (Wheeler and Ummel, 2008).

A combination of temperature and sea level rise would require the relocation of many of the world's greatest cities. The scenario concludes that the migration of populations would necessitate the development of high density, high rise cities in the temperate zones.

Sea level

James Hansen, referred to earlier, considers that a CO_2 concentration of 550ppm (387ppm at the time of writing) 'would be disastrous, certainly leading to an ice-free planet, with sea level about 80 metres higher [than today]'. Given the lack of an international consensus about the need to halt the rise in emissions, 550ppm is not just possible but probable. China, for example, will pursue

Source: the author, after *New Scientist*

Figure 1.5 Encroaching desert near Dunhuang, Southern China

economic growth even if this means carbon emissions in the atmosphere reach 700ppm.

In the opinion of Peter Cox, celebrated climate scientist from Exeter University, 'Climatologists tend to fall into two camps: there are the cautious ones who say we need to cut emissions and won't even think about high global temperatures; and there are the ones who tell us to run for the hills because we are all doomed... I prefer the middle ground. We have to accept changes are inevitable *and start to adapt now*' (quoted in Vince, 2009). That sums up the position of this book.

In 2008 a team led by Mark Lynas examined three scenarios based on differing CO_2 abatement performance. Even in the most optimistic case, Lynas concluded:

no politically plausible scenario we could envisage will now keep the world below the threshold of two degrees, the official target of both the EU and the UK. This means that all scenarios see the total disappearance of the Arctic sea ice; spreading deserts and water stress in the sub-tropics; extreme weather and floods; and melting glaciers in the Andes and Himalayas. Hence the need to focus far more on adaptation: these are impacts that humanity is going to have to deal with whatever happens now at the political level.

(Lynas, 2008).

These are some of the reasons why the 4°C outcome should be taken seriously and adaptation policies adjusted accordingly. It is understandable but unfortunate that policy documents are appearing based on some now outdated assumptions contained in the IPCC SRES scenarios. Since 2008 is the year when it is estimated that most of the Earth's population will live in towns and cities, it is vital that one focus for urgent adaptation should be the built environment. The next task is to expand on some of the expected climate impacts of this emissions scenario with a view to offering recommendations about how buildings and the urban infrastructure should prepare for the seemingly inevitable. Things may now seem relatively calm. How much better to gear up for the future storm than bask in the calm before it.

Four degrees and beyond:
A statement from the Met Office, 28 September, 2009

Dr Richard Betts, Head of Climate Impacts at the Met Office Hadley Centre, presented the new findings at a special conference this month '4 degrees and beyond' at Oxford University, attended by 130 international scientists and policy specialists. It was the first to consider the global consequences of climate change beyond 2°C.

Dr Betts said: 'Four degrees of warming, averaged over the globe, translates into even greater warming in many regions, along with major changes in rainfall. If greenhouse gas emissions are not cut soon, we could see major climate changes within our own lifetimes.'

In some areas warming could be significantly higher (10 degrees or more).

- The Arctic could warm by up to 15.2°C for a high-emissions scenario, enhanced by melting of snow and ice causing more of the Sun's radiation to be absorbed.
- For Africa, the western and southern regions are expected to experience both large warming (up to 10°C) and drying.
- Rainfall could decrease by 20 per cent or more in some areas, although there is a spread in the magnitude of drying. All computer models indicate reductions in rainfall over western and southern Africa, Central America, the Mediterranean and parts of coastal Australia.
- In other areas, such as India, rainfall could increase by 20 per cent or more. Higher rainfall increases the risk of river flooding.

2

Probable Future Impacts of Climate Change

Storms and floods

In the UK in 2008 the Department for Environment, Food and Rural Affairs (Defra) published a policy document entitled *Adapting to Climate Change in England: A Framework for Action*.

The report begins with the fact that seven out of the ten warmest years since records began have occurred since 1990. Apart from the direct victims, it is the insurance community that has born the brunt of the consequential costs. Claims have doubled to over £6 billion between 1998 and 2003. The Association of British Insurers (ABI) predicts that these costs will have tripled by 2050.

Economist Nicholas Stern (Stern, 2006) has concluded that under the high CO_2 emissions scenario (HES), formerly Business as Usual (BaU), the global loss of gross domestic product (GDP) per year will be 5–20 per cent in perpetuity. That is in parallel with rising world population. Furthermore, regardless of how successful the world will be at cutting CO_2, we are committed to 30–40 years of temperature and sea level rise. There have been a number of notable extreme events in the last six years:

- Summer 2003: 56,000 extra deaths across Europe with a temperature of <35°C in southeastern UK.
- 2004–2005: severe drought across Europe.
- 2005–2006: extreme flash floods, e.g. Boscastle (not mentioned in the Defra doc).

- 2007: unprecedented floods especially in Sheffield and South Yorkshire together with Gloucestershire.
- 2008: worst ever floods across the Indian State of Bihar with 100,000 hectares of land, much of it agricultural, under water and so far costing an estimated 2000 lives.

To understand the implications for the built environment, it is necessary to enter into greater detail regarding the principal expected impacts, such as storms. As stated above, the basis for predictions is the CO_2 HES.

Storms

Many countries have adopted the Beaufort Wind Force Scale, conceived initially for seafarers, as a measure of wind speed. The scale is divided from 1 to 12, with speeds becoming a cause for concern from force 7 (50–61kph; 31–38mph). Force 10 is a gale and force 12 a hurricane (118kph; 73mph). Force 12 corresponds to category 1 on the hurricane scale (below). Some countries, beginning with China, have extended the scale to 17 to cater for tropical cyclones.

Severe storms

Towards the end of August 2008 a hurricane named Gustav gathered strength from the warm seas in its path north to the US. Wind speeds of 150mph were recorded, making it a category

4 storm on the threshold of category 5. This caused the Mayor of New Orleans to order a complete evacuation of the city. Fortunately it subsided to a category 1 and only inflicted a glancing blow on the city where memories of Hurricane Katrina are still raw.

Severe storms go under various names. Wind speed becomes a storm when it exceeds 39mph; at this point meteorologists give it an individual name. If the wind speed exceeds 74mph it is termed either a tropical cyclone or hurricane in the Atlantic. The equivalent in the northwestern Pacific is a typhoon and a cyclone in the Indian Ocean. Hurricanes fall into five categories known as the Saffir–Simpson scale:

- category 1, 74–95mph (119–153kph)
- category 2, 95–110mph (154–177kph)
- category 3, 111–130mph (178–209kph)
- category 4, 131–155mph (210–249kph)
- category 5, 156mph (250kph) and above.

In general it is the sea surface temperature (SST) that triggers hurricanes and these can be generated when the temperature exceeds 26°C. In the summer of 2004 Florida was hit by an unprecedented four hurricanes. In Japan, ten typhoons beat the previous record by four. Then 2005 was a record season for hurricanes culminating in Katrina, which decimated New Orleans, and Rita. It seemed as though the connection between increasing storm frequency and intensity with global warming was then beyond dispute. This certainty was undermined by the fact that 2006 was unusually quiet, generating a flurry of theories from meteorologists.

Over the years scientists have devised increasingly sophisticated models of how hurricanes form. As mentioned, they need warm water, and therefore most originate in the tropics. Global warming is responsible for higher sea temperatures, which, in turn, increase evaporation. These two factors can set up the vortex motion characteristic of such storms. Quite small increases in sea temperature can turn a mere tropical disturbance into a hurricane.

In September 2008 the Texan port of Galveston was hit by hurricane Ike, comparable in strength to Katrina. It did not receive much publicity. Nevertheless, Ike inflicted US$21 billion of damage along the Texas coast. Three-quarters of Galveston's buildings were flooded leading to claims of US$2.3 billion from Federal funds. Sea level rises and severe storms pose an increasing threat along the Gulf of Mexico and the Atlantic coasts, so much so that the very viability of coastal cities like Galveston is being questioned. It is being argued that public money should no longer be used to pay for the recurrent damage to vulnerable towns and cities in the face of increasing impacts from climate change.

In addition to the overall warming of the oceans, a third factor is involved in creating conditions for hurricanes, the seasonal ocean pattern El Niño. This causes a warming of the tropical Pacific Ocean. It arises when there is a coupling between oceanic and atmospheric flows. In 2004–2005 El Niño was relatively weak, which led to sunny skies and moderate winds in the tropical Atlantic. Consequently there was less evaporative cooling, causing the ocean to warm by only 0.2°C. El Niño had collapsed by the summer, minimizing wind shear in the Atlantic, thus creating favourable conditions for hurricane formation. In contrast, La Niña, which caused a cooling of the Pacific, took hold during the winter of 2005–2006. This, in turn, led to stronger trade winds in the North Atlantic that drew heat out of the ocean.

During the summer of 2006, El Niño began to form again, contributing to greater wind shear in the Atlantic. In summary, lower sea surface temperature and unfavourable wind conditions fundamentally changed the condition of the tropical Atlantic compared with 2004–5.

The overriding pattern is that, since 1994, the number of named storms and hurricanes in the North Atlantic has steadily risen. The rise coincides with an increase in sea surface temperature in the latitude 10–20° north – the zone that spawns hurricanes. The trend is clear but now it is also obvious that El Niño and La Niña can cause temporary wobbles in the system.

Northern Europe was reminded that it is not immune to attacks from powerful tornados by the storm that hit the French town of Hautmont near the Belgian border. In August

2008 a storm cut a swathe of destruction through the town causing death and injury. It illustrated how, even in northern Europe, storms can devastate well built houses of traditional masonry construction.

Between 1987 and 2003 storms hitting the UK have cost 150 lives and €5 billion in insured losses (ABI, 2003). By 2100 the UK is predicted to experience a 25 per cent increase in severe winter storms. The intensification trend has already been evident in Scotland and Ireland over the last 50 years.

Is this further evidence of climate change due to global warming? Climate scientists have suggested that climate change may not increase the incidence of severe storms. In fact, numbers may decrease. What they affirm is that there will be more at the intense end of the scale. The reason for a possible decrease in numbers is because category 3–5 hurricanes draw considerable heat out of the ocean, thus delaying the conditions needed for a continuation of the cycle.

A Worldwide Fund for Nature (WWF) report discloses results of an investigation into

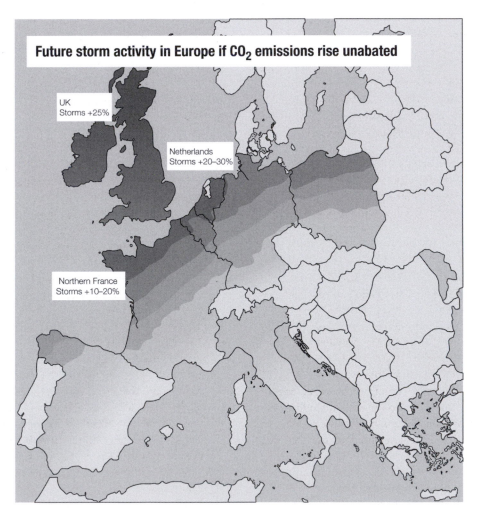

Increases in expected storm intensity in western Europe on the assumption that CO_2 concentrations reach 771ppm by 2090 (IPCC, 2000). This would correspond to an average global temperature rise of 3–5°C above the pre-industrial level.

Source: WWF (2006)

Figure 2.1 Future storm activity in Europe if CO_2 emissions rise unabated

the potential growth in storm activity in western and central Europe assuming the world continues on the Business as Usual (BaU) pathway (WWF, 2006). This predicts that very little attempt will be made to cut CO_2 emissions with the result that the atmospheric concentration will exceed 700ppm by 2100. (IPCC, 2000).

The North Atlantic is the generator of winter storms in western and central Europe. With CO_2 rising, it is inevitable that global heating will increase, resulting in more intense storms as the atmosphere becomes increasingly energetic. The WWF report concludes that, as the country, along with Ireland, being most exposed to the Atlantic, the UK is likely to experience the strongest increase in frequency and intensity of storms. The number of severe storms experienced by the country will probably increase by about ten over a 30 year timescale. Maximum wind speeds could increase by up to 16 per cent. The Netherlands can expect to experience the next largest increase in storm intensity and frequency with top wind speeds increasing by ~15 per cent. France is third in the scale of severe storm expectation (Figure 2.1).

Floods

In England in 2007, South Yorkshire, Humberside and Gloucestershire experienced unprecedented flooding. In Sheffield the River Don burst its banks, inundating large areas of the city, from the centre to the Meadowhall mega shopping complex. Many businesses were affected and some major companies went out of business. The river's expansion took in one of the City's main thoroughfares including the landmark Wicker Bridge. For Sheffield, some of the blame has been attributed to the fact that extensive developments like Meadowhall have increased rainfall runoff as well as building or paving over potential flood plains.

In residential areas of this region, for example Toll Bar, numerous households were still unable to return to their homes 16 months later due to extremely slow or defective remedial work. Serious health problems have been associated

with families having to live in caravans for this length of time.

Altogether in 2007, some 48,000 homes and 7300 businesses were flooded across England. Reservoir dams came under threat from the conditions and just outside Sheffield the Ulley reservoir was breached and a catastrophic flood was narrowly avoided.

Across eastern England one month's rain fell in one 24 hour period, inundating around $50km^2$. Those affected by this catastrophe needed no persuading of the reality of climate change. A few weeks later in Gloucestershire, the famous Abbey at Tewkesbury became an island of sanctuary as the town was overwhelmed.

In 2008, Sir Michael Pitt published a review containing transcripts of detailed interviews with the victims of these floods together with consequential recommendations. In summary these were:

- There must be a 'step change in the quality of flood warnings'. This would only be achieved by much closer cooperation between the Environment Agency and the Met Office combined with improved modelling of all forms of flooding. There must also be much greater public confidence in official information.

- The Environment Agency should widen its brief and local councils improve their technical expertise in order to take the lead in flood management.

- The event highlighted the need for much greater coordination between the responsible agencies, including those responsible for water and power. Higher levels of protection are needed for essential services (as was critically demonstrated in Gloucestershire). There must be greater involvement of private companies in planning to keep people safe in the event of a dam or reservoir failure.

- Finally, there is much to be learnt from good practice abroad where people receive advice on how to protect their families and homes. Levels of awareness must be raised through education and publicity programmes.

It was ironic that the UK government's Foresight Report on Future Flooding should have been followed so soon afterwards by the world's most expensive of the 200 floods that occurred worldwide in 2007.

The Foresight Future Flooding Report 2004

The *Foresight Future Flooding Report* is a detailed examination by experts from a variety of disciplines, chaired by the government chief scientist, Sir David King. It begins with an assessment of the future risks from flooding and the cost they incur. To quote from the report:

> Nearly 2 million properties in floodplains along rivers estuaries and coasts in the UK are potentially at risk from river or coastal flooding. Eighty thousand properties are at risk in towns and cities from flooding caused by heavy downpours that overwhelm urban drains – so-called 'intra-urban flooding'. In England and Wales alone, over 4 million people and properties valued at over £200 billion are at risk.
>
> (DTI, 2004, p12)

If average temperatures rise over 2°C above their 1990 level, millions will be at risk from coastal flooding (see flood maps). At an increase of 1.5–2.5°C, 20–30 per cent of all species risk extinction.

According to research by Groundsure (2008), independent environmental risk assessors, David King's estimate that almost 2.2 million homes and small businesses in the UK are at risk from flooding is accurate. The London area has the highest national percentage risk.

There is increasing consensus that the UK will experience a growing number of flash floods arising from 'tropical storm rainfall' such as that which devastated the village of Boscastle on 16 August 2004.

Rainfall

The UK is fortunate in hosting the Met Office Hadley Centre in Exeter. It is a world class centre for climate change research, especially as it now possesses one of the world's most powerful and fast super computers. This enables it to run even more sophisticated climate models, allowing scientists to refine estimates of uncertainty in their predictions. For the UK, winter rainfall is expected to increase by up to 30 per cent, especially in the south, with a consequent increase in the risk of flooding. However, summer rainfall could decrease by up to 50 per cent, again mainly in the south. The incidence of severe droughts is likely to increase, threatening water supplies.

On the global scale the Hadley Centre has modelled changes in precipitation from the 1960–1990 average to the 2070–2100 average. It not only features increases in rainfall in certain areas, but also the prospect of serious drought, notably in central Africa.

Future flooding costs

According to the former government chief scientist, Sir David King, if flood management policies and expenditure remain the same as in 2008, the following flood events can be expected in the UK, based on the HES:

- the increased annual cost will be about £27 billion by 2080 under the high emissions scenario;
- the average annual damage for all of the UK assuming flood management strategies and expenditure remain unchanged will be ~£28 billion by the 2080s;
- the average annual damage from flooding across UK as a percentage of GDP: 0.2 per cent.

Impact on infrastructure

By the 2080s the number of properties at a high risk from intra-urban flooding under the CO_2 HES will be about 380,000. The annual cost of the damage will be about £15 billion. At the same time average coastal erosion is predicted to be between 140 and 180 metres, resulting in an annual cost due to damage of £125 million.

The number of people at a high risk of river and coastal flooding at the present time amount to

1.6 million. By 2080 under the CO_2 HES of 700ppm this figure rises to between 2.3 and 3.6 million; 200,000 people are at risk of experiencing short-term duration flooding today; in 2080 this number could be as high as 700,000–900,000.

Summary of recommendations from the *Foresight Future Flooding Report*

The probability of flooding increases significantly in the high emissions scenarios … we could reduce the average damage by 25% if we achieve the low emissions scenarios … reducing climate change will not solve our future flooding problems by itself, but it could substantially ease them.
(Foresight Future Flooding Report, p39)

The urban challenge

The risk of flooding in towns and cities, as well as possibly being our greatest challenge in the future, is also the area of greatest uncertainty.
(Foresight Future Flooding Report, p40)

There are no easy options. If decisions are taken to build in areas at risk of flooding, the costs must be recognized and planned for.
(Foresight Future Flooding Report, p41)

One strategy would be to require developers to provide appropriate flood defences and therefore to let market forces determine where new housing will be located. However, against what yardstick for flooding will developers' tactics be judged? Will enough provisions have been made for future climate changes? For how long will the developer be required to maintain the defences? A period of 50 years has been mentioned. If the defences are breached, who will pay? Insurers might seek redress or the uninsured may resort to a class action. Insurance will be a major consideration, with renewal premiums for victims of the 2007 floods already showing considerable inflation. The *Foresight* report says: 'Government might have to consider how to respond to pressure to act as insurer of last resort if the insurance market withdrew cover from large parts of the UK, or if there was a major flood which the insurance market could not cover' (p45).

Finally, there is evidence that the UK is likely to be affected by a recently perceived change in the route of the jet stream – the high level, high speed jet of air that travels from east to west. This could lead to higher temperatures in the summer with more intense rainfall and flooding, together with warmer, wetter winters. This has been the case in 2007–2008. If this jet stream anomaly persists it could mean that long-term predictions will need to be modified. 'All adaptive strategies will need to know the behaviour of jet streams… The key question will be: what will our climate be thanks to jet streams? Getting it right will enable us to adapt to climate change; getting it wrong equals disaster' (Pieper, 2008).

Sea level rise

There is still controversy over the extent of sea level rise likely to occur towards the end of the century. The uncertainty is compounded by the fact that sea levels are also influenced by atmospheric pressure. In the UK this was demonstrated by the storm surge of 1953. This was England's first taste of a severe storm surge in modern times. It was particularly damaging to the coasts of Kent, Essex, Suffolk, Norfolk and Lincolnshire. Over 600km^2 were inundated, with the loss of 307 lives. The surge was formed by a combination of extreme low pressure and powerful winds reinforcing spring tides. What really made the difference on this occasion was that the low pressure caused the sea level to rise by around half a metre.

Deemed to be at a particularly high risk from a sea level rise and storm surge is the low lying land behind the Norfolk coast. In 2003 there was a warning that a large area of grade one agricultural land would be contaminated by flooding, with 83–100 per cent of an area adjacent to The Wash becoming unavailable for agriculture (Figure 2.2).

The biggest landowner in the UK is the National Trust. It manages some of the most scenic

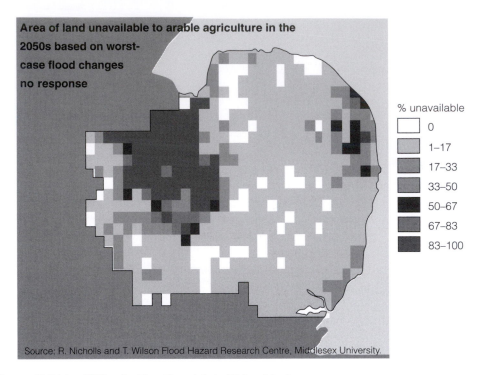

Source: R. Nicholls and T. Wilson Flood Hazard Research Centre, Middlesex University.

Source: Courtesy of R. Nichols and T. Wilson, Flood Hazard Research Centre, Middlesex University

Figure 2.2 Areas of Norfolk showing the percentage of land at risk of becoming unavailable for agriculture by 2050

coastal landscape in Britain and has come to the conclusion that some will be radically changed or lost. This is because the Trust now concedes that it is no longer possible to hold back the rising seas and prevent coastal erosion. In September 2008 it revealed the location of ten coastal 'hotspots' to demonstrate that the problem of climate change threatens about 70 sites owned by the Trust.

It is the rising cost of rectifying damage that has forced the Trust to come to this conclusion. For example, it states that, on just one site in Cornwall, it would cost about £6 million to build defences that would last only last 25 years. This statement by the Trust highlights the dilemma that will face many local authorities and governments worldwide as climate change gathers momentum, not least Greater London.

Storm surge risk

In 2005 the UK Met Office Hadley Centre compiled an assessment of the risk of storm surge inundation across northwest Europe by 2080. It indicated that the Thames Estuary is at the highest risk, causing Greater London to be highly vulnerable to future flooding (Figure 2.3).

When he was the government's chief scientist, Sir David King predicted that, if global warming continues at its present rate, London will be submerged by rising sea levels. His anxiety stems from the discovery from Antarctic ice cores that, during ice ages, the concentration of CO_2 in the atmosphere was 200ppm. At the peak of the ice age 12,000 years ago, the sea was 150m below the current level. When the CO_2 concentration reached 270ppm this produced a warm period and melting ice. The most recent measurement from the observatory at Mauna Loa (March 2008) shows the concentration to be 387ppm and rising at 3ppm per year, according to King (reported in the *London Evening Standard*, 14 July 2004).

Since David King sounded his warning, the impacts from global warming have accelerated, as mentioned in Chapter 1. This suggests that alarm

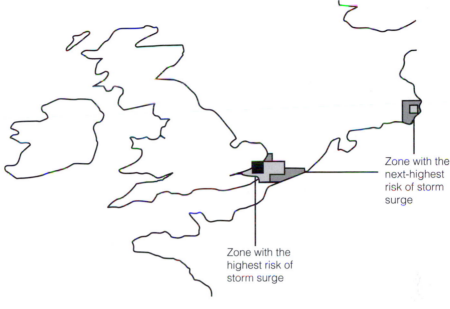

Zone with the
next-highest
risk of storm
surge

Zone with the
highest risk of
storm surge

Source: derived from Hadley Centre, 2005

Figure 2.3 Risk from storm surges in northwest Europe to 2080

bells should be ringing in cities like London and New York. For London, the only medium- to long-term solution is an estuary tidal barrage that could also generate considerable amounts of electricity (Figure 2.4). If the present barrier were to be overtopped by a storm surge, the cost to London would be £30 billion.

At the end of the last ice age, melting ice caused the seas to rise by around 1m per century. According to the Goddard Institute, New York City, the forces that led to this rate of rise 'are comparable to the forces we will experience this century' (Schmidt, 2008, p12). Some scientists now believe that a 1m rise in sea level by 2100 is an underestimate. The Tyndall Centre has produced a histogram predicting what this would mean in terms of the countries and populations under threat (Figure 2.5).

Temperature

Whilst uncertainties in climate change modelling are being reduced by the power of the latest computers, there are still those who use residual uncertainties as a 'wait and see' excuse.

However, there is no doubt about the average rise in global temperature especially over the most recent decades.

The temperature used by the Met Office to mark the start of a heatwave is 32°C. The summer of 1973 still holds the record for a heatwave with temperatures over 32°C being recorded in one or more places for 15 consecutive days. (*National Risk Register*, UK Cabinet Office 2008). In the hot summer of 2003 it is estimated that the heatwave resulted in 2045 excess deaths in the UK. As stated, across Europe the figure was said to be 56,000.

With long-life investments like homes, it makes sense to invest now in protective measures against the impacts of the high emissions climate scenario. This would be more cost-effective and efficient than resorting to remedial measures after the event. An example of such an 'event' has been identified by the Town and Country Planning Association (TCPA):

We must adapt to the 40 degree C city. Without very strong action we will see temperatures in many UK cities sitting above 40 degree C for long periods of the summer.

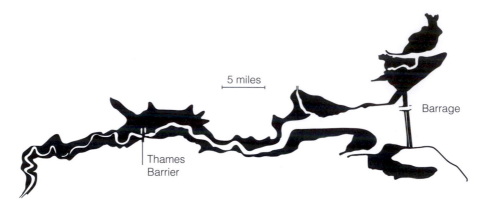

River Thames flood risk area below 5m contour

Figure 2.4 River Thames basin: the area below the 5m contour is subject to storm surge risk, making a compelling case for estuary barrages

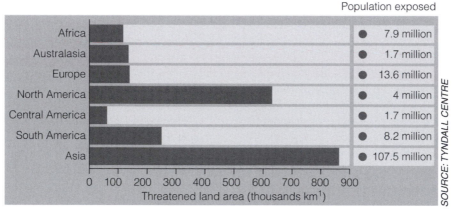

DROWNED OUT

The devastating impact of a sea-level rise of 1 metre

Source: The Tyndall Centre

Figure 2.5 Area of land and size of population under threat from a 1m sea level rise

The social, economic, not to mention environmental, implications of this will be far reaching and threatens to undermine the long term desirability of towns and cities as places to live and work.

(Robert Shaw, Director of Policy and Projects 2007)

It was the hot summers of 2003 and 2006 with their sustained high temperatures that gave a foretaste of summers that will become commonplace. Is it being premature to suggest that houses should be designed *now* for >40°C summer days and 35°C nights? Ironically the emphasis on building regulations has been on curtailing space heating through insulation and high levels of air tightness, whereas all the pointers are towards warmer winters and very much hotter summers. Later chapters will discuss the design implications of this probability.

According to a team led by Andreas Sterl of the Royal Netherlands Meteorological Institute, as climate change builds up, peak temperatures may rise twice as fast as average temperatures. They conclude that any point within 40° latitude of the equator will have a 10 per cent chance of peaking at over 48°C each decade. They add that the temperatures of 2003 in the forties will become commonplace (Sterl et al, 2008).

Studies by UKCIP predict that summer temperatures under the worst case scenario (World Markets, IPCC high emissions scenario) will increase 4.5° above average by 2080 in south and central England. In winter in the same region they will increase 3–3.5°.

Heat island effect

Urban areas modify their local climate and the urban heat island effect (UHI) is probably the most obvious manifestation of this feature in which temperatures are raised beyond their natural level by the release of accumulated local thermal energy in major conurbations.

Towns and cities face the twin challenge of adapting to localized micro-effects and globally driven macro-effects. The UKCIP projections demonstrate the difference between the north and south of the UK in terms of temperature impact. The UHI will significantly amplify this impact in the south with its high concentration of urban development. Another UKCIP study compares the percentage of hours of 'hot' discomfort in the bedroom of a new build house (25°C) is exceeded and the 28°C discomfort excess in offices. Figure 2.6 compares the expected difference from the 1980s to the 2080s in London, Manchester and Edinburgh.

In summary the predicted impacts of global warming for the UK are:

- periods of continuous high temperature;
- decreased summer rainfall leading to droughts and water stress;
- torrential rainfall incidents with severe flooding in excess of 2007;
- faster coastal erosion and related flooding;
- storm surges 20 times more frequent by 2100;
- sea level rise of 80mm around some parts of the UK by 2100 (others are more pessimistic – 3–4m expected if Greenland and West Antarctica go into serious melt);
- average summer temperature rise in south of England over 4.5°C by 2080;
- hotspots where several severe events impact simultaneously, especially in flood plains, estuaries and large conurbations;
- increased pressure on critical national infrastructure such as sewage and fresh water supply with an increased risk of summer water shortages and problems of water quality.

New build house: Bedroom

1960s Office: Mid floor

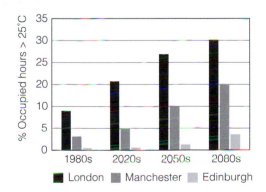
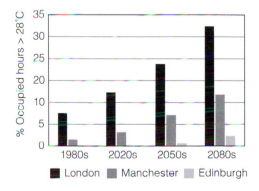

Source: UKCIP (2005); Shaw et al (2007)

Figure 2.6 Hours when heat related discomfort temperature is exceeded in homes and offices

In a paper 'Squaring up to reality' published in *Nature Reports – climate change*, May 2008, the authors state:

> *A curious optimism – the belief that we can find a way to fully avoid all the serious threats illustrated above – pervades the political arenas of the G8 summit and UN climate meetings. This is a false optimism, and it is obscuring reality. The sooner we recognise this delusion, confront the challenge and implement both stringent emissions cuts and major adaptation efforts, the less will be damage that we, and our children, will have to live with... [W]e know that immediate investment in adaptation will be essential to buffer the worst impacts.*
>
> (Parry et al, 2008)

It has been necessary to go into some detail about the probabilities of future climate impacts in order to justify the radical changes in planning and building practice that will offer protection in future decades. There are still uncertainties about the pace and extent of future climate change, but all the predictions so far have been underestimates. As the Parry and colleagues state: 'We have lost ten years talking about climate change but not acting on it' (Parry et al, 2008). Even if the world manages to improve on the CO_2 high emissions scenario, buildings and their inhabitants will still have to withstand severe climate effects. It will be far more cost-effective to build now to protect against the worst case scenario of climate change than retrofit buildings after the event. Action now offers a win–win opportunity.

Designing for an unknown future

It is the view of Mark Lynas that:

> *no politically plausible scenario we could envisage will now keep the world below the danger threshold of two degrees, the official target for both the EU and UK. This means the total disappearance of Arctic Sea ice,*

spreading deserts and water stress in the subtropics; extreme weather and floods... Hence the need to focus far more on adaptation; these are impacts that humanity is going to have to deal with whatever now happens at the policy level... At 4°C southern England temperature could reach 45°C – today in Marrakesh.

> (Lynas, 2008)

In a television interview James Lovelock, originator of Gaia theory, considered that global warming was already unstoppable (Malone and Tanner, 2008). It will run its course to its catastrophic conclusion, irrespective of reductions in CO_2 abatement. Emissions are virtually certain to cross the 450ppm CO_2 tipping point, marking the start of a new era in climate change impacts. However, it may still be possible to stabilize the concentration in the atmosphere at a level that is survivable for human society, albeit demanding massive adaptive strategies. It is the second tipping point that introduces runaway climate change and which ushers in the doomsday scenario. There is a view that 'irreversible' and 'runaway' climate change are synonymous. After a 2°C rise feedback systems will run their course until all ice has melted. That maybe a millennium away, so the argument for adaptation remains valid. Possibly the issue will be decided within the next 25 years. Meanwhile, the priority is to create buildings that will make life tolerable and secure against the predicted impacts which will be inevitable if the pace of Business as Usual is sustained.

In the industrialized countries, it is in the urban environment that adaptation will have to take place as a matter of urgency. This will mean fundamental changes in the way buildings and urban spaces are designed. Up to now policy concerning the design of buildings, as far as the environment is concerned, has been reactive. That is, regulations have been a response to problems that have already occurred. This has been the case in the public health sphere, and, in recent years, it has also been the case concerning the response to global warming and climate change. No less an organization than the IPCC has affirmed that 'immediate investment in adaptation will be essential to buffer the worst impacts' of global warming (IPCC, 2007).

In a press interview, Keith Clarke, chief executive of the engineering and design consultancy Atkins, argues that there has to be 'a fundamental change in the way we design the built environment.,. Just accept that climate change is a real and significant threat to mankind. It is quite clear it is already changing the standards we design to' (*Guardian*, 27 June 2008).

The aim of the book from here is to consider the design implications for buildings that will be proof against climate impacts that are beyond imagination. The next chapter illustrates some buildings that are well ahead of current best practice. However, buildings that could be considered genuinely climate proof, at least for this century, should be as much ahead of the leading examples of today, as *they* are ahead of current best practice standards. We are talking of designing to combat the unthinkable.

So far we have come to terms with the fact that it is virtually certain that the world will continue producing carbon emissions well beyond the threshold of irreversible climate change, namely the concentration of 450ppm. On 25 September 2008, the Global Carbon Project, which monitors worldwide emissions of the gas, reported that carbon emissions are rising four times faster than in the year 2000. This is mainly due to the fact that, year on year, emissions from developing countries are rapidly increasing, while emissions in the developed world are more or less static. So, perhaps even Nicholas Stern is understating it when he suggested that the average temperature may rise by 6°C by the end of the century, in which case the effects would be catastrophic (Stern, 2009). Therefore, this is where the precautionary principle urges that there is nothing to be lost by designing the built environment to cope with the worst case climate scenario.

3

The UN Carbon Trading Mechanism

There is another reason to be concerned about the chances of avoiding the extreme consequences of global warming. It centres on the principle that carbon can be a traded as a commodity. The belief that underpinned the carbon trading scheme was that it would spearhead the drive by developed countries to cut their carbon emissions in line with their Kyoto commitments. Has it worked?

Under the Kyoto Protocol, most industrialized nations except the US agreed to cut their emissions of carbon dioxide between 2008 and 2012. One mechanism for achieving this is to cap emissions from major industrial polluters. These companies are issued with permits allowing them to emit a fixed amount of CO_2 each year calculated against current annual emissions estimated by the companies. These permits are tradeable under the European Emissions Trading Scheme (ETS). The idea is that traders who cut their pollution can sell their surplus permits to companies that are failing to keep within their capped budget. The market will operate to set the price of carbon.

At the start of the present round of trading, some industries overstated their carbon requirements, flooding the carbon market, with the result that the price for carbon almost collapsed. It is currently trading at about $8 per tonne. Larry Lohmann, who has written extensively on carbon trading, describes it as a 'licence for big polluters to carry on business as usual' (Lohmann, 2006a). For example, the German utilities group RWE, with no carbon

penalties to pay for, made huge windfall profits from selling carbon credits in addition to the profits from the rising price of oil and gas.

Where the system enters into a grey area is in the fact that the Kyoto Protocol allows companies in industrialized countries to invest in emissions-reducing projects in developing countries. This happens under the certified emissions reduction scheme (CER). These are credits that can be used to offset a company's emissions, or can be traded on the open market. This is called the Clean Development Mechanism (CDM) and is judged to represent one tonne of CO_2 not emitted. By December 2007 the UN had approved over 1600 projects for CERs, which were sold to the highest bidders. Schemes approved included wind turbines in India, methane capture from landfill in Latin America and geothermal energy in central America.

A consortium of private companies led by energy company Centrica recently bought £400 million worth of carbon credits from China, a country that is outside the Kyoto Protocol and which is opening a new coal fired power plant every one or two weeks. That £400 million is already being passed on to consumers in higher gas prices. The danger is that the ETS is simply a method of shifting carbon around whilst allowing the major polluting firms to emit more and more carbon. As Lohmann puts it: 'It helps keep an oppressive, fossil-centred industrial model going at a time when society should be abandoning it' (Lohmann, 2006b, p18).

At the same time, plants that produce only a marginal carbon improvement over existing similar plants can claim offset income. For example, a new 4000MW coal fired plant in India is expected to claim CERs because its technology is a slight advance on its predecessors. It will nevertheless emit ~26 million tonnes of CO_2 per year over its 25 year lifespan and be paid for the privilege.

The most notorious abuse of the system centres on the gas HFC-23, a waste product from the production of refrigerants. A molecule of this gas is 11,700 times more potent as a greenhouse gas than CO_2, making it a potential gold mine. Because of this disparity, chemical companies can earn twice as much from creating then destroying the gas and selling the related CERs than from selling the refrigerant gas in the conventional market. There are concerns that manufacturers are producing an excess of HCF-23 in order to destroy it and claim CERs.

The general view is that carbon trading has created wealth but has had little impact on stemming the rise of atmospheric CO_2. Even when a CDM represents a real carbon reduction, there is virtually no global benefit and this was described by Patrick McNully[1] as 'a zero sum game'. If a mine in a recipient country cuts its methane emissions under the CDM, there will be no global benefit since the polluter that buys the offset avoids the obligation to cut emissions.

The logical outcome is that the majority of cuts in emissions supposed to be achieved under Kyoto will merely represent traffic in CDMs but no real cuts in carbon pollution. Analysts have estimated that two-thirds of the emissions demanded by the Kyoto agreement from developed countries may be met by obtaining offsets rather than decarbonizing their economies. So, claimed compliance may, in reality, be bogus. Of course there are other dodgy routes to compliance.

One stratagem is to export pollution. The UK excludes the CO_2 component of its imports as well as that generated by aircraft or shipping, claiming that, to account for them would be too complicated. So, cars from Japan or clothes from China imported by Britain that could produce a CO_2 liability escape the net. Whilst the UK government claims to have reduced carbon emissions by 16 per cent since 1990, it is claimed that greenhouse gases for which it is actually responsible have risen by 19 per cent over this period (Helm, 2007).

In addition to the CDM there is an unofficial offsetting carbon market that has not been subject to the UN accreditation scheme. Airlines are doing this with a modest conscience surcharge on tickets that helps to plant a tree or two or preserve a portion of rainforest. For a short time BP promoted its offsets schemes on its Targetneutral website by telling its customers 'it is now possible to drive in neutral'.

It has to be questioned whether it is possible to achieve any degree of accuracy in measuring the sequestration capacity, for example, of a tree. A young tree will make a net contribution to CO_2 abatement, but how much is debateable. As it gets older it may well be a net polluter.

Additionality

One problem is that two-thirds of the emissions reduction obligations of countries that ratified Kyoto are said to have been met by buying offsets rather than making actual carbon reductions.

(Patrick McNully quoted in the *Guardian*, 21 May 2008, p9)

The problems of offsets have been widely aired, especially on the question of 'additionality'. Would the development paid for by CDM funds have happened anyway? Proof of additionality is extremely hard to verify. Additionality also creates a perverse incentive for developing countries not to legislate for carbon reductions. Why should a government enforce energy efficiency measures when these then become 'Business as Usual' and thus not eligible for CDM income?

More than 60 per cent of official CDM projects approved by April 2008 were for hydroelectric dams, mostly in China. As these substitute for coal fired plants it is a legitimate destination for funds. However, the non-governmental organization (NGO) Climate

Action Network, has reported that most of the projects issued with CERs were either completed or under construction before the application for CERs was made. This suggests there was already a commitment to build them, which implies there was inadequate scrutiny on the part of the UN. The environmental writer Oliver Tickell claims (2008) that 96 per cent of carbon credits for hydroelectric dam construction were issued after construction had begun. Even if the problem of additionality is addressed, some countries may hold back projects they intended to build so that they would qualify for CERs.

To prove additionality it is necessary to show that, if a developer or factory owner did not receive offset income they would not build their project or switch to a greener fuel and that they would not do so within a decade from the start of the offset funding.

A new profession of carbon consultant has emerged as a result of the growth in carbon trading and because, generally, companies do not have the expertise to know where to place their CER credits. This has given rise to a new field of creativity in conjouring up reasons why a development would be impossible without CDM offsets. Apparently consultants are expert at showing how a project would be non-viable on its own. It was alleged by an NGO based in California (International Rivers, 2007), that scores of hydro developers have claimed that their projects will produce less than half the electricity expected of a dam of a given capacity, which means the sums do not add up; the solution is a CDM. 'Offsets are an imaginary commodity created by deducting what you hope happens from what you guess would have happened' said Dan Welch (2007) in a report for *Ethical Consumer* magazine. There is claimed to be evidence that almost 75 per cent of projects approved by the CDM Executive Board as non-additional were already complete at the time of approval. For example 'the majority of … hydro projects in China, South America and Africa are using "Alice in Wonderland" arguments to pretend they are cutting emissions' (International Rivers, 2007).

There are carbon brokers who buy credits and then find appropriate markets, such as a Chinese wind farm project. In 2007 the value of carbon deals reached $60 billion, which includes the brokers' percentage. It is clear why major financial institutions are now becoming involved.

It is ironic that the negotiations for the next phase of Kyoto after 2012 are coinciding with the worst global economic recession for many decades. Predictably the rapidly growing constituency of carbon brokers and consultants is lobbying for the CDM to be expanded and its rules weakened. The evidence above is merely a small sample of the problems besetting the ETS. In the short term it must be radically reformed. After 2012 it must be replaced by a mechanism that is, as near as possible, proof against fraud. The sub-prime crisis has demonstrated how the whole banking and investment system can be corrupted when there is insufficient government surveillance and control. The unfettered market is not an appropriate mechanism for saving the planet from catastrophic global warming consequences.

There are further anomalies. The system offers a mechanism whereby emissions are cut, but at the price of increasing them elsewhere. For example, carbon credits can be obtained by reverting to biofuels. However, the crops may grow in fields formed by draining peat bogs, thus releasing methane or cutting down forests. Even an executive in the steel industry has recognized that European carbon pricing 'is not going to curb emissions. It will just move the emissions elsewhere' (Ian Rogers, director of the trade association UK Steel, quoted in Pearce, 2008). 'Many fear … that carbon capitalism is already out of control, delivering huge profits while doing little to halt global warming. They are deeply sceptical of the notion that market forces can fix climate change.' According to Tom Burke, former director of Friends of the Earth: 'To believe that is to believe in magic' (Pearce, 2008).

Feed-in tariffs should create a real incentive to cut carbon, and likewise the purchase price should offer a profound disincentive to companies to overshoot. We cannot allow the future of the planet to be held to ransom by international big business, which is what is happening now.

The German environmentalist Hermann Scheer refuses 'to accept the idea of issuing emission rights that can be traded. It is like giving rights to trade in drugs, and saying drug dealers can buy and sell those rights' (Scheer, 2008, p44).

Beyond 2012

There needs to be fundamental reform of the ETS and the first task would be to 'nationalize' carbon. At present the UK has 60 or so carbon trading companies, few of which seem to be fit for purpose. It is unacceptable that carbon should be just another component of the commercial free market. It is much too important to be regulated by market opportunism.

The EU Environment Commissioner should have the power to set the mandatory carbon emissions for EU members based on international commitments and reducing year on year. Individual member nations would be allocated their ration by the Commissioner, probably on a per capita GDP basis, possibly adjusted according to the relative contributions from the private, commercial and industrial sectors. Sale and purchase prices for carbon would also be set on an annual basis by the Commissioner who would fix both floor and ceiling for prices. For the market to succeed it is necessary that there should be a high price for carbon and confidence in the long-term viability of the market. It should not be market forces that determine the price of carbon but the rate at which emissions must be cut to avoid catastrophic climate impacts. One suggestion is that the initial price of carbon should be based on a scientific analysis of the damage likely to be inflicted by climate change under the IPCC's medium emissions scenario, ~450ppm by 2050. This would provide a basis for attributing damage to a tonne of CO_2 assuming that it contributes roughly 75 per cent of all greenhouse gases. Every member nation would have its own carbon exchange with responsibility for buying and selling carbon units within the union and distributing money to validated causes. Countries failing to meet their targets would have to buy carbon credits.

A problem that is fundamental to carbon trading is that the measurement of carbon is an imprecise science. This undermines confidence in the carbon said to have been emitted by a polluter, especially when it is based on the polluter's own estimate. Since energy is the prime source of human CO_2 emissions, the only secure way of measuring emissions is by determining the carbon content of the fuel mix used by a consumer within a set period, either a quarter or a year. David Miliband is on record as favouring individual carbon budgets. This may claim the moral high ground but it was relegated to the long grass by the prime minister. The best medium-term solution would be to target the two sectors responsible for the majority of emissions: the built environment and transport. It is also important that the pain of carbon abatement should be spread evenly and also that the carbon content of energy should be accurately accounted for. Meanwhile, 'the European Union's Emissions Trading Scheme has resulted in no net reductions in carbon emissions to date' (Ainger, 2008, p34).

The appendix to this chapter offers a suggestion for a building-centred carbon budget strategy.

Appendix

The carbon budget principle for buildings

Houses

There is no better time than now to introduce a mandatory system for accounting for CO_2 emissions due to the use of buildings. A carbon budget system that embraces all properties is the answer. A home would have a fixed 'ration' of carbon initially based on the current annual average for the type of property and the level of occupation. Smart meters with an indoor display would show the electricity and gas consumed and state of the CO_2 budget The display could be a pi diagram indicating the daily level of remaining carbon credits. Unused carbon credits could be sold to the official carbon exchange at the price set by the Commission, which would constitute a significant incentive to save energy. If carbon units had to be purchased to meet the budget they would carry a surcharge plus the cost of administration. A domestic carbon budget system would have to take account of a number of variables:

- habitable area;
- location: urban or rural;
- climate zone;
- number of occupants;
- access to energy (e.g. those without mains gas would have a higher allowance);
- age of the property;
- age of the occupants;
- disabilities;
- special relief for low income and single parent families.

Non-domestic buildings

In commercial and institutional buildings the carbon budget should be based on overall energy use of, say, 120kWh/m^2/year with a target of the current best practice standard of 90kWh/m^2/year. There might also be a limit set on the amount of excess carbon units that could be purchased, say 20 per cent of the annual budget. An individual building's budget would take account of:

- area of occupied space;
- climate zone and possibly micro-climate;
- age of the property;
- its historic importance, e.g. listed building status;
- type of operation and level of electronic appliances;
- level of occupancy, e.g. 24/7.

For both domestic and commercial/institutional buildings this is a sample of factors to be considered in determining carbon budgets.

Transport

A cost-effective way of curbing the carbon generated by road vehicles is the carbon smart card. When a vehicle obtains its road fund licence a card is supplied loaded with appropriate carbon credits for the period of the licence. Factors taken into account for private cars would include:

- category of vehicle, say 3 categories based on CO_2g/km but tapering down to a low emission vehicle level within say 5 years;
- location of owner: urban or rural;
- special needs: disability, age;
- chronic health problems;
- access to public transport;
- ratio of private to occupational use;
- multiple vehicle adjustment.

The fastest growing emissions are from aircraft. The EU is proposing that they should come under the carbon trading umbrella whether in terms of flights or individual passengers. This would only be legitimate were it to be universally applied. The chances of this are remote. The only robust strategy would be for a carbon tax, based on average occupancy or freight and according to the length of flight, to be levied on either take-off or landing. The EU would need to brace itself for the consequences, especially opposition from national, commercial and industrial interests. If only these interests would recognize that their future existence depends on the world achieving rapid and drastic cuts in CO_2.

Note

1   Patrick McNully is Executive Director, International Rivers, a US think tank.

4

Setting the Pace Towards Climate-proof Housing

There have been isolated examples of design in housing that respond to the Atkins' challenge of what Keith Clarke defines as 'carbon critical' design (see Chapter 2). It was in Germany that the challenge was first taken up with inception of the PassivHaus programme.

Case studies

PassivHaus, Darmstadt, Germany

In 1990, Germany launched its PassivHaus programme with an ultra-low energy demonstration project in Darmstadt. This involved walls with a U-value[1] of $0.10-0.15W/m^2K$, with wall insulation of 300–335mm. Roof insulation was 500mm and triple glazing achieved a U-value of up to $0.70W/m^2K$ (Figure 4.1).

The basic principles of PassivHaus design are illustrated in Figure 4.2.

The emphasis of the PassivHaus is on retaining heat, mostly as measured by U-values. In the future the emphasis for much of the year may well be on keeping cool.

The US Department of Energy has established a private/public partnership with the title 'Building America: Developing Energy Efficient Homes in the US'. Its goals include:

- producing homes on a community scale that use on average 30–90 per cent less energy;
- integrating onsite power systems leading to 'zero-energy' homes (ZEH) that will

ultimately produce as much energy as they use by 2020;
- helping home builders reduce construction time and waste;
- improving builder productivity;
- providing new product opportunities to manufacturers and suppliers;
- implementing innovative energy and material saving techniques.

Whilst not yet aiming to produce homes to the PassivHaus level, it does incorporate several features of that standard. The principal aim of the programme is to encourage 'whole systems engineering'; what in the UK is called 'integrated design'. The purpose is 'to unite segments of the building industry that traditionally work independently'. In other words, the design and construction teams should work together from the inception of the design. Post-completion prototypes will be rigorously tested before the programme goes into volume production.

Autonomous House, Southwell, UK

Soon after the PassivHaus prototype was completed, two architecture lecturers at the Nottingham University School of Architecture embraced the PassivHaus challenge with their vernacular style Autonomous House in Southwell, UK (Figure 4.3). Completed in 1993, its style was dictated by the fact that it was close to Southwell

Source: Wikipedia

Figure 4.1 PassivHaus, Darmstadt, Germany 1990

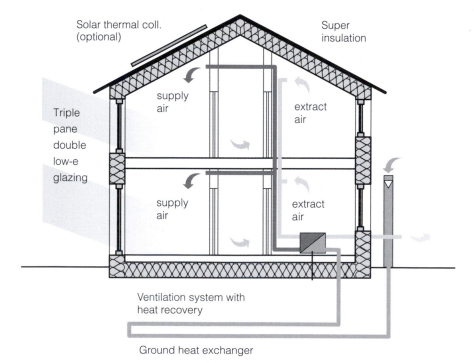

Source: Wikipedia

Figure 4.2 PassivHaus characteristics

- space heating: passive solar plus 4kW wood stove;
- water supply: stored and filtered rainwater collected through copper rainwater goods;
- a 2.2kW PV array is positioned in the garden and solar thermal panels on the roof.

Figure 4.3 The 'Autonomous House' Southwell, rear view with 2.2kW photovoltaic cell array

Minster, an outstanding Norman cathedral surrounded by venerable domestic buildings. The architects were Robert and Brenda Vale.

This three-storey house was designed to be not only net zero carbon but also independent of most mains services, justifying the title 'Autonomous House'. It was connected to the grid in order to export excess power from the photovoltaic (PV) cells. The only other external link was a telephone line. The environmental credentials of the house still place it in the vanguard of current practice. These are the essential elements:

- there is a two-storey conservatory on the west, garden side of the house;
- construction is heavyweight with high insulation and thermal mass properties (Figure 4.4);
- heat recovery is by natural ventilation;
- water heating: solar thermal with ground source heat backup;

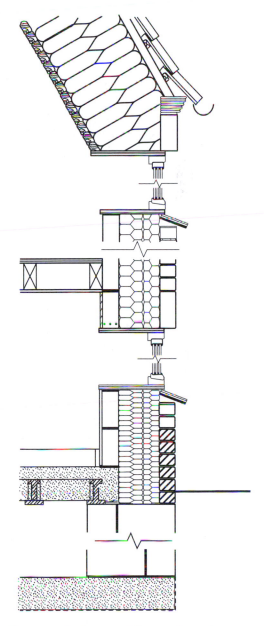

Figure 4.4 Roof, wall and floor section of the Autonomous House

The U-values (in W/m²K) are as follows:

Area	U-value	Construction
Ground floor	0.6	
Walls	0.14	100mm dense concrete blocks, 250mm insulation, bricks exterior
Roof	0.07	500mm cellulose fibre
Windows	1.15	triple-glazed in wood frames
Conservatory	2.1	double-glazed argon filled and low emissivity coating

The construction materials were rigorously chosen to minimize embodied energy. Energy use, excluding the wood stove, solar thermal and PV panels was 17kWh/m²/y. If these figures are taken into account, its performance surpasses the Darmstadt PassivHaus prototype.

Hockerton Housing Project (HHP)

In addition to designing the Autonomous House in Southwell, the Vales designed a group of ultra-low energy houses near the village of Hockerton in Nottinghamshire (Figures 4.5 and 4.6). HHP is the UK's first earth-sheltered, self-sufficient ecological housing development, with homes amongst the most energy efficient dwellings in Europe.

It comprises a narrow plan single aspect group of houses, fully earth sheltered on the north side with the earth carried over the roof. The south elevation is completely occupied by a generous sun space across all the units.

This is designed to be a partially autonomous scheme using recycled grey water and with waste products being aerobically treated by reed beds.

Figures 4.5 Passive solar houses 1998, Hockerton Self-Sufficient Housing Project south elevation and conservatories, exterior

PVs and a wind generator supplement its electricity needs. It is described as a net zero energy scheme, which is defined as a development that is connected to the grid and there is at least a balance between the exported and imported electricity. Like the Autonomous House in Southwell, this development meets all of its electricity needs onsite and therefore is not reliant on the grid, making it an autonomous development.

Hockerton is a project designed for a special kind of lifestyle, which will only ever have minority appeal. For example it plans to be self-sufficient in vegetables, fruit and dairy products employing organic-permaculture principles. One fossil fuel car is allowed per household and 8 hours support activity per week is required from each resident. It is a demonstration of what it means to create a symbiotic link between living and architecture.

The Hockerton project has a number of key features:

- 90 per cent energy saving compared with conventional housing;
- self-sufficient in water, with domestic water collected from the conservatory roof and reed bed treated effluent for purposes that require EU bathing water standard;
- considerable thermal storage due to earth sheltering;
- 70 per cent heat recovery from extracted warm air;
- triple-glazed internal windows and double-glazed conservatory;
- 300mm of insulation in walls;
- a wind generator to reduce reliance on the grid;
- roof mounted photovoltaics.

Solar House, Freiburg, Germany

In 1992 a house was completed for the Fraunhofer Institute for Solar Energy Research in Freiburg im Breisgau (Figure 4.7). Described as a self-sufficient solar house, it was an experimental design to test the viability of energy self-sufficiency. It was well ahead of its time in terms of thermally efficient construction, with south, east and west elevations constituting a Trombe wall. This consisted of 300mm calcium silicate blocks behind acrylic glass honeycomb transparent insulation material (TIM) with integral blinds between the TIM and external glazing. With the blinds closed the U-value was $0.5W/m^2K$ and $0.4W/m^2K$ with

Figure 4.6 Passive solar houses 1998, Hockerton Self-Sufficient Housing Project south elevation and conservatories, interior

Figure 4.7 Solar House, Freiburg, Fraunhofer Institute for Solar Energy Research

them open. The unglazed north wall comprised 300mm calcium silicate blocks supporting 240mm of cellulose fibre insulation protected by timber boarding.

Roof mounted PV cells provide electricity and solar thermal panels serve the domestic hot water system. A unique feature of the house was that the PVs were connected to an electrolyser that produced hydrogen for a fuel cell to provide continuous electricity. Triple-glazed low-E (low emissivity) windows of U-value $0.6W/m^2K$ completed the specification for a highly innovative house well ahead of its time. The only serious problem that the experiment exposed was that the fuel cell capacity was inadequate during periods of extreme cold.

State of the art housing 2009

The experimental solar house is proof that, in the 1990s, the city of Freiburg was a pace setter in terms of exploiting solar energy, which, in 2008, caused the *Observer* to describe it as possibly 'the greenest city in the world' (*Observer Magazine*, 23 March 2008). As its significance extends beyond the characteristics of individual buildings, it will be considered in some detail in Chapter 8, concerned with eco-towns.

The result is that Freiburg has achieved a high level of energy efficiency in its buildings, with a significant number realizing the PassivHaus energy consumption standard of $15kWh/m^2/year$ (Figures 4.8 and 4.9).

Source: Wikipedia

Figure 4.8 Sonnenschiff Energy Plus development

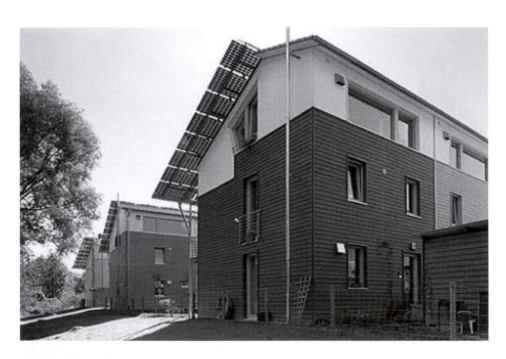

Figure 4.9 Solar Village (Solarsiedlung), Freiburg

Sustainability and the Solarsiedlung

The Solarsiedlung is a mixed development of commercial units and housing. The houses are designed to PassivHaus standard. This includes:

- 400mm of insulation in the walls and 450mm in the roof;
- 1000m² of roof mounted PVs providing 135kWp electricity;
- no air conditioning – the project relies on passive cross ventilation with night time purging; coloured panels projecting 400mm from the facade allow cool air to enter the building via grilles that offer security;
- a community combined heat and power (CHP) plant, with 80 per cent of its fuel provided by the adjacent Black Forest and 20 per cent from gas; there is supplementary heat from solar thermal vacuum tube panels on the roofs;
- ground source heat pumps provide heat in winter and cooling in summer.

All the terraced houses face south, with large windows to maximize solar gain. The space between blocks ensures insulation in winter. The aim of the scheme is for a combination of energy efficiency and renewable sources to provide all the energy demands of the scheme. In some cases there is an energy surplus. Where electricity is exported to the grid, the owner receives €0.42/kWh for 20 years.

Developments in the UK

There is an eco-project still under construction is the satellite community of Upton in Northampton. Its homes all reach the BRE Environmental Assessment Method (BREEAM) standard of excellence. This means they all represent significant improvements over the current building regulations. BREEAM has now been supplemented by the Sustainable Building Code as outlined below. Some houses feature PVs and others solar thermal panels. Nevertheless, the contrast with eco-homes in Freiburg is stark (Figure 4.10). There is little doubt that the influence of the Prince of Wales Architecture

Figure 4.10 Eco-homes in Upton, Northampton, UK

Institute has been decisive in determining the style. It is no coincidence that it echoes the architecture of the Institute's blueprint for one of the proposed government eco-towns.

There are two notes of architectural defiance in Upton. The first is sounded by the new primary school, the second is the ZedFactory terrace of RuralZed houses (Figure 4.11), designed by the Bill Dunster team that produced the mould-breaking BedZed scheme in south London. To understand the significance of this small island of excellence in Upton, it is necessary to explain how the UK government is bent on reaching the goal of zero carbon homes by 2016 in response to accelerating climate change. To be precise, it has declared its intention to exceed the PassivHaus standard with level 6 of the Sustainable Homes Standard. In December 2006 the Department of Communities and Local Government of the UK issued its standards for sustainable homes on a scale of 1–6.

UK Sustainable Building Code

Under the Code for Sustainable Homes (CSH) there are nine categories of compliance. Table 4.1 refers to standards for CO_2 emissions. Table 4.2 describes the nine environmental categories involved in compliance.

The last level in Table 4.1 is meant to represent a net 'zero carbon home', inclusive of heating, lighting, hot water and all other energy uses in the home. This, of course, means that there must be an onsite source of renewable energy (electricity and heat).

Table 4.1 Star ratings for mandatory minimum standards in CO_2 emissions under the Code for Sustainable Homes representing improvements over the Building Regulations Part L

Code Level	Minimum percentage reduction in dwelling emission rate over target emission rate
Level 1 (∗)	10
Level 2 (∗∗)	18
Level 3 (∗∗∗)	25
Level 4 (∗∗∗∗)	44
Level 5 (∗∗∗∗∗)	100
Level 6 (∗∗∗∗∗∗)	'Zero Carbon Home'

Source: Code for Sustainable Homes – setting the standard in sustainability for new homes; Department for Communities and Local Government, 2006

The Bill Dunster RuralZed design for a three-bedroom house in basic kit form for a medium density development achieves Code level 3 (Figure 4.11). As such it represents a 25 per cent improvement over the current building regulations. It has a timber frame structure that contains 50mm concrete panels forming the inner face of the walls. Further thermal mass is provided by vaulted terracotta ceiling panels supported by first floor joists. The surface of the ground and first floors comprises waxed concrete slabs that create a smooth surface. Altogether 21 tonnes of concrete provide substantial thermal mass. In the external walls, studwork between the structural members contains 300mm of rockwool insulation. Mandatory air tightness is achieved with a high performance vapour-permeable membrane. The area of the basic home is 88m².

To meet Code level 4 the design employs passive ventilation with heat recovery, together with solar water heating and a wood chip boiler.

Figure 4.11 RuralZed homes in Upton, Northampton, UK

Table 4.2 Summary of the environmental categories and issues of the Code for Sustainable Homes

Categories	Issue
Energy and CO_2 emissions	Dwelling emission rate (mandatory) Building fabric Internal lighting Drying space Energy labelled white goods External lighting Low or zero carbon (LZC) technologies Cycle storage Home office
Water	Indoor water use (mandatory) External water use
Materials	Environmental impact of materials (mandatory) Responsible sourcing of materials – basic building elements Responsible sourcing of materials – finishing elements
Surface Water Run-off	Management of Surface Water Run-off from developments (mandatory) Flood risk
Waste	Storage of non-recyclable waste and recyclable household waste (mandatory) Construction waste management (mandatory) Composting
Pollution	Global warming potential (GWP) of insulants NO_x emissions
Health and Well-being	Daylighting Sound insulation Private space Lifetime homes (mandatory)
Management	Home user guide Considerate constructors scheme Construction site impacts Security
Ecology	Ecological value of site Ecological enhancement Protection of ecological features Change in ecological value of site Building footprint

Source: Code for Sustainable Homes – setting the standard in sustainability for new homes; Department for Communities and Local Government, 2006

Level 5 would need the addition of seven south facing 180W PV panels and a green roof on the north slope. Rainwater harvesting completes the specification. To achieve level 6 requires the addition of a sunspace plus 21 more PV panels to meet the needs of lighting and appliances. This brings the area to 100m^2.

As mentioned, the forerunner to RuralZed was the Beddington Zero Energy Development (BedZed) in south London. It was the first sizeable community development to be based on ultra low energy principles. It is described in detail in Smith, 2007, pp157–162.

BRE Innovation Exhibition 2007

In 2007 housing developers were invited to contribute to an exhibition site at the Building Research Establishment (BRE) in Watford. Each was to illustrate how its design fulfilled the requirements of the Code at levels 4–6. The Innovation site, was also intended to illustrate the versatility of 'offsite' or factory fabricated construction. They were all designed to fit on a compact site, which meant that some went to three storeys (Figure 4.12). Part of the intention was to expose some of the problems that might arise under such demanding conditions and, among others, the following two issues came to light.

The first was that several examples initially failed to meet the required level of air tightness. This was understandable in a project that was experimental (Olcayto, 2007). It also demonstrated that some types of construction make it easier to realize this goal.

The second problem concerns thermal mass. Surviving the future will not just require high standards of energy efficiency but also high levels of thermal mass and structural robustness. This raises questions about the long-term viability of lightweight structure homes like the Osborne example in Figures 4.12 and 4.13.

The Hanson 2 example on the BRE site was much more in tune with the needs of the future, being of heavyweight construction for walls and floors (Figures 4.14 and 4.15).

Composite brick and concrete insulated panels were fabricated offsite. This, plus a concrete

Figure 4.12 Osborne House at BRE with lightweight construction and low thermal mass

Figure 4.13 Wall sections, Osborne House

Figure 4.14 Hanson 2, Architects T P Bennett

Figure 4.15 Hanson 2, first floor living room

change. But maybe things are changing if the latest demonstration home at BRE is anything to go by.

In May 2008, BRE unveiled a demonstration house that it claims to be Sustainable Building Code level 6 and therefore genuinely zero carbon. But here's the rub. A house to this standard with its high level of thermal mass could cost up to £500,000 to be constructed, plus site costs. It could end up costing three quarters of a million (Figure 4.16).

Returning to the zero carbon debate, there are conflicting views. Homes can be designed to be near zero carbon in terms of space heating and cooling, but there are numerous other systems in a home that have carbon consequences: lighting, cooking, white goods, TVs and so on. If a house is to be truly carbon neutral it must receive sufficient power from renewable technologies to meet these associated demands. The government seems bent on insisting this must be generated from either integrated or onsite renewable systems. Is this realistic?

plank first floor, gives the house the thermal mass that will make 40°C summers tolerable as well as give it the structural robustness to cope with expected 140mph storms.

For a start, creating volume housing that is genuinely future-proof will require a radical shift in design standards compared with current building regulations and even compared to the standards demonstrated at the BRE Offsite exhibition. So far the building industry has not demonstrated its willingness to adapt to radical

Figure 4.16 Zero Carbon house by Barratt Homes and Architects Gaunt Francis

If future-proof homes are to be zero carbon in an absolute sense, this means that they must employ integrated or onsite energy production from PVs, Ground Source (GS) heat pumps, solar thermal and possibly micro-wind if conditions allow.

Department for Communities and Local Government Case Studies: Code for Sustainable Homes 2009

Mid-Street, South Nutfield, Surrey, CSH level 5

This is a development of 2 × two-bedroom flats. The construction is of prefabricated timber structural insulated panels (SIPS). The SIPS system incorporates mineral wool and expanded polystyrene insulation. The floor is concrete beam and block with mineral wool and expanded polystyrene insulation (Figure 4.17). The key sustainability features of this development are:

- passive solar design;
- low flow rate sanitary ware;
- rainwater recycling;
- low energy lighting;
- PV array;
- biomass pellet boiler;
- low energy rated white goods;
- FSC certified timber;
- mechanical ventilation with heat recovery;
- windows are triple-glazed with low-e glass.

Area	U-value	Construction
Walls	0.14	SIPS panels with 50mm external insulation
Roof	0.13	Timber with concrete tiles and 400mm mineral wool
Floor	0.14	Concrete beam and block with 75mm insulation
Windows	0.80	Triple-glazed low-e
Doors	1.2	Fully insulated

Source: Department of Communities and Local Government

Figure 4.17 DCLG case study: 4 Mid Street, South Nutfield, Surrey, achieving Code Level 5

The original intention was to design for air permeability at the PassivHaus standard of 1m³/h@50Pa. This was relaxed to 3m³/h@50Pa due to achieving trade-offs through other CSH requirements. Final tests resulted in 4.9m³/h@50Pa. This echoes the problems at the BRE Innovation exhibition with SIPS construction and seems to be inherent in this form of system building in addition to its deficiencies regarding thermal mass.

Energy Homes Project, Nottingham University

The PassivHaus principle is behind the decision of Nottingham University to promote the construction of six demonstration houses under its Energy Homes Project on its campus. The benchmark is the PassivHaus standard for energy consumption of 15kWh/m²/year. The first to be completed was the BASF funded example (Figure 4.18). The second, the Stoneguard house, is nearing completion and two further houses will be built by Tarmac. Another home illustrates how a 1930s semi-detached house may

Figure 4.18 BASF PassivHaus, Nottingham University

be upgraded to near PassivHaus standard. The BASF house is expected to achieve near zero carbon energy efficiency. Its cost is expected to attract first time buyers.

The U–values (in W/m^2K) are as follows:

Area	U-value	Construction
Internal glazed screen to sun space	1.7	
Double-glazed external screen to sun space	2.7	
Walls and roof	0.15	
Windows	1.66	Double-glazed to north elevation

The notable design features of this house include:

- efficient compact plan;
- extensive passive solar gain with sun space – in winter it contributes to heating through controlled solar gain and underground air pumped in to preheat the space; in summer underground air contributes to cooling;
- high insulation levels and small openings to north, east and west;
- ground source heat pump for heating and cooling;
- ground floor construction consisting of insulated concrete formwork (Figure 4.20);
- first floor comprises 150mm polyurethane foam insulated structural panels;

- air tightness and thermal bridging is improved by 90 per cent over current practice;
- thermal mass is enhanced by phase–change material designed for lightweight buildings;
- first floor and roof are finished in Corus Colorcoat Urban cladding with the roof coated in heat reflective pigments achieving a U-value of $0.15W/m^2K$; the roof is certified as 'drinking water safe';
- solar thermal panels should provide 80 per cent of hot water needs;
- biomass boiler to provide extra heat when needed, fuelled by wood pellets;
- rainwater is fed via a fine filter to a 3300l tank for use in the garden and non–potable purposes in the home.

The energy use is expected to be roughly $12kWh/m^2/y$ compared with $15kWh/m^2/y$ for the PassivHaus.

The Stoneguard C60 house (Figures 4.19–4.21) has four bedrooms and a basement. It will be occupied by staff and students who will monitor the building's performance. It features a steel frame structure together with many of the ecological and environmental features of the BASF house. In addition it employs sunpipes to maximize natural lighting. It has a grey water management system to reuse shower/bath water for flushing as well as a rainwater harvesting system. It is expected to be completed by early 2010.

The real challenge for the future will be how to reduce the energy consumption of the existing housing stock in the UK, currently responsible for 27 per cent of all CO_2 emissions. According to Dr Mark Gillott, research and

Figure 4.19 Stoneguard House, Nottingham University

Figure 4.21 Steel frame, Stoneguard house

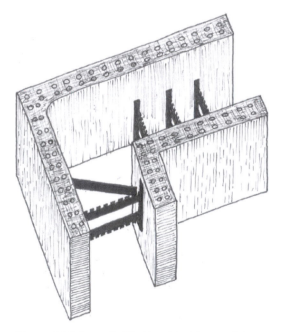

Figure 4.20 Concrete filled insulated formwork to the ground floor

project manager for Creative Homes in the university, 21 million homes, or 86 per cent of the current total, will still be in use in 2050.

As with the high standards set by Parker Morris for social housing in the 1960s and 1970s, so today a way has to be found to build affordable homes that will nevertheless be able to tolerate torrid summers and cold and stormy winters. In many locations they will have to be proof against flash floods as torrential rain episodes and storm surges multiply in frequency and intensity. The aim should be to produce buildings that are as far ahead of Code level 6 as that level is above current building regulations. Will it be possible?

Note

1   U-value is the rate at which the heat flows from a unit of area (usually $1m^2$) through an element at 1°C of temperature difference. The lower the value the better the level of insulation.

5

Future-proof Housing

Advancing from the small handful of zero carbon homes currently being built to 240,000 homes a year within nine years will challenge everyone connected with the industry... There are major risks which the market, on its own, will not resolve.

(Callcutt Review, *An Overview of the Housebuilding Industry*, 2007, p88)

This is a clear admission that the goal of achieving the zero carbon standard for homes across the board by 2016 will be impossible without the help of government. What form this help might take has still to be revealed. First it is necessary to distinguish between 'carbon neutral' and 'zero carbon'. The first can be achieved by offsetting carbon emissions through investment, for example, in renewable energy projects or securing sustainable tree planting, usually in developing countries. 'Zero carbon' usually only applies to buildings and means that there are no net CO_2 emissions per year. Buildings are allowed to emit CO_2 provided it is offset by renewables, either integrated or onsite.

However, *zero carbon is not enough*, for reasons to be explained. In an article published in the *Guardian* on 1 October 2008, Vicky Pope, head of climate change research at the Met Office, claimed there are now relatively firm predictions to the year 2100 regarding impacts of climate change. Assumptions come under four scenarios.

Scenario One

- CO_2 emissions start to decrease worldwide by 2010.
- Reductions soon reach 3 per cent per year.
- This produces a 47 per cent decrease by 2050.
- Global average temperature by 2100 is between 2.1° and 2.8°C above 1990 level.

Even this could be crossing the threshold into irreversible climate change. The impacts could include 20–30 per cent of species at a higher risk of extinction. There is a likelihood of increased damage from storms and floods. In addition, above 2°C plants and soils begin to lose their capacity to absorb CO_2; warmer seas are also less able to soak up CO_2.

Scenario Two

- There is an early but slow decline in emissions.
- Action starts in 2010.
- Reductions average 1 per cent per year.
- Emissions return to 1990 levels by 2050.
- Temperature rise is between 2.9° and 3.8°C by 2100.

The impacts of this scenario include up to a 30 per cent loss of coastal wetlands; a sea level rise of several metres due to melting ice sheets; heat waves, floods and droughts causing significant loss of life.

Under this scenario there is every chance that the temperature will rise above 4°C, which is regarded as the tipping point into accelerating climate impacts due to the release of methane from permafrost and ocean hydrates. It should be remembered that methane is not included in current IPCC calculations.

Scenario Three

- There is a delayed and slow decline in emissions.
- Action starts in 2030 with reductions in line with scenario two.
- Emissions would increase by 76 per cent above 1990 level by 2050.
- Temperature rise is 4–5.2°C.

The impacts of scenario three include up to 15 million people being at risk from flooding and 3 million facing water stress. The heat would impact on food production worldwide, especially in low latitudes.

Scenario Four

- The present situation of BaU is maintained throughout the century.
- CO_2 emissions increase by 132 per cent above 1990 level by 2050.
- Temperature rise is 5.5–7.1°C.

In terms of impacts this is unknown territory but by 2100 there would be major extinctions, severe coastal erosion, flooding of low lying land and 10–20 per cent loss of ice in the Arctic tundra.

At the current rate of progress in international achievements in tackling climate change, there are good reasons for believing that adaptation policy in terms of the built environment should assume the third or fourth scenarios. Even if this proves to have been too pessimistic, there is also the energy situation to consider, meaning that extra costs will soon be recovered in energy efficiency gains.

The design determinants for climate-proof housing

In certain respects, housing standards in the developed world have been raised as a *reaction* to current climate change impacts. The time has come to be *proactive* because the world's climate is changing for the worse at a pace that exceeds expectations. Consequently housing deserves special consideration because it is the one area of building that most affects the quality of life and is also intergenerational. It is estimated that 87 per cent of the housing existing today will still be standing in 2050. In fact, in the UK, at the present rate of replacement, it will take at least 1000 years before all homes have been replaced. With such a long-life investment at stake, it is wise to consider *now* the features of homes that will be necessary if the worst case climate predictions of impacts materialize. This means setting standards for design that will be valid for decades ahead, including features that do not figure in either the passive house programme or the UK Code for Sustainable Homes.

Current progress in achieving international agreement to curb CO_2 emissions would suggest that it is logical to consider the design features that will soften the blow if the IPCC high emissions or worst case scenario materializes. At present, this is the odds-on favourite. We must therefore consider what our housing stock will be likely to have to withstand as the century progresses.

Even in the unlikely event that the world manages to stabilize CO_2 emissions before fossil fuels run out, extreme impacts are almost inevitable. These can be summarized as:

- extreme storms in the hurricane and tornado category;
- extremes of temperature, possibly cold as well as hot, if the jet stream route changes and/or the Gulf Stream circulation breaks down;
- episodes of extreme rainfall producing flash floods;
- alternatively, extended droughts affecting structures;

- storm surges leading to extended flooding especially in flood plains;
- rising sea level amplified by low pressure, currently running at 3mm/year.

Many places in the world are already experiencing hurricanes or typhoons in category 4. This means wind speeds between 131 and 155mph. Recent experience shows that the US is not immune from such events. Even northern Europe has not escaped as demonstrated by the localized but devastating storm that demolished most of the village of Hautmont in northern France in August 2008. As such storms are likely to be more widely distributed and possibly more frequent in the future, the precautionary principle dictates that we should be considering now how houses should be designed to withstand such an onslaught from nature.

Many of the features required for our houses to withstand wind storms will, in fact, be relevant to several of the extreme impacts. To fully appreciate the scope of the changes that will be necessary, it will be logical, first, to consider the elements of a house.

Walls

The shift away from masonry to lightweight construction, usually with timber, but also featuring pressed steel members, is not just confined to the UK. The increasing trend in the US to achieve the PassivHaus standard is, in many cases, being realized through timber frame construction. More than anything, this is an economy measure.

The 2008 Innovation exhibition at the UK Building Research Establishment (BRE) has highlighted how developers see the route to achieving Code for Sustainable Homes levels 4–6, as is soon to be required by government regulations. The common feature of all the houses is that they were largely fabricated offsite. Only one, the Hanson 2 house, featured fully brick and block construction for its external walls.

From the point of view of storms, climate-proof homes will need to be of heavyweight masonry construction. The recommendation is that the masonry component of external walls should add up to at least 240mm, for example, external element 140mm dense concrete blocks and internal leaf, 100mm. Alternatively, offsite concrete construction can meet the standard, provided the cross section is robust and quality control impeccable. If insulated offsite panels are to be employed, then they would be suitable if supported within steel frame construction (see Figure 5.4 below). A suggestion as to how such techniques could be employed in masonry are illustrated in Figure 5.5.

External walls alone will not suffice. Internal partitions should be of concrete block construction at least 112mm thick. Structural stiffness is as important as the strength of external walls. Ground and first floors ideally should be made of concrete, either formed in situ or as precast units that can accommodate services.

Roofs

Both pitched and flat roofs are the first to go when it comes to succumbing to storm damage. Even the relatively modest storms experienced by the UK have revealed the weaknesses in much modern roof construction. Timber sections are frequently reduced to a minimum for reasons of economy.

Whilst timber mostly has excellent sustainability credentials, it is not being used in sections that are robust enough to withstand extreme storms. It is not only absolute wind speed that does the damage but also sudden changes of direction, as is characteristic of tornados. Cross-section standards for roof timbers should be revised to take account of anticipated loading. Joints between key members should be made using steel connectors and bolts in place of the gang-nail trusses that are currently popular.

Storms generate huge suction forces, so it is essential that roof members are firmly attached to external walls. In the early 1960s Sheffield experienced extreme winds that wrought havoc with domestic roofs and resulted in changes in building regulations so that that roofs were required to be anchored to walls with steel straps. Future risks have increased by orders of magnitude. In the examples that are illustrated, it is suggested that a ring beam in concrete or steel should cap the external walls and create a robust connection to roof members as well as providing anchorage to the walls.

The 30° pitch is the optimal angle for PVs and solar thermal panels. High pitch roofs considerably increase the wind load during storms. However, this means that conventional roof tiles are mostly inappropriate. In this circumstance, metal sheet covering is the most common alternative, particularly zinc with standing seam joints[1] finished in heat-reflective paint. This would also facilitate the later addition of solar panels if they are not installed at the outset.

Windows and doors

Triple glazing in timber frames should be standard throughout, achieving a U-value of less than $1.0 W/m^2 K$. However, even these may be vulnerable to failure in super-storms. This is one of several reasons for recommending a return to the traditional practice of fitting external shutters, which also protect against extreme temperatures. 'Concertina' type shutters regularly feature in new buildings in mainland Europe (Figure 5.1).

Sustainability approved hardwood external doors should exceed current thermal building

regulations and feature a window in toughened glass only large enough for identification purposes.

Where possible, houses should be orientated with their gable ends east–west with minimum openings. This will offer protection from prevailing winds. Where possible, natural wind breaks should be exploited. There is even a place for the Leylandii hedge, provided it is kept in check.

Temperature

In the formulation of building regulations like the UK's Part L, the emphasis up to now has been on conserving warmth. In the future it is probable that keeping cool will be as important as retaining heat. In the government's Planning Policy Statement: Eco-Towns, concerning standards for proposed eco-towns, it states that houses should 'incorporate best practice on overheating'. This throws into doubt the viability of lightweight structures that can be efficient at retaining heat but are deficient in avoiding overheating.

A Met Office report commissioned by the Department of Works and Pensions in 2008 concluded that 'the weather may become so hot that Britain's poor and elderly will need state help to pay their summer energy bills as they reach for air conditioners to prevent themselves dying from heat exhaustion'. The report concluded that, by 2050, summers of the intensity of 2003 will occur every other year (*Guardian,* 8 January 2009, p9). It is worth repeating the TCPA warning in Chapter 2 to expect 40–48°C summers.

The UK has adopted the target of 2 million new homes by 2016 and 3 million by 2020. This was repeated at a time when the construction of new homes had almost come to a halt as contractors were denied loan facilities. The official view is that the only way such targets can be realized is if offsite, factory prefabrication is optimized. This favours timber frame lightweight construction as demonstrated by the Innovation exhibition at the BRE, featured in Chapter 4. The advantages are speed of erection and cost.

Figure 5.1 Folding sliding shutters

The overriding disadvantages are that such construction techniques will be vulnerable to failure in hurricane scale storms, as mentioned, and that, as demonstration examples have shown, it can be difficult to achieve the Code level of air tightness.

Above all, the poor thermal mass of these buildings will create interiors that amplify the peaks of outside temperature but do not respond to the troughs. In others words high temperatures are sustained overnight. The killer factor in the 2003 heatwave was the persistence for weeks of night temperatures at around 35°C. This means that the zero carbon credentials of such houses will be compromised by the use of room-size air-cooling units in high summer, especially at night.

As discussed in Chapter 4, the Hanson 2 house at the BRE exhibition was the only one that achieved anything approaching a significant capacity of thermal mass. This capacity is where the specification for storm protection coincides with the need for thermal mass and is an issue that should be considered separately from thermal efficiency as defined by U-values. This reinforces the argument in favour of at least 240mm of masonry in external walls. At least 150mm of insulation should be incorporated to meet Code 6 thermal requirements (see Figure 5.5 below).

A further advantage of masonry construction is that it is more efficient at achieving the mandatory level of air tightness than lightweight structures, which, as mentioned have encountered difficulties in this respect.

Thermal mass, or volumetric heat capacity (VHC), is the ability of a material to store heat or cooling when subject to a temperature change, without undergoing a phase change. It is measured in kilojoules/m² K. Typical values are: concrete 2060 and brickwork 1360. So, high thermal mass evens out the peaks and troughs of the external temperature. In winter it stores heat and in summer reduces heat absorption whilst also facilitating night time purging. In houses this can be achieved passively. The BedZed and RuralZed projects

employ rooftop cowls that have vanes that orientate the cowl to the prevailing wind. This means that the ventilation inlet faces upwind and exhaust air is extracted by suction downwind. In winter a heat exchanger transfers the warmth from the exhaust air to the incoming fresh air (see Figure 4.11).

It has been estimated that the 'thermal lag' in a high thermal mass office building can be six hours. As climate impacts gather momentum, it will be likely that building regulations will have to include minimum standards for thermal mass (RIBA, 2007).

Phase change materials (PCMs) can supplement thermal mass. PCM plaster contains nodules of wax that change from a liquid to a solid and vice versa according to the temperature, thereby absorbing or releasing heat. PCMs can be located in ceiling voids into which air is drawn by a fan, either to be recirculated in during the day or released to the exterior for night time cooling.[2]

There may be objections to these recommendations on the grounds that heavyweight construction involves substantially more embodied energy than the lightweight counterpart. The repost is that it will have a long life expectancy as a whole and in respect of its components. This comes at a price. However, according to engineering consultants Atelier Ten, 'High mass, conventional buildings with tested conventional materials have a much longer life in use than lightweight construction. The lifespan of many lightweight buildings, with their reliance on mastics and exposed metals, is often quite short – as little as 25 years is not uncommon. On the other hand, conventional and traditional buildings have been shown to last hundreds of years.'

In many instances the on-costs could be offset by lower insurance premiums. Where homes are due to be built on flood plains only radical measures may make properties insurable. There is always the 'peace of mind' factor of a property that will appreciate in value as the effects of climate change become ever more apparent.

Source: Architect: the author

Figure 5.2 Passive solar house, 1968

Passive solar gain

Not all environmental impacts come with a price tag. In the 1960s, passive solar gain became the first step on a journey that has culminated in the idea of zero carbon homes (Figure 5.2).

Solar gain from a low angle winter sun is still a valuable commodity that should be incorporated in design. Triple-glazed windows and insulated shutters offer protection when the cold is not alleviated by solar gain.

Torrential rain and flash floods

Here again, there is a contrast between lightweight and masonry houses. The combination of rain and high winds has proved too much for some timber framed residential developments in Europe. In the future, structural robustness will be a much prized virtue for homes.

The UK, mainland Europe and the US have all experienced severe disruption caused by episodes of torrential rain, usually in the hills where runoff discharges into rivers and streams. The ground is unable to soak up such intensive inundation with the result that watercourses downstream overflow and overwhelm rural and urban drainage systems. With a house building programme as ambitious as that declared by the UK government, it is inevitable that homes will be built in areas that have experienced severe flash flooding, as illustrated in Chapter 2. In this case additional measures must be adopted, both in terms of individual homes and the wider environment. For example, in the eco-village of Upton in Northampton, the risk of flooding has been reduced by a network of substantial drainage channels running parallel to the houses (Figure 5.3).

The flash flood problem has been exacerbated by extensive developments requiring large areas of hard surface with runoff consequences. In new developments, like supermarkets, it must become mandatory for hard surfaces other than roads to be porous. This should also apply to the paving over of domestic gardens to create parking in areas where on-street parking is becoming more difficult and/or expensive.

Building over flood plain areas is particularly hazardous, yet, as mentioned, the pressure for new homes makes such development inevitable. This is why special measures need to be taken to enable such homes to remain habitable and to obtain insurance. Speaking at an Institute of Economic Affairs conference *The Future of General Insurance*, Dr Paul Leinster, chief executive of the New Environment Agency, warned the insurance industry that flood-hit houses should be rebuilt to be better prepared for flooding. 'Where homes are flooded, we want them rebuilt to more flood resilient standards.' He told the conference that the annual cost of damage from flooding could rise from the present £1 billion to £25 billion by 2080. The number at a high risk from flooding could rise from 1.5 million to 3.5 million. He went on to advise that insurance companies could offer incentives to people to take flood protection measures. This should be equally, or more, true for new developments.

Figure 5.3 Storm ditch between rows of houses, Upton, Northampton, UK

Structural recommendations

The most obvious flood protection strategy is to raise buildings on stilts. This would be most straightforward with a steel frame option that would serve both individual houses and multi-storey apartments. The open ground floor would provide parking space that could be evacuated on the announcement of flood warnings (Figure 5.4).

Alternatively, there are numerous waterproofing systems available, some of which consist of a surface coating. For example, a paint-on material Penetron creates a tight crystalline web within the structure of concrete, making it watertight. However, traditionalists will claim that the only reliable, long-life technique able to withstand the pressure from serious flooding is tanking. Figure 5.5 illustrates how this is achieved in a high thermal mass structure.

At the same time, doors and windows that extend below dado height should have watertight seals. The most fail-safe method would be inflatable seals triggered manually by the same mechanism as that used in vehicle air bags.

The most effective design for flood-prone areas involves the inclusion of a semi-basement. This can be reasonably cost-effective if the excavation adopts the cut-and-fill method, avoiding earth removal. This method has the advantage of raising the ground floor at least one metre above ground level. The BREEAM Eco-homes recommendation is:

> *Where assessed development is situated in a flood zone that is defined as having a medium annual probability of flooding, the ground level of all dwellings and access to them and the site are designed so that they are at least 600mm above the design level of the flood zone.*
>
> (EcoHomes and the Code for Sustainable Homes, BRE, 2007)

In either case, the problem of access for the disabled remains to be resolved.

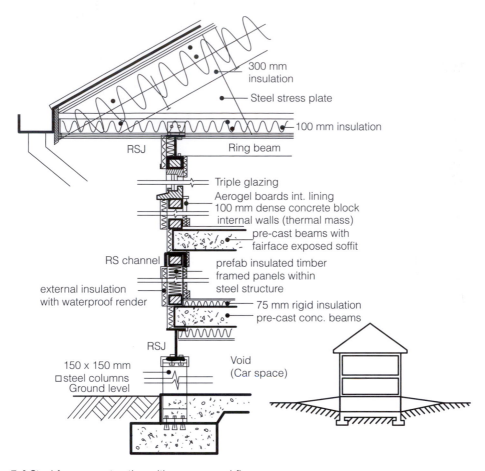

Figure 5.4 Steel frame construction with open ground floor

A detailed cost analysis will be necessary to determine which is the more cost-effective between the steel frame and masonry systems. The advantage of the former is that much of it can be prefabricated, whereas the latter has better thermal mass.

In Holland there is a growing appetite for homes with in-built flotation chambers. However, these are mostly intended as permanent floating homes which can rise and fall as water level dictates. The time may come when the shortage of land following sea level rise will make this an option for the UK. It would seem to be an extravagance at present.

Appliances will need special attention. A retrofit flood protection programme in South Yorkshire has provided 'bung' seals for WCs; not elegant but presumably effective, pending design changes. Sanitary ware manufacturers will have to be persuaded to provide basins, baths and showers with screw-down plugs and without overflow openings.

In the 2007 floods in Gloucestershire the inundation of a major electricity substation was just avoided. Had it been flooded, thousands of homes would have been without electricity perhaps for weeks. In flood risk areas like the Severn and Thames valleys it would be prudent for roof PVs to serve dual AC/DC appliances and fittings as well as keeping a bank of batteries fully charged.

The rising demand for new houses and the pressure to bring many of them within the range of first-time buyers highlights the dilemma facing developers and designers on the one hand and the government responsible for standards on

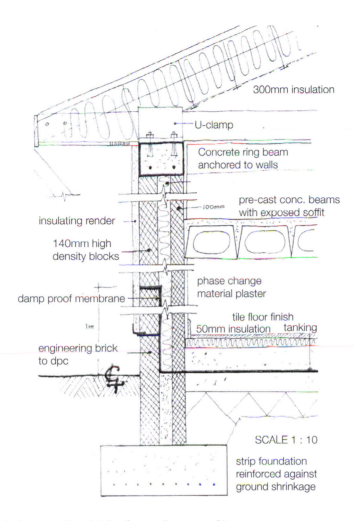

Figure 5.5 Suggested construction details of near-climate-proof houses

the other. Is it a case of the best being the enemy of the good? The purpose of this and subsequent chapters is to consider the design challenge assuming the worst case climate change outcome. Given a near miracle, CO_2 emissions may be stabilized before runaway climate change is triggered. However, the prospect of peak oil and rapidly diminishing reserves is beyond the scope of miracles. Energy efficiency and fossil free alternatives for power are not options but inevitabilities.

Some home buyers will be aware of the value of investing in a near climate-proof home, 'but this translates only weakly into buying preferences: it ranks well behind the key requirements of price, size and location. This is insufficient to motivate housebuilders or, through them, the rest of the market' (Callcut Review, 2007, p89).

Only radical revision of the building regulations will succeed in delivering the quality of homes that will withstand the impacts of the coming decades.

Figure 5.5 is an outline idea of the kind of construction that should protect against high temperatures and all but the worst of flash floods. It has traditional tanking to at least 1m above ground level and inflatable seals to doors and marine-type seals to windows. There would also be measures to protect against upsurge via appliances. High thermal mass is provided by external walls, floors and partitions. PCM plaster could enhance the thermal mass.

Extra structural strength, such as a reinforced concrete ring beam securing the roof members, is provided to protect against hurricane level storms. Reinforced foundations protect against damage through ground shrinkage, which can be an effect of a severe drought – also one of the predicted impacts of climate change. Folding shutters protect quadruple-glazed windows. Masonry construction guarantees that the highest air tightness standard will be achieved in conjunction with heat recovery low power mechanical ventilation. The warm air could be enhanced by a ground source heat pump. The extended south facing 30° roof would be covered with PVs and solar thermal panels. Substantial eaves overhangs will offer solar shading in summer. In winter the south elevation would make the most of passive solar gain. This could be the nearest we ever get to a zero carbon house.

There will be those who argue that such building practices will involve much greater embodied energy than the timber frame alternative. Expended energy is a function of materials and construction on the one hand and life expectancy on the other. On this basis high thermal mass masonry homes could show a much better balance in their energy account than their timber counterparts. Then there is the matter of robustness.

Advocates of timber may point to Tudor timber frame buildings that are still standing after 500 years. However, these were usually constructed of hardwood, mostly oak, often of a cross section with a massive margin of safety (redundancy). Even so, oak is not infallible. In 1983 I was commissioned to carry out a restoration survey in the President's Lodge in Cloister Court at Queens' College, Cambridge. This included a timber long gallery placed above a brick cloister. A massive oak 'keel' beam running the length of the centre of the cloister was supporting the floor of the long gallery. I discovered this had split along its length at the point where floor joists were halved into it. Engineers consulted on the matter considered that there could have been a catastrophic collapse at any time, given the right wind loading. In mitigation, the beam was at least 400 years old (Smith, 1983).

Solar assisted desiccant dehumidification with air conditioning

In periods of high temperature it will be necessary for high thermal mass homes to expel daytime accumulated heat by night purging. This can be achieved by solar-driven desiccant cooling, which involves a cycle including a desiccant wheel and thermal wheel in tandem to provide both cooling and dehumidification (Figure 5.6). A more detailed explanation of the system is given in the Appendix to this chapter.

An argument that continues to be raised against add-on costs due to climate change is that there is still uncertainty in the science. Therefore it is imprudent to invest now in future impacts that may never arise. This view is countered by the chief scientist at the Met Office.

> *One should not over-state uncertainty… Some features in current predictions for the UK are expected on physical grounds and are consistent across a range of models, including significant warming, rise in sea level and increased winter rainfall… The aim, [of the Met Office] as ever, is to ensure that government and industry have the best available climate advice to guide future investment.*
>
> (Mitchell, 2008, p26)

It is inevitable that additional costs of construction making these sorts of provisions will be significantly higher than for lightweight constructions, but these should be offset by reduced insurance costs and the inherent value of a climate-secure investment. There is also the avoided cost of energy/CO_2 that is likely to be incurred by portable air conditioning units that

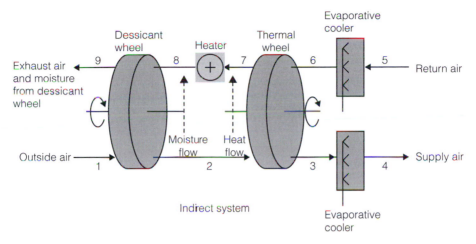

Figure 5.6 Desiccant wheel and thermal wheel dehumidification and cooling

lightweight frame structures will need during torrid summers.

Finally, there is rising concern that Level 6 of the Code for Sustainable Homes can only be achieved with energy from onsite renewables. An alternative is a renewable energy levy per kg of CO_2 paid by the developer according to a desk top calculation of the annual per m² CO_2 in excess of zero carbon. The levy should be administered by a Trust independent of government with its income earmarked for the provision of utility scale renewables. Each house would have its energy monitored showing its CO_2 equivalent. After one year a post occupancy evaluation (POE) would adjust the levy amount as necessary, with any excess added to energy bills. This would be more efficient and reliable than offsetting schemes, which have thrown up numerous problems.

Appendix

Desiccant dehumidification and evaporative cooling

In some environments a combination of high temperature and high humidity defies a remedy by conventional air conditioning that is biased towards temperature rather than humidity.

Dehumidification is merely a by-product of bringing the temperature down to below the dew point of the air causing condensation.

A desiccant is a hygroscopic material, liquid or solid, which can extract moisture from humid air, gas or liquids. Liquid desiccants work by absorption – moisture is taken up by chemical action. Solid desiccants have a large internal area capable of absorbing significant quantities of water by capillary action. Examples of efficient desiccants are:

- silica gel;
- activated alumina;
- lithium salts;
- triethylene glycol.

This method of dehumidification requires a heating stage in the process to dry or regenerate the desiccant material and requires a temperature range of 60–90°C. One option is to supply the heat by means of evacuated tube solar collectors, backed up by natural gas when insolation is inadequate. Alternatively waste heat, for example from a Stirling CHP unit, may be exploited.

As a full alternative to air conditioning, desiccant dehumidification can be used in conjunction with evaporative cooling. After being dried by the revolving desiccant wheel, the air passes through a heat exchanger such as a thermal wheel for cooling. If necessary further cooling may be achieved by an evaporative cooler before the air is supplied to the building.

The exhaust air at room temperature also passes through an evaporative cooler and then through the thermal wheel, chilling it in the process. This enables the thermal wheel to cool the supply air. After passing through the thermal wheel, the air is heated and directed through the desiccant wheel to remove moisture and is then expelled to the atmosphere.

There are problems with the system. It is not amenable to precise temperature and humidity control and it is not as efficient in dry climates. On the positive side it does provide a full fresh air system. (For further explanation see Smith, 2007, ch. 3).

Notes

1   Alternatively a Kingspan KS1000 kingzip standing seam roof system.
2   A fuller description of cooling in buildings is contained in Chapter 3, 'Low energy techniques for cooling' of Smith (2007).

6

Building-integrated Solar Electricity

The UK government's target is to make all new homes zero carbon by 2016. Is this a credible objective? In the case of photovoltaic cells (PVs) an average household would need about 10m² of cells mounted on a south-facing roof to be able to meet a reasonable fraction of its electricity needs. This is high grade energy. But a substantial part of a household's energy needs are met in the form of low grade energy for space heating and domestic hot water. Economically, the installed cost of solar thermal panels is only one quarter that of PVs. The average house does not have the roof area to provide for both solar electric and solar thermal energy. At the present state of technology, it would be difficult for the average home to be zero carbon. Even the most energy efficient house will still need an additional source of energy either in the form of offsite electricity or from a combined heat and power (CHP) unit from a local grid or power from the national grid.

The problem is even clearer on the national scale. For the country to be totally served by renewable energy, which excludes nuclear and coal with carbon capture and storage (CCS), huge areas of land and sea would be consumed by any one of the main technologies. For example, take biomass: even if 75 per cent of the country were to be covered with energy crops, this would still not be nearly enough to meet the energy needs of the nation. Meeting electricity demand from PVs would require PV farms covering an area the size of Wales.

The bottom line is that in the transition from the era of oil and gas to renewables, we will be compelled to make drastic reductions in energy consumption from buildings, industry and transport. As far as houses are concerned, they will have to make minimal demands on external energy sources, which means achieving levels of energy efficiency well in excess of level 6 of the Sustainability Code.

At present the capacity of the UK national grid is around 75GW, allowing for a peak demand of 60GW. By the 2020s around 30 per cent of UK generating capacity will have been decommissioned.

At the present rate of replacement by renewable technologies, there will be a considerable energy black hole in that decade if not before. A spokesman for the Association of Electricity Producers has stated: 'We are fast approaching a generation gap and at least £100 billion needs to be spent on new and greener power stations.' This was endorsed by the Parliamentary Business and Enterprise Committee, which has warned that 'new capacity to store and generate electricity must be created if a disastrous energy shortfall is to be avoided' (Parliamentary Business and Enterprise Committee, 2008).

Homes account for 27 per cent of UK energy, therefore they should be designed to make minimum demands on the grid. There is a good chance that within the next decade, the capacity of the grid will be reduced from the present ~75GW, so energy-light homes will be as much a matter of social responsibility as of self-interest. An optimum assessment by the UK Energy Saving Trust is that domestic building integrated renewables could meet 40 per cent of the UK's electricity demand.

In future decades the role of houses as micro-power stations will be crucial. The Tyndall Centre estimates the UK potential from renewables is 5.7MWh/person/year. David Mackay puts the figure at 6.6MWh/person/year assuming public opposition is eliminated (MacKay, 2008).

The UK government's requirement is that Code level 6 new homes should obtain supplementary energy either from onsite or integral renewable sources. The most obvious source is solar energy. But first there are some fundamental issues to be considered. The benefits of solar radiation are affected by latitude, orientation and angle. Figure 6.2 compares variations between Barcelona, Florence, Zurich, Bristol, Den Haag and Malmo. For example, a

30 degree south-facing pitched roof in Barcelona receives ~1650kWh/m²/year of solar radiation. Bristol, on the other hand, can only expect ~1200kWh/m²/year. A 30 degree east-west pitched roof receives in both cases 200kWh/m²/year less; similar to flat roofs.

As a further example, Cambridge in the UK is on latitude 52° and the sunlight hitting the earth at noon on a spring or autumn day is ~60 per cent of that at the equator. In this city a typical domestic roof array of crystalline silicon (cSi) cells would have a peak output of about 4kW and a yearly average of 12kWh/day. A case study cited by Mackay is a 25m² crystalline silicon (cSi) array on a house roof in Cambridgeshire installed in 2006. It produces a year-round average of 12kWh per day, which amounts to 20W/m² of panels (Mackay, 2008, p41).

Figure 6.2 illustrates the efficiency of average PV cells at different angles and orientation.

What it shows is that PV facades may make a significant solar contribution in combination with roof mounted cells.

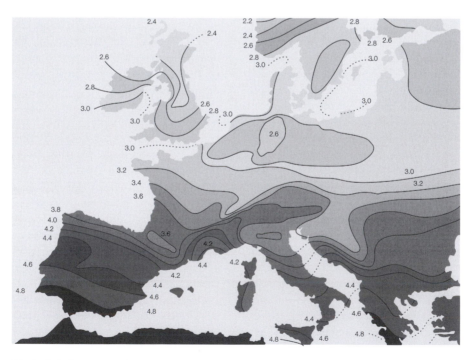

Source: Energie Institut Cerda, Spain 2001 and TFM, Barcelona

Figure 6.1 European solar radiation map in GJ/m²/year

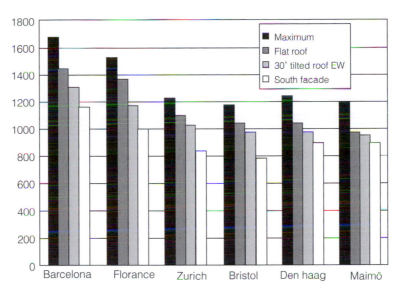

Source: Solar ElectriCity Guide – new solutions in energy supply, Energie, 2001, p23

Figure 6.2 City comparisons of solar radiation (kWh/m²/year); 30–36° south-tilted roofs, flat roofs, and 30° tilted roofs east or west on south-facing facades

Photovoltaic cells

Whilst PVs are not the most cost-effective form of domestic renewable energy, the idea of producing high grade energy in the form of electricity has a psychological appeal. In this regard the UK is still at a serious disadvantage compared with other EU partners in that it has still to implement a feed-in tariff (FIT). This is when renewable energy fed to the grid receives a premium price above the supply price to consumers. No doubt the day will come when we follow the example of Germany and Spain where FITs have spawned a vibrant manufacturing sector to meet burgeoning demand.

First generation solar cells

As yet, the market is dominated by first generation cSi cells, which have a peak efficiency of around 20 per cent. They are expensive and their payback time is well in excess of their expected lifetime, it is only with a generous FIT that they become attractive.

Historically there have been problems. A large scale urban 1.35MWp cSi PV project was completed in The Netherlands in 1999 in the new town of Nieuwland, near Amersfoort, comprising 550 houses, an elementary school, a kindergarten and a sports complex. This project has exposed problems that can arise in large-scale community PV projects, for example, 11 per cent of respondents in a survey were unaware that their houses were connected to PVs (*Renewable Energy World*, Sept–Oct 2008, pp114–123).

Despite its worldwide fame, some residents are even asking for their cells to be removed. There have been complaints about the standard of maintenance over the years. This is partly due to a change in the political complexion of the Dutch government, which no longer has a commitment to PVs, offering no incentives for their energy between 2003 and 2008. Changes in home ownership and ownership of the utilities has added to the project's problems. At the same time, incoming tenants or owners may be less committed to the project and therefore it is essential that from the outset, there is a robust maintenance contract in place. This may be a remote monitoring service that can check yield and performance with the aim of optimizing energy output and system maintenance. In contrast, when individual home owners install PVs, they are committed to maintaining them to safeguard their investment and achieve peak performance.

Second generation solar cells

Thin film technology

Market analysts predict that cSi technology will soon be overtaken by second generation thin film systems. These are mostly less efficient than cSi cells but are much cheaper to produce on a rolling process. Therefore they may well win on a cost per watt basis and consequently this is where most commercial research is focused because of the capability of mass production and market competitiveness. Thin film technology comprises semiconductor compounds sprayed onto a flexible substrate. It is claimed that they use as little as 1 per cent of the volume of material that cSi cells require. By adjusting the ingredients of the film, the system can capture energy from different wavelengths of light. For example, cells that use copper, indium, gallium and selenium (CIGS) can reach an efficiency of 19 per cent for a fraction of the cost of cSi cells. It is expected they will achieve grid parity in cost within five years. Cadmium telluride (CdTe) cells are also among the successes in this category.

Another product among the second generation of solar cells are dye-based cells that mimic the process of photosynthesis. Developed by Michael Gratzel and Brian O'Regan of the University of Lausanne, these cells use a dye containing ruthenium ions that absorb visible light analogous to chlorophyll in nature. The dye is applied to nanocrystals of the semi-conductor titanium dioxide or 'titania'. The titania have the electronic property of being able to draw electrons from the ruthenium and propel them off into an electrical circuit.

The construction of the cell involves sandwiching a 10 micrometre thick film of dye-coated titania between two transparent electrodes. The tightly packed nanocrystals form a porous film that maximizes the light absorbing capacity of the cell. The space between the electrodes is filled with a liquid electrolyte containing iodine ions. These ions replace those knocked out of the dye by the action of the photons. The two electrodes are connected to form a circuit that carries the electrical discharge.

The conversion efficiency is around 10 per cent in direct sunlight but up to 15 per cent in the diffuse light of cloudy days, which makes these cells especially suitable for northern climes. The cost is claimed to be only 20 per cent of the price of crystalline silicon, and may be even less since huge deposits of titanium have been discovered in Australia.

Third generation solar cells

The future will tend to be dominated by improving the performance and lowering the cost of second generation cells such as the Gratzel PVs. The University of Washington is responsible for a step change in the technology of dye-sensitized solar cells. Researchers have found that using tiny grains of photo-sensitive material ~15 nanometres across and combining them into larger 'clumps' about 300 nanometres across causes light to be scattered. This means the light travels a longer distance within the solar cell. The complex internal structure of these balls creates a surface area of about $1000ft^2$, which is coated with a dye that captures light. By using titanium oxide-based dye-sensitized solar cells, the expectation is that this 'popcorn ball' technology will push efficiency well over the 11 per cent of the Gratzel cell (Figure 6.4).

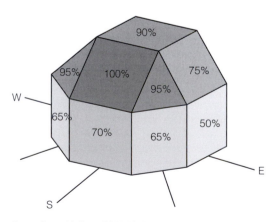

Source: *Renewable Energy World*, July–Aug 2005, p242

Figure 6.3 PV efficiency according to angle and orientation

Plastic solar cells

Plastics that are able to conduct electricity allow incoming light to liberate electrons. Cells are made by a plastic in liquid form being applied to a substrate, somewhat analogous to a printing process. The immediate goal is to achieve 10 per cent efficiency. Even at this efficiency such cells should be attractive to the market because of their very low manufacturing costs.

Another strand of research seeks to optimize the capabilities of silicon by multiplying the level of sunlight falling into a cell. Concentrated solar cells focusing on PV crystals can achieve efficiencies of 40 per cent. At the University of Delaware, scientists using a concentration of 20 suns (20 times the power of the sun) have achieved 42.8 per cent efficiency. This is done by splitting the incoming light into its constituent wavelengths and directing each wavelength to a chemical that optimizes its electricity conversion. The disadvantages of such cells are, first, that they require direct sunlight to operate efficiently, and, second, that they continue to be expensive.

The Fraunhofer Institute for Solar Energy Research is also breaking new ground in concentrating solar cell technology with multi-junction cells that reach 37.9 per cent efficiency. This is realized through a solar concentration of between 300–600 suns.

A technology with integrated cooling for concentrated solar PVs has been patented by SUNGRI and will be available for both on-and-off-grid by 2010 (Figure 6.5).

An alternative version of concentrator technology has been developed by scientists at MIT. This system does not involve tracking or cooling systems. The principle is that light is collected over the area of a multi-layer assembly of glass forming a solar cell. The solar energy is then transported to the edges of the glass where it encounters PV cells positioned round the edges of the window. Dye molecules are coated on the layers of glass and they work together to absorb light across a range of wavelengths. Light is then re-emitted at a different wavelength and transported across the pane to solar cells around

Source: Department of Materials Science and Engineering, University of Washington

Figure 6.4 'Popcorn-ball' clusters comprising grains 15 nanometres across

the perimeter of the glass. This way solar energy collection is optimized at each wavelength. It is claimed that concentrating light around the boundary of a solar panel in this way increases the electricity obtained from each solar cell by a factor of 40. In addition, the nature of the cells also enables them to function as a window, albeit with reduced transmission efficiency.

Source: *Renewable Energy World,* May–June 2008, p12

Figure 6.5 SUNRGI XCPV system of concentrated solar cells with proprietary method of cooling the cells

The development team at MIT believes that because the system is straightforward to manufacture, it could be ready for market within 3 years and at a considerably reduced cost compared with conventional PVs.

The battle lines are now being clearly drawn between the upgrading of crystalline silicon technology through solar concentration and thin film technologies. Writing in the *New Scientist* with regard to the latter, Bennett Daviss states: 'perhaps that's where the true promise of solar power lies, not in expensive high-efficiency cells, but in clever new designs that are dirt cheap to produce' (Daviss, 2008, p37). The co-inventor of PV plastics, Allen Heeger, believes that 'The critical comparison is dollars per watt' (Daviss, 2008, p37). There is a growing perception that this is where the future of PVs lies.

Photovoltaics and urban design

Towns and cities present an ideal opportunity for the exploitation of PVs. They have a high concentration of potential PV sites with a heavy energy demand. At the same time the physical infrastructure can support localized electricity generation. It is estimated that installing PVs on suitable walls and roofs could generate up to 25 per cent of total demand. The biggest opportunity for PVs is as systems embedded in buildings. It is expected that building integrated PVs (BIPVs) will account for 50 per cent of the world PV installations by 2010, with the percentage being significantly higher in Europe.

The widescale adoption of PVs in the urban environment will depend on the acceptance of the visual change it will bring about, especially in historic situations. There is still a barrier to be overcome and planning policy guidance may have to be amended to create a presumption in favour of retrofitting PVs to buildings.

The efficiency of PVs in a given location will depend on factors such as:

- fairly consistent roof heights – compact developments are ideal for roof mounted PVs;
- orientation;

- openness of the aspect – a more open urban grain may allow the potential of facade PVs to be exploited;
- overshading – especially in the context of seasonal changes in the sun's angle.

Surface to volume ratio

The surface area available for either facade or roof PV installation is largely determined by the surface to volume ratio. A high ratio of surface to volume suggests opportunities for facade integrated PVs. However, in high density situations overshading will limit facade opportunities. On the other hand, lower values indicate opportunities for roof PV installation.

The spacing between buildings is also an important factor in determining facade PV opportunities. Wide spaces between buildings with a southerly aspect will be particularly suited to facade BIPV. Also, wide streets and city squares provide excellent opportunities for this PV mode. A tighter urban grain points to roof mounted PVs. The suitability of BIPVs is dependent upon a variety of factors. For example, flat roofs are the most appropriate sites in city centres, combining flexibility with unobtrusiveness. When considering pitched roofs, the orientation, angle of tilt and aesthetic impact all have to be taken into account.

Reflected light is a useful supplemental form of energy for PVs. Many facades in city centres have high reflectance values offering significant levels of diffuse light for facade PVs on opposite elevations, thus making orientation less important. In glazed curtain wall buildings solar shading is now de rigueur. Here is a further opportunity to incorporate PVs into shading devices. When office blocks are refurbished the incorporation of PVs into a facade becomes cost-effective.

In conservation areas there are particular sensitivities. The next generation of thin film PVs look like offering opportunities to integrate PVs into buildings without compromising their historic integrity.

The conclusion to be drawn from this section is that places on the latitude of the UK will benefit the most from thin film solar technology, which optimizes light rather than just sunlight. In southern Europe concentrated solar PVs on a domestic scale may be cost-effective since a relatively small cell area may provide adequate electricity. Chapter 14 discusses how southern Europe is beginning to exploit concentrated solar energy at the utility scale.

Retrofit building integrated PVs

A building that featured in *Sustainability at the Cutting Edge* (Smith, 2007) is the CIS Tower (Co-operative Insurance Society) in Manchester (Figure 6.6). It is illustrated here because it is still the most ambitious example of retrofitted PVs in the UK. Whilst PVs are not yet cost-effective without an attractive feed-in tariff, where extensive facade refurbishment is needed, the additional cost can get closer to being an economic option. This is one factor that caused the CIS management to turn the service tower of its HQ into a vertical power station. It was designed to produce 800,000kWh/year. Despite the proliferation of tower blocks in the city, the CIS Tower remains a landmark building, illustrating how retrofit PVs can also make it a signature building.

Source: Pam Smith

Figure 6.6 CIS Tower, Manchester, with retrofitted PVs

7

Sun, Earth, Wind and Water

Solar thermal energy

Solar radiation is the most abundant source of energy at 219,000TWh per year. Solar thermal and photovoltaics (PVs) are the two technologies that directly exploit it. PVs tend to attract most attention, probably because it is a 'high tech' and modern technology that generates a product that can serve a variety of purposes. It is at the cutting edge of science and still has considerable developmental potential. Solar thermal, on the other hand, is a comparatively low tech system that has a long history in countries with generous sunshine. Another problem for solar thermal is that it does not contribute directly to reductions in CO_2, nor is it linked to major industrial companies. Excess energy cannot be exported to the national grid. It is significant that the International Energy Agency omitted it from its 2008 report on renewables to the G8 countries.

Under the 2008 EU agreement to produce 20 per cent of energy from renewables by 2020, the UK's proportion is 15 per cent. The government's Renewable Energy Strategy suggests that, in order to meet the 15 per cent target, it might be easier to increase the share of renewable heat rather than increase the level of renewable electricity. This is partly because heat does not create complications for the grid and also because the UK's heavy reliance on wind generation leaves it potentially with a considerable renewables shortfall. In the UK heat accounts for 49 per cent of final energy demand and 47 per cent of CO_2 emissions. Space heating,

ventilation and water heating are the main constituents. The Renewable Energy Strategy concludes that it will be necessary to 'develop a completely new approach to renewable heat, providing substantial incentives to jump-start this new market' (DECC, 2008a).

This represents a paradigm shift: promoting renewable heat into the pantheon of the renewables gods such as PVs and wind. The government acknowledges that subsidies will be necessary, for example a Renewable Heat Incentive Scheme in the form of a feed-in tariff measured in £/MWh thermal. These are some of the components of a recommended Renewable Heat Incentive regime so that it makes a significant contribution to CO_2 abatement.

Even in the UK, on a south-facing roof in southern England vacuum tube collectors can achieve 50 per cent efficiency compared with a peak of 20 per cent for current PVs. Depending on location, a 10m² array of solar collectors would generate 4MWh of heat per year. Figure 7.1 shows the results of an experimental 3m² solar thermal panel producing average solar power of 3.8kWh/day. The experiment assumed a consumption of 100 litres of water at 60°C per day. The graph shows a 1.5–2kWh/day gap between total heat generated (black line) and hot water consumed (red line). The green lines represent the solar thermal power generated. The magenta line at the bottom is the electricity used to power the system (Mackay, 2008, p40). This area of solar panel would be typical for an average family house.

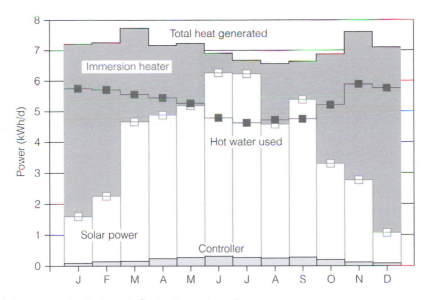

Figure 7.1 Solar power outputs from 3m² solar thermal panels

Central solar heating plants for seasonal storage (CSHPSS)

Banking heat in summer to meet winter expenditure is the principle behind seasonal storage. There are three principal storage technologies.

- Aquifer heat storage – Naturally occurring aquifers are charged with heat via wells during the warming season. In winter the system goes into reverse and the warmth is distributed through the district network.
- Gravel/water heat storage – A pit with a watertight plastic liner is filled with a gravel–water mix as the storage medium. The storage container is insulated at the sides and top, and at the base for small installations. Heat is fed into and drawn out of the storage tank both directly and indirectly.
- Hot–water storage – This comprises a steel or concrete insulated tank built partly or wholly into the ground.

Central solar plants with seasonal storage aim at a solar fraction of at least 50 per cent of the total heat demand for space heating and domestic hot water for a housing estate of at least 100 apartments. The solar fraction is that part of the total annual energy demand that is met by solar energy. For all these installations it is necessary to receive authorization from the relevant water authority.

By 2003 Europe had 45MW of installed thermal power from solar collector areas of over 500m². The ten largest installations in Europe are in Denmark, Sweden, Germany and The Netherlands, mostly serving housing complexes. Germany's first solar assisted district heating projects, launched as part of a government research project 'Solarthermie 2000', were at Ravensburg and Neckarsulm. These have already proved valuable test beds for subsequent schemes.

One of the largest projects is at Friedrichshafen and it serves well to illustrate the system (Figure 7.2). The heat from 5600m² of solar collectors on the roofs of eight housing blocks containing 570 apartments is transported to a central heating unit or substation. It is then distributed to the apartments as required. The heated living area amounts to 39,500m².

Surplus summer heat is directed to the seasonal heat store, which, in this case, is of the hot water variety, capable of storing 12,000m³.

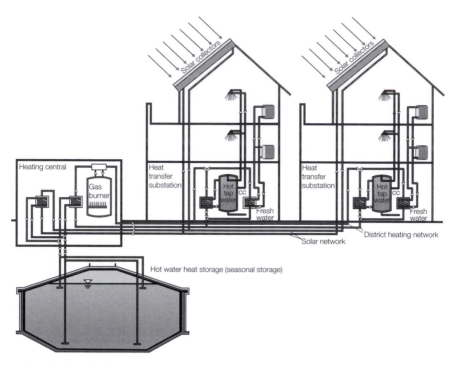

Source: Courtesy of *Renewable Energy World*

Figure 7.2 Diagram of the CSHPSS system, Friedrichshafen, Germany

The heat delivery of the system amounts to 1915MWh/year and the solar fraction is 47 per cent. The month by month ratio between solar- and fossil-based energy indicates that from April to November inclusive, solar energy accounts for almost the total demand, being principally domestic hot water (Figure 7.3).

Hybrid technology

The fusion of solar electric with solar thermal energy is the ultimate destiny of both technologies. Hybrid PV/thermal systems can achieve the maximum conversion rate of absorbed solar radiation. Heat is extracted from the PV modules and used to heat either water or air whilst, at the same time, keeping the PVs at maximum efficiency by cooling the cells. A pioneering scheme in the UK was installed at

Beaufort Court Renewable Energy Centre, created by Studio E Architects. A PV/thermal (PVT) roof comprising 54m² of PVT panels was constructed over a biomass store. The 170m² solar array comprises 54m² of hybrid PVT panels and 116m² of solar thermal panels. The PVT panels consist of a photovoltaic module, which converts light into electricity, and a copper heat exchanger on the back to capture the remaining solar energy. The panels have been developed by ECN in The Netherlands, incorporating Shell Solar PV elements and Zen Solar thermal elements. They produce electricity and hot water (Figure 7.4).

An alternative approach has been devised by Heliodynamics. Their units surround small, high grade gallium arsenide PV cells with arrays of slow moving flat mirrors. These focus sunlight onto the PV, which can deliver both electricity and hot water. This could be a technology with a big future.

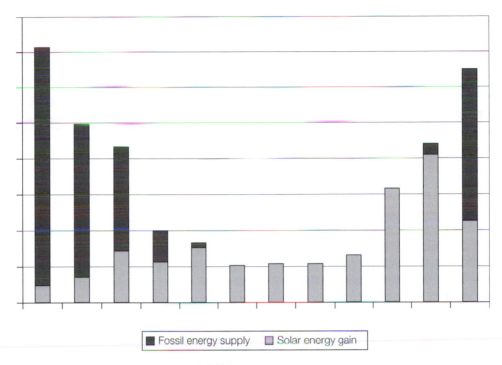

Fossil energy supply   Solar energy gain

Figure 7.3 Friedrichshafen delivered energy in MWh per year

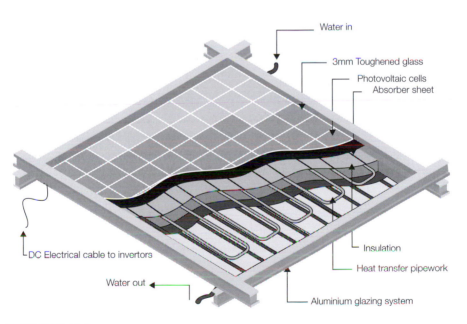

Water in

3mm Toughened glass

Photovoltaic cells

Absorber sheet

Insulation

Heat transfer pipework

DC Electrical cable to invertors

Aluminium glazing system

Water out

Source: Courtesy of Studio E Architects

Figure 7.4 PV/thermal hybrid panels

Seasonal underground heat store

The underground heat store is an 1100m³ body of water that stores the heat generated by PVT and solar thermal panels for use in buildings during the colder months. The top of the store is insulated with a floating lid of 500mm expanded polystyrene. It is hinged around the perimeter to allow for the expansion and contraction of the water and the design also incorporates a suspension system to support the roof should the water level reduce. The sloping sides are uninsulated. As long as the ground around the store is kept dry, it will act as an insulator and additional thermal mass, increasing the capacity of the store. The high specific heat capacity of water (4.2kJ/kg°C) makes it a good choice for storing heat.

During the summer there will be little or no demand for heat in the building, so the heat generated by the PVT array will be destined for the heat store. In the autumn some of the solar heat generated will be used directly in the buildings and the excess will be added to the heat store. The temperature of the water in the store will gradually rise over the summer and early autumn. During the winter the solar heat generated will be less than the building's heat load, and heat will be extracted from the heat store to heat the incoming air to the building. The temperature of the water in the store will drop as the heat is extracted. Some heat will also be lost to the surroundings. This is estimated to be about 50 per cent of the total heat put into the store over the summer. The relatively low grade heat from the store can be used to preheat air coming into the building, as the outside air will be at a lower temperature than the water.

So far polycrystalline and amorphous crystalline cells have been used in this way and trials have been successful in a domestic thermosyphonic system (as opposed to a pumped system). The recovered heat is used for domestic hot water. Larger systems have been devised, suitable for apartment blocks and small offices.

This dual capability had the additional benefit of improving the cost-effectiveness of each technology when utilized separately.

Small-scale wind

It is unlikely that micro-wind power will play a significant role in bringing about the energy revolution of the coming decades. Three factors are involved: first the capacity or 'load' factor of turbines as a whole; at best this is around 30 per cent. This is the proportion of the rated capacity of a machine that can be delivered to a household or the grid. Second, wind speeds in a built-up area are unreliable and turbulent due to the configuration of buildings, streets and open spaces. Third, it is generally considered that an average wind speed of 7m/second or 16mph is necessary for the commercial success of wind power. Only about 33 per cent of the UK land area has such speeds (Mackay, 2008).

Figure 7.5 shows the distribution of average summer and winter wind speeds in the UK. The figure concentrates mostly on Scotland where the greatest concentration of wind farms is to be found. Very few cross the economic viability threshold of 7m/second.

The performance of a micro-turbine with a 1.1m diameter, assuming an above average wind speed of 6m/second, should deliver ~1.6kWh/day. Mackay (2008) describes an Ampair 600W micro-turbine positioned on a roof in a small town in the midlands of the UK. The average power generated is 0.037kWh/day.

Larger machines can serve a group of houses and an excellent case study is the Hockerton Housing Project in Nottinghamshire. It has installed two 5kW free-standing turbines as well as roof-mounted PVs over its four earth-sheltered homes. From June to September their output per month is mostly under 200kWh. What stands out from this record is that PVs have an important part to play in the energy mix at the domestic level, especially in combination with small-scale wind (6kW and above).

The triple helix vertical axis turbine (Figure 7.6) is appearing in increasing numbers of urban situations, such as the waterfront of Albert Dock, Liverpool. The machines produced by quietrevolution are rated at 6kW, producing an average of 10,000kWh/year assuming average wind speeds. Machines are 14m high and 3m in diameter, but need only be 8m high when

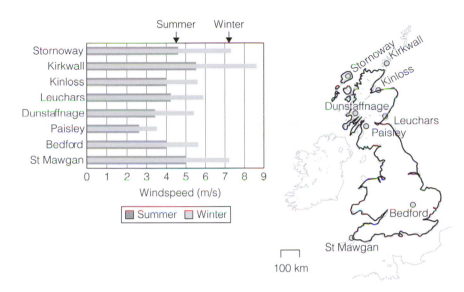

Source: Mackay (2008, p264)

Figure 7.5 Average summer and winter wind speeds in the UK over the period 1971–2000 at a height of 10m

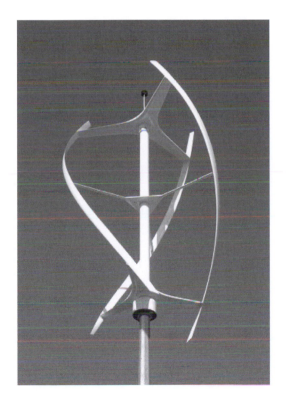

Source: Courtesy of quietrevolution Ltd

Figure 7.6 Triple helix wind generator by quietrevolution (qr5)

mounted on the roofs of high buildings such as the Fairview apartments in Croydon (Figure 7.7).

The wind energy company Altechnica has patented a number of building integrated turbines that are deigned to accelerate wind velocity. Collectively they are known as *Aeolian Planar* or *Wing Concentrators*. They are designed to exploit the cubic relationship between wind speed and power output. This would mean that an increase of 25 per cent in wind speed would double the power output. These could also be described as 'building augmented wind energy systems'. The development of this technology means that:

- wind turbine size for a given output can be reduced;
- annual output of a wind turbine can be increased substantially;
- wind turbine capacity factor can be increased substantially;
- wind turbines will 'cut-in' at a lower wind speed;
- simpler fixed yaw wind turbines become more feasible;
- sites with lower wind speed characteristics become more viable;
- urban sites become more viable;

Figure 7.7 Quietrevolution helical turbines, Fairview Homes, London Road, Croydon

- wind turbines can be productive for a greater proportion of a year;
- substantial CO_2 emissions are abated from what is effectively a 'new' energy source.

The 'Aeolian roof' combines a suitably profiled roof with a shaped fairing or plane designed to enhance wind speed along the apex of the building. The fairing or wing also protects the rotors. The system can accommodate cross-flow or axial turbines (Figure 7.8) and can generate power even at relatively low wind speeds and when there is turbulence. Structurally this is a robust system that minimizes roof loading. The prototype currently under test also indicates that vibrations are not transmitted to the structure.

The Building-Augmented variants of the patented Aeolian Wing™ Wind Energy Concentrator Systems family include several options including Aeolian Roof™ systems that are appropriate for a variety of roof profiles including curved, vaulted, shell and membrane roofs as well as dual-pitched, mono-pitched and flat roofs. The system is not only suitable for new buildings but also for retrofit application (Figure 7.9).

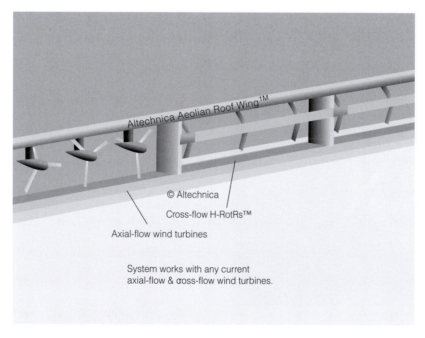

Source: Courtesy of Derek Taylor, Altechnica

Figure 7.8 Roof ridge accommodating cross-flow or axial turbines

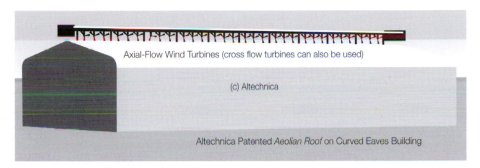

Axial-Flow Wind Turbines (cross flow turbines can also be used)

(c) Altechnica

Altechnica Patented *Aeolian Roof* on Curved Eaves Building

Source: Courtesy of Altechnica

Figure 7.9 Aeolian system for terrace housing

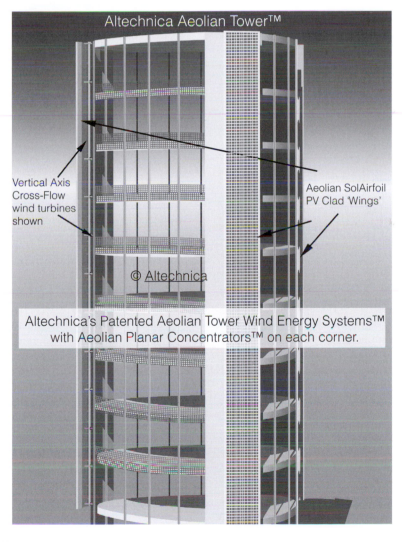

Altechnica Aeolian Tower™

Vertical Axis Cross-Flow wind turbines shown

Aeolian SolAirfoil PV Clad 'Wings'

© Altechnica

Altechnica's Patented Aeolian Tower Wind Energy Systems™ with Aeolian Planar Concentrators™ on each corner.

Source: Courtesy of Altechnica

Figure 7.10 The Aeolian Tower

Altechnica has also designed the system to be adapted to high rise buildings (Figure 7.10).

Aeolian Tower™ systems are designed to be incorporated into the sides and/or corners of buildings – particularly tall structures. Height increases the productivity of wind technology and side or corner installations reduce the visibility of wind energy exploitation on tall buildings. Again there is the potential for new-build and retrofit.

Heat pumps

Heat pumps may seem an unlikely candidate for inclusion in the major renewables for the future. In fact their popularity in mainland Europe suggests it is a technology that will have an important role to play in the race for zero carbon energy.

Heat pumps are an extension of refrigeration technology. Their principle is that they extract residual heat from the ground, air or water, which can then be used to supplement space heating or provide domestic hot water. Ground source heat pumps (GSHP) exploit the fact that the Earth at a depth of 6m maintains a constant temperature of 10–12°C. At 3m it fluctuates between 8° and 15°C. In reverse mode GSHPs can also provide cooling. The technology exists to allow heating and cooling to occur simultaneously in different parts of a building. There is a body of opinion that considers that heat pumps will lead the field in low energy technology for buildings. It is relatively low cost, and economical to run.

If PVs with battery backup provide the power for pumps and compressors, then it is a zero energy system. The co-efficient of performance (COP) is, at best, 1:4. This means that 4kW of heat are obtained using 1kW of electricity. If the ground loop is located in an aquifer, an even higher COP can be obtained due to the rapid recovery rate of the water temperature. Heat pumps can be used to supplement the heat gained from ventilation systems with heat recovery.

In the sphere of social housing there is a growing trend to retrofit GSHPs to replace oil-fired central heating. One system that is extensively used is the HeatGen™ package. The following is taken from the specification in its brochure:

> *HeatGen™ is a ground source heat pump package specifically matched to UK housing, capable of providing all the heating and hot water needed without using supplementary direct electric heating.*

Typically each house is fitted with a single borehole within the curtilage of the property, coupled to a Dimplex ground source heat pump located either within the dwelling or housed in an external enclosure in the garden. EarthEnergy undertakes all the works necessary to 'replace the boiler' so that the heating engineer has a similar scope of works to that of a traditional system.

This 'one borehole per house' solution provides a bespoke designed ground loop matched to the heat loss of the house providing:

- onsite renewable energy;
- low running costs;
- low CO_2 footprint;
- unobtrusive – not visible externally;
- no flames or combustible gases;
- no emissions or noise nuisance;
- no fuel handling/storage requirements;
- no fire/explosion hazard;
- doesn't require planning permission;
- only requires electrical infrastructure;
- available 24 hrs a day 7 days a week;
- long lifetime;
- no reduction in performance over time.

> *HeatGen™ is an affordable way to address fuel poverty in existing housing stock with no mains gas available; reducing fuel bills, improving the quality of life of tenants and significantly reducing carbon emissions.*

> *New housing developments can readily incorporate HeatGen™ to meet planning*

obligations for onsite renewable energy and achieve compliance with Building Regulations and the Code for Sustainable Homes.

Heat pump technology is being scaled-up to serve large buildings. For example, one of the largest GSHP systems in the UK, at 4MW, is destined to provide all the heat and cooling for the Churchill Hospital, part of the Oxford Radcliffe Hospitals NHS Trust. The design load is 2.5MW with the remainder as essential reserve capacity.

Air source heat pumps (ASHP) are very popular in mainland Europe, especially Sweden, despite its extreme winter temperatures. They are much cheaper to install than GSHPs and have a COP of ~3.5:1. Their drawback is that they freeze up when the outside temperature falls to 4°C in conditions of high humidity. These conditions are common in the UK but not so often in Sweden. Therefore, in the UK, the energy balance has to take into account a heating element to keep it operational in frost conditions.

Air source technology is proving popular for large buildings and, whilst there are unlikely to be radical improvements in its technology, economies of scale will bring down costs for a robust and 24-hour reliable source of low grade heat or cooling. As thin film PV technology crosses the grid parity threshold, their use in conjunction with heat pumps will provide a genuinely zero carbon, low maintenance, long life source of heat and cooling. (A more detailed description of heat pump technology is given in Smith, 2007, ch. 4 'Geothermal Energy'.)

Micro-fuel cells

Micro-fuel cells are now beginning to appear among the domestic scale technologies for the future. Chapter 15 offers a description of the Ceres 1kW fuel cell, which would seem to have much to offer in the domestic buildings sector.[1]

For some time the technology of the future on the domestic scale was Stirling combined heat and power. This is an external combustion engine in which heat is applied to one end of a cylinder whilst the opposite end is cooled. The piston is set in motion by the difference in pressure at the cylinder's extremities. In the first machines for the domestic market, the vertical action of the pistons was converted to rotary action connected to a generator. Next generation systems employed a free-piston Stirling engine that produced electricity by the interaction of magnetic fields in the walls of the sealed cylinder and in the piston. The heat generated was used for domestic hot water, supplemented by a gas burner (Smith, 2007, ch. 9). Up to the present it has been beset by engineering problems concerning the extremely fine tolerances needed in the manufacture of the piston and cylinder.

With the support of a major utility like British Gas, the Ceres Power fuel cell is likely to offer serious competition to the Stirling option in the domestic combined heat and power market. It is compact, it has no moving parts and it generates heat rather than imports it.

Small-scale and micro-hydro generation

Micro-hydro generation has not featured much in the pantheon of renewables. However, an initiative in New Mills, Derbyshire, is set to change perceptions of this technology. The installation at New Mills consists of an adaptation of the Archimedes Screw that was initially designed to raise water. Used in reverse, its rotary action drives an electricity generator. Built in Germany, the Screw is the centre piece of the Torrs Hydro Scheme (Figure 7.11). It is 11m long, 2.6m wide and weighs 11.3 tonnes. It is used to harness power from the River Goyt to be delivered to the nearby Co-operative supermarket as well as to local homes. The project was backed by the Manchester-based Co-operative Group and a grant from the Co-operative Fund helped establish this community-owned power enterprise. It began operation in 2008 and now generates ~240,000kWh per year, enough to power 70 homes.

Plans are well advanced to install a similar scheme in Settle, Lancashire. Other locations are being considered, including Sheffield. The Co-operative Group is set to extend support to other projects across the country.

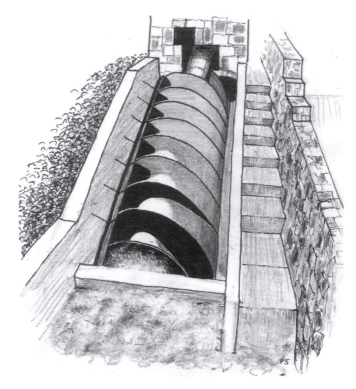

Figure 7.11 Archimedes Screw in the River Goyt at New Mills, Derbyshire

Biofuel

Biofuels have not been included in the list of front runners in renewables. This is because biofuel resources will be monopolized by the demand from vehicles and in contributing to the fuel mix for thermal power stations. Pellets will have a role to play in the domestic sector, but space constraints suggest this will be only marginal. The technologies covered are the ones that have the potential to play a central role in the drive towards zero carbon buildings. However, it has to be said that the goal of absolute zero carbon buildings per se is unattainable.[2] Onsite renewable energy will never be sufficient to counter the carbon released in the construction process and the building in use. However, *offsite* renewable energy is another matter.

Notes

1   www.cerespower.com

2   The net zero carbon target for homes and all appliances set for 2016 will only be achievable with power from renewable sources. Government regulations state that 'Calculations (re zero carbon) can include onsite renewables and offsite where renewable energy is supplied to a dwelling via a private wire arrangement.' ('Definition of Zero Carbon Homes and Non-domestic Buildings', DCLG, Dec 2008, p10.)

8

Eco-towns: Opportunity or Oxymoron?

The starting point of this chapter echoes the underpinning idea of Chapter 5:

> *Given the long lifetime and cost of the built environment, it is important that we plan for, and create, communities that are robust in the face of climate change. New developments must be designed to cope with future rather than historic climates. [We] will need to cope with changing climate over decades even centuries.*
>
> (Shaw et al, 2007).

In 1992 the town of Gussing in Austria was a declining place close to the Iron Curtain. By 2001 it was energy self-sufficient due to the production of biodiesel from local rapeseed and used cooking oil, together with solar heat and electricity. In addition, it installed a biomass-steam gasification plant that sells surplus electricity to the grid. Not only has this produced significantly higher living standards, new industries have created 1000 new jobs. As a result, the town has cut its CO_2 emissions by 90 per cent.

This is an example of a growing number of towns that are seizing the opportunity to become near-carbon-neutral, motivated as much by the price of fossil energy as the need to cut carbon emissions. In the UK they are the 'transition towns'. However, the focus of this chapter is on the UK's programme of ten eco-towns.

Eco-town case studies

Vauban, Freiburg im Breisgau

Much of the inspiration behind the UK's eco-town concept comes from Freiburg in southwest Germany and, in particular, the sector of Vauban.

The beginning of the 'solarization' of Freiburg can be traced to 1975 when the community successfully lobbied against the construction of a nuclear power plant in fairly close proximity to the city at Wyhl. The risk of a consequent energy shortfall caused the citizens to take advantage of Freiburg's location as the sunniest region of Germany. A stimulus to the evolution of Freiburg as the solar capital of Germany was the foundation of the Fraunhofer Institute for Solar Energy Research in 1981. This was perhaps the driving force behind the solar revolution in Freiburg and is now Europe's largest solar energy research institute.

The French occupied Freiburg in 1945 and maintained a military presence there until 1991, when they finally withdrew from their Vauban base. The city then created the Forum Vauban Association in 1994 to involve public participation in the development of the former French army base with the aim of creating the ideal eco-city of the future. In many ways it constitutes a social as well as an architectural and urban design revolution. In Vauban, green living is compulsory. For example:

- All buildings had to be constructed to achieve an energy consumption of 65kWh/m^2/year six years before this became the overall German standard in 2002.
- The energy standard for the city is set to be reduced to 40kWh/m^2/y (the national standard is now 75kWh/m^2/y). The preferred energy benchmark for houses is the PassivHaus standard of 15kWh/m^2/year. Triple glazing is mandatory with a minimum U-value of 1.2 W/m^{2}K.
- Ecological building materials such as walls of compressed natural materials are used extensively.
- Solar energy is maximized. The flagship solar development is the mixture of 'Plus-energy' housing and commercial use (Chapter 4). The architect was Rolf Disch.
- Priority has been given to pedestrians and cyclists as well as public transport. A tram system and buses have made it convenient to be largely car free.
- There are powerful disincentives to car use with strict limits on car ownership in the 'passive' zone. Owning a car incurs a fee of £12,000 for parking plus a monthly management fee.
- Although the development is high density, there is room for allotments to enable residents to cultivate fruit and vegetables.

The city of Freiburg is served by a district heating scheme that includes contributions from a wood fired co-generation plant, anaerobic digestion of bio-waste, a rape co-generation plant and a wood-chip CHP plant.

For some the image of Vauban is that it is a ghetto for green extremists. A resident has admitted that 'some people are very anti-car, and there have been conflicts in some streets. There is also a stigma … in living in Freiburg's most militant green quarter' (*Observer*, 2008a).

However, the outstanding positive feature of Freiburg is the exploitation of solar energy, mainly through PVs. The City's 'SolarKonzept 2000' together with the Lander (county) provides a grant of up to 40 per cent to a limit of DM8000 equivalent per household for the installation of solar power and heating. In addition there is a generous feed-in tariff offered by the federal government under the Renewable Energy Law. The result is that the city generates 4.3MW of electricity together with 10,000m^2 of solar collectors. It is no surprise that Freiburg is home to a leading PV manufacturing company, SolarFabrik, and its spin-off distribution company Solarstrom AG.

The result is a city that is an outstanding example of public participation and a world showcase for solar power as shown by the Plus Energy project (Plusenergiehaus) (see Figures 4.8 and 4.9). Designed by architect Rolf Disch, the 60 homes in the Sonnenschiff are designed to produce a surplus of energy, currently earning the community €6000 per year thanks to the subsidy.

Hammarby Sjostad, Stockholm

A more recent eco-development admired by the UK government is Hammarby Sjostad, Stockholm. The brief was to design a development that combined the traditional inner city character of Stockholm with modern architecture in sympathy with the natural environment. It includes 9000 apartments housing 20,000 people. There were guidelines that emphasized the need to integrate key buildings, public spaces and pedestrian routes. In fact the list of guidelines was most comprehensive, which might have been inhibiting; instead, the result was a city sector that was visually inspired.

Eco-towns for the UK

The UK specification for its eco-towns has more in common with Vauban than Hammarby. It is as much about dictating lifestyle as prescribing design and construction specifications. Eco-towns represent a response to three challenges:

- climate change;
- the need to develop more sustainable living;
- the requirement to increase the supply of housing.

The government's conditions

The government's definition of an eco-town is that, 'over a year, the net carbon dioxide emissions from all energy use within buildings on the development are zero or below. Planning applications should demonstrate how this will be achieved.' All buildings will be included: commercial, public sector as well as housing.

The eco-towns are intended to be demonstrations of:

- a zero-carbon and sustainable approach to living by means of new design at the whole town scale;
- the role of well-designed new settlements as an element in increasing the supply of housing alongside growth in existing towns and cities;
- exploiting the opportunities to design and deliver affordable housing. Eco-towns will include 30–50 per cent of affordable housing and a mix of tenures and family sizes.

Summary of requirements

The government's objectives for planning are set out in Planning Policy Statement 1 (PPS 1) and include:

- **to promote sustainable development by:**
  - ensuring that eco-towns achieve sustainability standards significantly above equivalent levels of development in existing towns and cities by setting out a range of challenging and stretching minimum standards for their development, and in particular by: providing a good quantity of green space of the highest quality in close proximity to the natural environment; offering opportunities for space within and around the dwellings; promoting healthy and sustainable environments through 'Active Design' [**www.sportengland. org/planning_active_design**] principles and healthy living choices; enabling opportunities for infrastructure that make best use of technologies in energy generation and conservation in ways that are not always practical or economic in other developments; delivering a locally appropriate mix of housing type and tenure to meet the needs of all income groups and household size; and taking advantage of significant economies of scale and increases in land value to deliver new technology and infrastructure such as for transport, energy and community facilities.
- **to reduce the carbon footprint of development by:**
  - ensuring that households and individuals in eco-towns are able to reduce their carbon footprint to a low level and achieve a more sustainable way of living.
  (DCLG, 2009)

The conditions are that an eco-town should be:

- a new development;
- of sufficient size to support the necessary services and establish their own identity;
- of sufficient critical mass to deliver much higher standards of sustainability;
- able to make provision for between 5000 and 20,000 homes;
- able to provide green space to a high standard through their link with the natural environment;
- provide space within and around buildings especially for children;
- able to provide healthy and sustainable environments through 'Active Design' principles and healthy living choices;
- able to provide easy access to workplaces and be a viable local economy;
- provide communities resilient to climate change;
- be in close proximity to existing or planned employment and have links to a major town or city.

Eco-towns should deliver a high quality local environment and meet the standards on water, flooding, green infrastructure and biodiversity set out in this PPS, taking into account a changing climate for these, as well as incorporating wider best practice on tackling overheating and impacts of a changing climate for the natural and built environment (DCLG, 2009).

The most contentious condition relates to onsite renewable energy:

> *[Buildings should] achieve through a combination of energy efficiency, onsite low and zero carbon energy generation and any heat supplied from low and zero carbon heat systems directly connected to the development, carbon reduction (from space heating, hot water and fixed lighting) of at least 70% relative to current Building Regulations Part L 2006.*
> (DCLG, 2009, Part 2)

Large parts of the towns will be car free. Car-sharing will replace car ownership. One potential initiative is that staff in the eco-towns will offer residents and businesses personalized travel planning to enable them to adapt to the largely car-free environment. By capturing rainwater and reusing treated grey water for toilets, the towns should be 'water-neutral'. In other words, the development will make no more demands for water than was the case on the undeveloped site. To summarize: as a minimum all houses must achieve at least level 4 of the Code for Sustainable Homes.

There is even the suggestion that retailers should provide plenty of products with low meat and dairy content. This is following reports showing that a significant reduction in the consumption of meat could cut the ecological footprint due to food by 60 per cent. All this is to achieve the target of 'one planet living'. At present the British lifestyle, if it were to be universal, would consume the resources of three planets (the figure for the US is 4).

The stringent conditions laid down for the eco-towns has already had consequences. Nine of the ten sites finally selected for development at the first stage have so far not met all the conditions laid down in the invitation for bids. The successful one is Rackheath, northeast of Norwich, which obtained a Grade A in the assessment. However, the government is not being deflected from its eco-ambitions, and it plans for construction to begin in 2010.

Eco-towns: a critique

There are several concerns about the eco-towns project and one is that in all probability developers will resort to lightweight timber frame construction to meet the zero carbon standard required within the cost contraints. This could conflict with the requirement to use best practice to tackle overheating and the impacts of a changing climate, as discussed in Chapter 4.

Even more serious is the fate of the flagship Hammarby Sjostad project and its wide use of lightweight construction. A headline in the journal *Building Design* sounded the alarm: problems with moisture penetration between the timber frames and their plasterboard cladding is causing the town to face 'a ticking time bomb' according to Professor Per Ingvar Sandberg of the Technical Research Institute of Sweden (Hurst, 2007). His report highlights a fundamental fault that can occur in this type of construction. It was also pointed out that it is uncertain that the mandatory level of air tightness can be achieved in this system simply through reliance on an air-tight membrane (Sandberg, 2007b).

This has significance for the UK eco-town programme. One such town is likely to be Bordon Whitehill in East Hampshire. The chief executive of the District Council Will Godfrey is on record as saying: 'Homes could be built from prefabricated wooden panels sourced from local managed woodlands' (*Observer*, 2008b).

In Chapter 4 it was argued that lightweight frame and panel structures lacking thermal mass would be unsuitable for the temperatures we can expect if climate change continues on its present trajectory. Engineers Atelier Ten also argued that such structures might only last 25 years, not the centuries that the TCPA recommends.

Concern has been voiced that the government is being advised by the Commission for Architecture and the Built Environment (CABE) and an environmentally conscious development company Bioregional that residents should be monitored to ensure that their carbon footprint is at least three times less than the British average. This could mean monitoring the number of car journeys made and the type of waste generated by homes and businesses. They are also recommending that thermographic imaging should be employed to determine which homes are wasting energy. They are also calling for all homes to be powered by renewables, with gas serving only as a backup fuel.

In announcing the eco-towns initiative, housing minister Caroline Flint summed up the intention: 'We will revolutionise the way people live.' It is becoming clear what she meant.

The government claims that the programme of eco-towns is entirely different from the new towns programme culminating in Milton Keynes. It isn't. Yet the underlying utopian ideals, which have underpinned all 'clean sweep' urban endeavours since the Garden City prototype of Letchworth, persist. Eco-towns are its latest manifestation.

This latest version is more extreme than all its predecessors. The arch-critic of the idea is probably Simon Jenkins. Writing in the *Guardian* he points out that, according to the Empty Homes Agency, 'building new houses emits 4.5 times more carbon than rehabilitating old ones'. He goes on: 'An eco-town has to build houses, roads, sewers, shops and all services from scratch. It is absurd to pretend that this is more carbon-efficient than expanding and "greening" existing settlements.' He concludes: 'The way to preserve the green of the countryside and maximise the carbon-efficiency of human habitation is to make today's cities work better. They are full of usable land… Cities are the new green' (Jenkins, 2008).

This chimes with the objections of Professor Anne Power, one of the key members of Lord Rogers' Urban Task Force, and John Houghton: 'The only sustainable solution to the housing crisis lies in "recycling" cities, not building on greenbelt.' Their article concludes: 'Cities, large, difficult and ambitious stretch human capacity to its limit, yet within their small, crowded spaces we find myriad signs of regrowth. In this lies our hope for the future' (Power and Houghton, 2007).

Writing in the *Guardian* (25 June 2008) architectural critic Jonathan Glancey suggests 'These ecotowns are a far from being benign project. The scheme is more of a land grab in favour of developers and retailers.' He concludes: 'Ecotowns reflect an utter failure of imagination. There is no commitment to design, no concern for urbanistics.'

Architect Lord Rogers is unequivocal: eco-towns are 'one of the biggest mistakes the government can make' and one that is due to be magnified in scale in the Thames Gateway project. Lord Rogers recently said in the House of Lords: 'There is something wrong when the Thames Gateway – Europe's biggest regeneration project – is still peppering the banks of the beautiful river Thames with shoddy, Toytown houses and Dan Dare glass towers. I fear that we are building the slums of tomorrow' (*Guardian*, 28 December 2008, p13). Reported in the same article, property developer Sir Stuart Lipton added his voice of criticism speaking to The Thames Gateway Forum: 'Will this be one of the biggest projects in UK history that has been dumbed-down by Noddy architecture?' (Figure 8.1).

1. Basildon
   10,700
2. Thurrock
   9,500
3. Barking & Dagenham
   20,000
4. Lewisham
   10,000
5. Greenwich
   19,000
6. Dartford
   15,500
7. Gravesham
   9,200
8. Medway
   16,000

Figure 8.1 Thames Gateway main housing projects

The verdict

The aims behind the eco-towns may be laudable but they are misplaced. The government's rationale is that they will influence towns and cities throughout the country; a classic trickle-down effect. This doesn't work in finance, and it is extremely unlikely to work in the built environment. The specification that is appropriate for eco-towns should also be good for all towns and cities. It is better to direct funding towards upgrading conurbations towards the eco-town standard than have a few shining examples that may become another case of the best being the enemy of the good. At worst they may fulfil the threat voiced by the Local Government Association: 'they will be the eco-slums of the future if they are built without regard to where residents can get jobs or training' (*Observer*, 13 July 2008).

This view has also been expressed by one of the original architects of Milton Keynes, Michael Edwards: 'They've pitched it all far too small. It's extremely difficult to make towns of 20,000 people the slightest bit self-sufficient' (*Guardian*, 28 December 2008).

In a time of economic recession developers will tend to favour prestigious developments on greenfield sites with easy access over urban brownfield sites possibly with remediation problems. The result could be that existing towns and cities may be starved of limited development resources. The evidence is manifest at the time of writing in the forest of abandoned cranes.

In addition, to suggest that any town can be genuinely zero carbon is to make considerable demands on energy efficiency and presumes an energy intensity of onsite renewable energy that is not yet available. Eco-towns could be an opportunity to demonstrate how the best of design can satisfy the highest ecological goals. Instead all indications point to a contradiction in terms.

Adaptive action for towns and cities

Across the population there is increasing pressure on individuals to make lifestyle changes. Figure 8.2 shows the extent to which the average individual contributed to the global warming problem in 2005; space heating and car travel clearly make the biggest contribution, accounting between them for almost 60 per cent of the total.

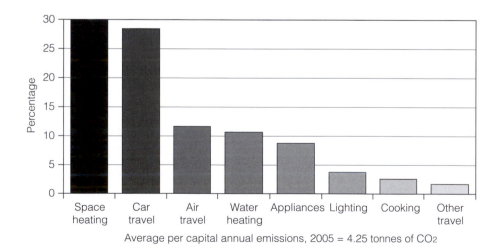

Average per capital annual emissions, 2005 = 4.25 tonnes of CO_2

Source: Defra, 2006

Figure 8.2 The average individual's contribution to annual CO_2 emissions

In response to this situation, at the grass roots level there is a parallel initiative to the eco-towns programme called the Transition Towns movement. The initiating principles behind this are a lack of confidence that governments will take appropriate action against climate change and the imminence of peak oil. Consequently communities are coming together to take action. The inspiration came from Rob Hoskins, a lecturer in sustainable living, in 2003. The first Transition Town was Totnes in Devon. It presented inhabitants with a 12 step guide to sustainable living. Step 1 was to establish a steering group to take the project forward. Steps 2–11 are about raising awareness, initiating working groups to discuss topics like food and fuel and the techniques for liaising with local government. Step 12 is the final challenge to create an energy action plan. Totnes has even established its own currency, accepted only by local businesses.

Totnes was followed by Lewes in East Sussex where the project has been so successful that it has formed the Ouse Valley Energy Service Company. Government grants have helped it to launch subsidized renewable energy technologies across the area. There are now 100 Transition Towns, the latest being Fujino in Japan. Such a movement is probably more in tune with the bottom-up spirit of the times than the idea of eco-towns, which will represent an implied rebuke against all lesser eco-aspirants. However, for the latter, help is at hand.

The TCPA guide for sustainable communities referred to at the start of the chapter drew attention to the *Adaptation Strategies for Climate Change in the Urban Environment* (ASCCUE) project, which has sought to quantify the potential of green space to moderate the impacts of climate change in the urban context. The project has produced a conurbation scale risk and adaptation assessment methodology to support policy in moderating climate change impacts. As a policy tool it begins by broadly analysing the impacts at the large urban scale to pave the way for neighbourhood scale analysis (Gwilliam et al, 2006).

At the conurbation scale the ASCCUE report makes several recommendations:

- High quality greenspace, made up of a linked network of well-irrigated open spaces that can be used by a range of people (a 'green grid'), which has additional ecological, recreational and flood storage benefits. Green infrastructure within urbanism includes green roofs and walls as well as the obvious features. In connection with plant health, there has to be access to water. Also, climate change means a longer growing season and changing species.
- Evaporative cooling through fountains, urban pools and lakes, rivers and canals.
- Shading will become increasingly important, achieved with trees, (deciduous) greater overhanging of eaves, narrow streets (canyon ventilation) and canopies.
- Passive ventilation through intelligent building form and orientation.

Managing temperature at the neighbourhood scale

The key measures that can be taken at a local level to manage changes in temperature include:

- Maximizing evaporative cooling from border planting, street trees, green roofs and elevations, for example. The ASCCUE project indicates that a 10 per cent reduction in urban greenery results in increased maximum surface temperatures in Manchester by the 2080s under the high emissions scenario.
- Evaporative cooling from ponds, roadside swales, flood alleviation lakes, fountains, rivers and canals.
- The orientation of buildings and arrangement of windows to minimize solar gain.
- Facade materials that are less heat absorbent.
- Light coloured finishes to pavements, roads and parking areas to minimize heat absorption.

- Porous pavements to facilitate rainwater infiltration.
- As an alternative to green roofs, reflective finishes to minimize thermal gain and help reduce internal temperatures.

Heat island effect

Increasing attention is being paid to the way built environments can amplify ambient temperature. In central London the 'heat island effect' can add 6°C to the temperature prevailing in open countryside (Figure 8.3).

According to the Met Office the heat island is the result of:

- the release (and reflection) of heat from industrial and domestic buildings;
- the absorption by concrete, brick and tarmac of heat during the day, and its release into the lower atmosphere at night;

- the reflection of solar radiation by glass buildings and windows – the central business districts of some urban areas can therefore have quite high albedo rates (proportion of light reflected);
- the emissions of hygroscopic pollutants from cars and heavy industry act as condensation nuclei, leading to the formation of cloud and smog that can trap radiation – in some cases a pollution dome can also build up;
- recent research on London's heat island has shown that the pollution domes can also filter incoming solar radiation, thereby reducing the build-up of heat during the day; at night the dome may trap some of the heat from the day, so these domes may be reducing the sharp differences between urban and rural areas;
- the relative absence of water from urban areas means that less energy is used for evapotranspiration and more is available to heat the lower atmosphere;

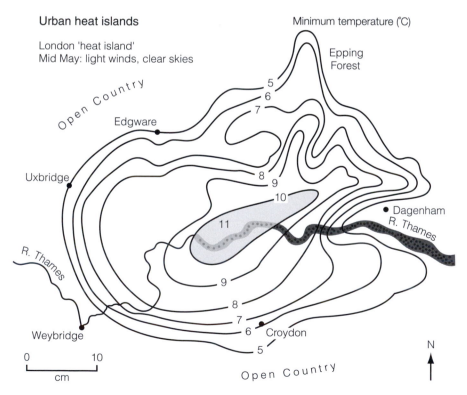

Figure 8.3 Six degree heat island effect in London

- the absence of strong winds to both disperse the heat and bring in cooler air from rural and suburban areas – urban heat islands are often most clearly defined on calm summer evenings, often under blocking anti-cyclones (Figure 8.4).

Even a small city like Chester can experience a sharp heat island effect that falls off rapidly at the city boundary (Figure 8.5).

Responding to the call for innovative use of space within and around buildings, Robert Shaw of the TCPA counters with the warning that 'ill-thought through promotion of high density development in order to save land can do much to exacerbate heat island problems. Space needs to be left or created for large canopy trees combined with green spaces and green roofs that can help to keep summer temperatures in cities cooler and minimize the risk of urban flooding' (TCPA, 2007, p2).

A diagram from the TCPA report (Figure 8.6) encapsulates many of the strategies that can alleviate problems arising from high temperatures (TCPA, 2007, p19). This chapter ends with an emphasis on temperature because this is an impact that will bear on inhabitants on an international scale as demonstrated in 2003. Floods and even storms can be localized events but high temperatures are widespread and inescapable.

Masdar City Abu Dhabi

It seems appropriate to end this chapter with a project that promises to set the standard for zero-carbon towns and cities of the future, regardless of climate zone. It is the energy crisis rather than global warming that has inspired the most ambitious plans for a city 'where carbon emissions are zero'. Masdar City (Figure 8.7) is the centrepiece of the Emirate of Abu Dhabi's plans to be a leader in renewable energy as a hedge against the time when oil and gas reserves expire. In many of its forms it will echo the

Figure 8.4 Inversion producing a pollution dome

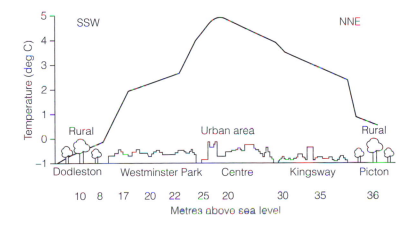

Figure 8.5 Extreme heat island effect, Chester, UK

Menu of strategies for managing high temperatures

The diagram summarizes the range of actions and techniques available to increase adaptive capacity.

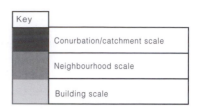

Key

Conurbation/catchment scale

Neighbourhood scale

Building scale

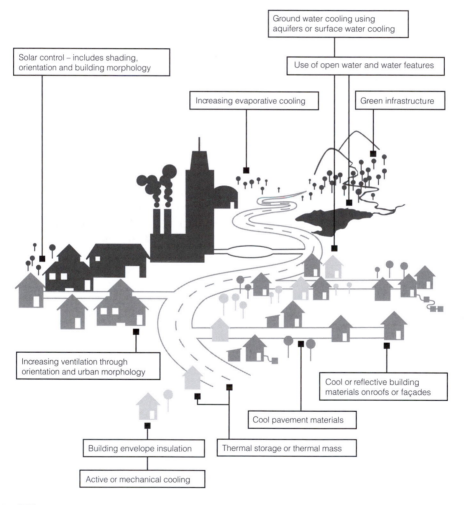

Ground water cooling using aquifers or surface water cooling

Use of open water and water features

Solar control – includes shading, orientation and building morphology

Increasing evaporative cooling

Green infrastructure

Increasing ventilation through orientation and urban morphology

Cool or reflective building materials on roofs or façades

Cool pavement materials

Building envelope insulation

Thermal storage or thermal mass

Active or mechanical cooling

Source: Courtesy TCPA

Figure 8.6 Managing high temperatures on an urban scale

traditional Arab city with narrow streets and extensive shaded walks (Figure 8.8). The city will be powered by photovoltaics, solar thermal, wind power and bio-energy. The city plan is orientated to the northeast to minimize the amount of direct sunlight falling onto buildings' elevations and windows. It will house about 50,000 permanent residents plus a considerable

Source: Masdar Masterplan Development, Abu Dhabi, UAE, 2007. Client: Masdar-Abu Dhabi Future Energy Company Mubadala Development Company. Business Plan: Ernst and Young. Architect: Urban Design: Foster + Partners. Renewable Energy: E.T.A. Climate Engineering: Transsolar. Sustainability-Infrastructure: WSP Energy. HVAC Engineer: WSP. Transportation: Systematica. Quantity Surveyor: Cyril Sweet Limited. Landscape consultant: Gustfason Porter.

Figure 8.7 Masdar City, Abu Dhabi

Source: Masdar Masterplan Development, Abu Dhabi, UAE, 2007. Client: Masdar-Abu Dhabi Future Energy Company Mubadala Development Company. Business Plan: Ernst and Young. Architect: Urban Design: Foster + Partners. Renewable Energy: E.T.A. Climate Engineering: Transsolar. Sustainability-Infrastructure: WSP Energy. HVAC Engineer: WSP. Transportation: Systematica. Quantity Surveyor: Cyril Sweet Limited. Landscape consultant: Gustfason Porter.

Figure 8.8 Street in Masdar City

transient population of students, academics and technologists. The city will be car free, cars being replaced by a personal rapid transit (PRT) system. Each car carries six people and is powered by batteries charged by solar power. These vehicles would run beneath the city. The cars can be programmed by passengers to target any one of approximately 1500 stations.

There is a good chance that this will be a genuinely zero carbon city and there is a touch of irony in the fact that it has been designed by UK architect Norman Foster and its carbon profile calculated by Bioregional. Even though Masdar is sited in a very different climate to the UK (although potentially not so different by 2050) there are numerous features that are relevant to Europe. Lord Foster is designing eco-cities in the Middle East and China, but eco-towns in the UK will be largely at the mercy of developers. It seems we have graduated from being a nation of shopkeepers to one of spec builders.

Appendix

Extract from Planning Policy Statement: eco-towns under consideration

Sustainability appraisal, habitats regulations assessment and impact assessment

Q5 Do you have any comments on the accompanying Sustainability Appraisal/ Habitats Regulations Assessment or the Impact Assessment?

Q6 Do you have any comments on the issues identified in the Sustainability Appraisal/ Habitats Regulations Assessment of the locations for eco-towns?

Q6.1 Penbury (Stoughton)

Q6.2 Middle Quniton

Q6.3 Whitehill-Bordon

Q6.4 Weston Otmoor and Cherwell

Q6.5 Ford

Q6.6 St Austell (China Clay Community)

Q6.7 Rossington

Q6.8 Marston Vale

Q6.9 North East Elsenham

Q6.10 Rushcliffe (Nottinghamshire)

Q6.11 Greater Norwich

Q6.12 Leeds City Region

Although SA of the locations for Manby, Curborough and Hanley Grange have been undertaken, these locations are not being taken forward as a result of promoters withdrawing schemes from the programme.

Q6.13 Curborough

Q6.14 Manby

Q6.15 Hanley Grange and Cambridgeshire

9

The Housing Inheritance

Britain has a unique mass housing inheritance, thanks to its role in initiating the industrial revolution. Many were built in haste to house the labour force for the rapidly expanding economy. There were exceptions: some houses were built by philanthropic mill owners who assumed responsibility for the welfare of their employees. World famous examples include Saltaire near Leeds and Port Sunlight near Birkenhead. For much of the rest of the 19th-century housing stock, the official view from the 1950s–1980s was to consider them prime candidates for demolition. Liverpool provides a classic example of this attitutde.

The policy of demolition was deemed cost-effective because it was considered that getting rid of the poorer quality housing and rebuilding would be cheaper than upgrading. In major UK cities the demolition and replacement of older terraced properties began in the 1930s, a process ably assisted by the Luftwaffe in the 1940s. The irony is that, of the 27 million or so existing homes in Britain in need of extensive upgrading, a significant proportion are the ones that replaced these demolished properties under the post-war rebuilding and development policies.

Statistics

Case study: England

According to the English House Condition Survey 2006, there were 22 million homes in England of which 70 per cent were owner-occupied and 2.6 million privately rented. Pre-1919 homes accounted for 22 per cent with 94 per cent being privately owned and 71 per cent owner-occupied.

Over the second half of the 20th century the greatest change that occurred in the composition of households was the rise of single person occupancy. In 1971 it comprised 17 per cent of the total and by 2000 this had risen to 32 per cent. Single occupancy homes are also the least energy efficient (Energy Saving Trust, 2006). According to the Department for Communities and Local Government (DCLG, 2006) it is estimated that the number of homes will increase by 209,000 per year until 2026 and that 75 per cent will be single person households. This will have a direct effect on the stock profile and will exert pressure on construction costs. The result will be an emphasis on quantity rather than quality (Figure 9.1).

Housing condition

In England 9.2 million houses are considered to be 'hard to treat' (HTT). This adds up to 43 per cent of the total stock. A HTT dwelling is defined as one that, for whatever reason, cannot accommodate 'staple' or 'cost-effective energy efficiency measures' (Defra, 2008b). 'Staple' measures consist of loft insulation, cavity wall insulation and improvements to a heating system, such as installing gas central heating.

In 2008, the government agreed to accept the recommendation of the Energy Efficiency Partnership for Homes that carbon emissions attributable to housing should be reduced by 80 per cent by 2050. The UK Green Building Council (UK-GBC) was given responsibility to lead the project. What needs to happen now is that UK-GBC is actually allowed to lead the process. The Council is forthright in its view that

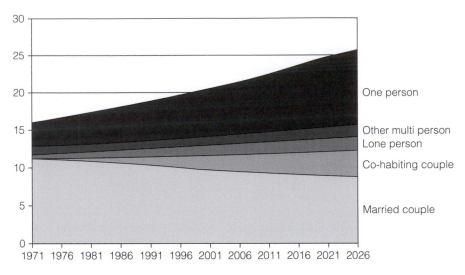

Source: Department of Trade and Industry (2006)

Figure 9.1 Breakdown of household growth in England 1971–2026

there is 'broad agreement that current levels of activity will not deliver the savings required for ambitious carbon reduction targets in the long term' (UK-GBC, 2008). Meanwhile the Parliamentary Committee on Climate Change has set out interim targets to 2020. These will be in the form of three five-year targets. The government was due to respond to these proposals in the spring of 2009. The scale of the challenge is shown in the histogram in Figure 9.2.

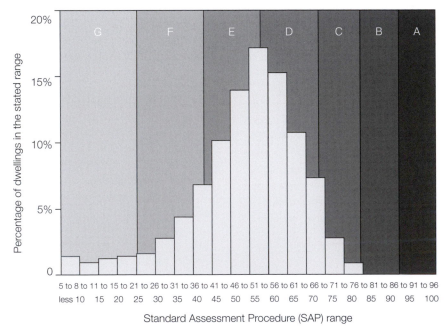

Source: based on BRE (2007a)

Figure 9.2 The challenge is to shift 90 per cent of the housing stock to Energy Performance Certificate (EPC) bands A and B

Proposed solutions

> *Demand reduction measures which are not currently cost effective will have to be delivered to achieve the 2050 target, for example, solid wall insulation. Low to zero carbon (LZC) technologies will be needed in the majority of, if not all, homes.*
>
> (UK-GBC, 2008)

The report recommends that the government should:

- set a long-term carbon reduction target for the household sector of a least 80 per cent by 2050, with interim targets every five years;
- establish mandatory targets, phased over time, to upgrade the energy performance of existing homes;
- provide financial incentives to support low carbon homes;
- review the roles and scope of existing delivery bodies;
- explore the feasibility of developing targeted 'low carbon zones', supporting improvements through a district- or area-based application of a whole house approach to refurbishment.

The complexity of the housing stock and the range of occupancy conditions presents a daunting challenge. However, under Article 7 of the EU Energy Performance in Buildings Directive, implementation of Energy Performance Certificates (EPCs) should offer a mechanism for focusing on the details of the problem.[1] The mandatory requirements mentioned in the second point above should include a statutory obligation on local authorities to require all home owners and landlords to obtain EPCs for their properties within a set time, say 2 years. This would provide a measure of the problem, broken down to a neighbourhood scale.

The key question is: what are the operational implications of an 80 per cent CO_2 reduction strategy? Setting targets is the easy part; how to roll out an effective upgrading programme to this standard across the nation will require government intervention at a level normally confined to war time.

Operation and management

The UK-GBC recommends that 'alongside targets for emissions reductions from homes … Government should develop a national strategy for delivery, to provide clarity around roles and responsibilities including what is expected of local authorities, individuals, communities and the supply chain' (UK-GBC, 2008, p9).

This is in tune with an Engineering and Physical Sciences Research Council (EPSRC) research programme designed by the author earlier in the decade, which recommended that, for a scheme on a national scale, the operational structure will have to be consistent across the country (Smith, 1998). The Energy Saving Trust (EST) would be the obvious body to have oversight of the programme, being accountable to the government for the efficient operation of the scheme. It would compile the retrofit specification and set the standards of performance.

The next tier of management should be the local authority. Councils would be responsible for delivering the statutory carbon savings within their boundary and within a definite timescale. A member of the EST might be positioned within the local authority for the duration of the project. Using the EPC data, councils could fine-tune the operation according neighbourhood characteristics. The median cost of energy across households within a postal district would be the basis for a contract that would ensure an average gain of 15 per cent over the combined cost of energy and refurbishment.

The operational responsibility would be delegated to specialist project management companies that have demonstrated competence in this field. The contractors for the operation would be approved energy service companies (ESCOs) who would assume responsibility both for the supply of energy and the installation of the energy-saving measures. It is suggested that a contract would embrace a postal district with a local authority (LA) agreeing a contract price for both the delivery of energy and retrofit operation, the latter being on a fixed price basis according to house type. Householders would be locked-in to the ESCO for the duration of the specific neighbourhood contract with the LA, with the latter ensuring that the ESCO did not abuse its monopoly position. The work would be carried out on a rolling programme, neighbourhood by neighbourhood, beginning with the poorest quality housing. As an incentive to owner-occupiers and landlords to participate, a subsidized loan scheme would be made available, but only for the duration of the specific neighbourhood programme.

Currently, the government commitment is limited to the Carbon Emissions Reduction Target (CERT), which delivers subsidies for cavity wall and loft insulation and low energy lighting up to 2020. The UK-GBC comments: 'However, there remains the issue about how to deliver and fund measures once the "low hanging fruit" of cavity wall and loft insulation and low energy lighting have been addressed. Currently there is only a niche market for higher cost measures and this is unlikely to change *without major policy intervention*' (UK-GBC, 2008, p2, italics added).

The scale of the 'major policy intervention' necessary is summarized in The Oxford University Environmental Change Institute report *Home Truths*, 2007. This suggests that achieving the target of 80 per cent carbon savings in the housing sector by 2050 would incur an annual cost of £11.95 billion. This is broken down into:

- £3.65 billion/year for a low interest loan programme;
- £3.3 billion/year to tackle fuel poverty through targeted low carbon zones;
- £2.6 billion/year to fund a coordinating role for local authorities for other programmes and to develop heat networks;
- £2.4 billion/year to provide tax incentives to encourage participation in upgrading programmes.

For the present author all this has a touch of déjà vu. The main objective of the EPSRC research was to test the hypothesis that a vigorous upgrading programme of the housing stock would ultimately yield net savings to the Exchequer (Sharples et al, 2001). This was prompted by the claim by Brenda Boardman of the Oxford Environmental Change Unit (in a

lecture to the Institute of Housing in 2000) that bad housing was incurring a cost to the health service of £1 billion per year.

At that time (c.2000) the backlog in repairs to the housing stock in England was put at £19 billion (*The Economist*, 5 May 2001). The UK-GBC report estimates that the annual repair and maintenance bill now amounts to £24 billion. The additional cost of upgrading the stock is put at £3.5–5 billion per year. The positive aspect of this is that these costs represent retrofit business opportunities that can be especially beneficial in times of recession in the new-build sector.

Unavoidable policy imperatives

The fuel poor

The first priority is to address the needs of the fuel poor, that is, families or individuals who incur energy costs exceeding 10 per cent of their income.

In the past much of the grant support for social housing was targeted at installing energy efficient central heating with condensing boilers. However, it has been shown that installing energy efficient central heating in homes that are inadequately insulated is wasteful since the fuel poor cannot afford to use the system to full advantage. The truth is that if the wall insulation is not improved, central heating exacerbates problems of condensation by increasing the temperature difference between the internal air and the walls.

In this sector of the community there is no alternative but for grant aid to be at 100 per cent of the cost of the upgrading package. There would have to be a 10 per cent/year claw back agreement with homeowners who qualify for the 100 per cent to deter them from selling the home to exploit the added value of the upgrade.

Options for the fuel secure

For those for whom energy costs are easily managed, there seems to be little appetite for thermal improvements. In 1999 the Co-operative Bank offered its customers low interest loans to 'green' their homes. Out of a six figure circulation about 60 responded and just over 30 took up the offer. Companies carrying out projects under the Energy Efficiency Standards of Performance (EESoP) regime of the government of that time had difficulty persuading householders to accept energy efficiency improvements even when they were free. Things are not very different today.

There is no avoiding the fact that, if there is to be robust participation in a voluntary upgrading programme by homeowners, there has to be a financial incentive. Aside from the fuel poor, many in this sector, even today, do not perceive the cost of energy to be a major problem. To make an upgrading package attractive to the fuel secure and to compensate them for the disruption, the annual cost of energy plus repayments for the improvements should be at least 15 per cent *less* than previously paid for energy alone on a 'same warmth basis'. For housing at the lower end of the SAP/EPC scale we could be talking of an 80–90 per cent improvement in the thermal efficiency of the property so that 'same warmth' energy bills would show a substantial reduction, leaving a significant margin for increased comfort. It is evident that, for many properties, raising the thermal standard to economic comfort levels would incur excessive repayment costs if market rates of return are included.

One outcome of the EPSRC research was that the fuel-secure homeowners will only come on board in significant numbers if 10–15 year loans for upgrading are available at low interest and can be paid off if a house is sold before the redemption of the debt. This means there would need to be a subsidy to bridge the gap between the cost acceptable to the homeowners and a market rate of return on the loan with perhaps half met by the government and the remainder by the energy companies. This would be a logical destination for receipts from carbon trading. For some it might be necessary to seek low start loans with repayments linked to inflation, thus keeping the real repayment cost more or less constant.

To summarize, the attractions for the homeowner are:

- an increase in house value;
- diminishing real cost of retrofit repayments over 15 years if based on a fixed repayment basis;
- reduced maintenance costs;
- increased comfort;
- improved health;
- substantial reduction in energy costs once the loan has been repaid;
- a permanent relative cushion against steeply rising energy prices, especially after 'peak oil'.

Private rented homes

Undoubtedly the most challenging problem concerns the private rented sector where tenants normally meet all their energy costs. There may be no way of avoiding coercive legislation. First, legislation will be needed to require local authorities to obtain proof of satisfactory heating standards as a condition of releasing housing benefit, bringing private landlords more into line with registered social landlords.

Second, there should be a requirement that accommodation offered for rent should achieve a minimum of EPC level C by a target date, say 2020. In the meantime, there should be rigorous application of the regulation that if a property is materially altered then the whole property should be raised to current building regulations standards.

Unfortunately, properties at the bottom end of the 'hard to treat' category will be beyond even the most generous cost-effective upgrading and here the only option will be to demolish and rebuild.

Cost estimates

The cost of upgrading by overcladding existing terraced, solid wall homes with 75–100mm of insulation is currently ~£8–10,000; the average unit cost of central heating is ~£4–5000. However, as explained above, installing energy efficient central heating in homes that are inadequately insulated is inefficient. Professor Paul Elkins (cited in Green Alliance, 2009) has this prescription for the housing stock: 'The ultimate goal of this programme [CERT] should be to make one million homes per year super-efficient, which is likely to entail, on relatively conservative assumptions, expenditure of about £10,000 per home, totalling an investment of about £10 billion per annum. Even then it would take a quarter of a century to bring the UK housing stock up to the levels of energy efficiency implied by the 80 per cent reduction target', which is the UK commitment for 2050.

However, when benefits are factored in, the picture becomes less daunting. The EPSRC research programme cited above suggested that a 15 year programme, assuming a 6 per cent discount rate, would yield a net social benefit of around £2.4 billion. It will now be greater. Further benefits should accrue when the next round of the carbon trading scheme is implemented in 2013.

Benefits to the Exchequer

- more disposable capital from reduced energy costs;
- reduced demands on social services;
- National Health Service (NHS) savings with fewer cold and damp related illnesses;
- the CO_2 emissions reductions assisting the UK target;
- in 2001 employment gains were estimated at one new job for every £39,000 directly and a further job for each £80,000 due to the indirect creation of employment (the respend factor). These figures should be adjusted for inflation. In a time of high unemployment in the construction industry, there is also the avoided job seekers' allowance.

In summary, there are six key points.

- For there to be a significant uptake in the private sector (over 50 per cent) the credit allowed over 15 years for the upgrading element should be at low interest.
- Once the upgrading is complete, there should be a minimum of a net 15 per cent reduction in combined energy and repayment costs as against former energy costs alone.

- For the fuel poor (on the formula of disposable income) grants should meet the total cost of upgrading.
- The implementation should be on a once-and-for-all rolling programme basis, starting with neighbourhoods with the highest incidence of fuel poverty.
- Private landlords must be obliged to provide proof of satisfactory heating standards with the requirement that their properties should reach the standard of EPC level C by 2020.
- The skills shortage means that a training programme should be instituted as a matter of urgency to create an army of retrofit operatives qualified to a national standard.

The problem with setting standards like 80 per cent carbon reduction is that they do not relate to a fixed baseline. Households are almost infinitely variable in their pattern of energy use as well as the thermal efficiency of their properties. It would be better to establish what are the optimum technical measures that can be afforded over, say, a 15 year upgrading programme.

Whilst the overall costs estimated by Boardman (Boardman, 2005, pp100–101) are substantial, it can be argued that they are justifiable in the light of the billions spent on rescuing financial institutions from the results of their avarice and irresponsibility.

Eco-renovation of historic houses

Between 2009 and 2014 the National Trust is embarking on a programme to renovate over 5000 buildings to meet a set of minimum environmental standards. These will include installing maximum loft insulation, double or secondary glazing, thermostatic heating controls, efficient lighting systems, water saving devices and rainwater storage. This is a formidable challenge for a property stock that includes castles, stately homes, churches, farm cottages, urban terrace and semi-detached houses and public houses. The majority of buildings have historic value, which means that eco-renovation has to be sensitive to both their historic and aesthetic qualities. Since most of the stock is Victorian and older, environmental interventions can have a significant impact on the way buildings perform as well as their long-term integrity.

The Trust is committed to achieving significant reductions in energy use and the incidence of waste. Where possible local materials will be used and local services engaged. As a charity the Trust is constrained regarding available funds. However, it recognizes that many of these undertakings will reduce its operational costs. For example, it is working with its partner npower to instal biomass heating systems and solar technology.

Technical recommendations

There is only space here to offer a flavour of the technical options currently available to refurbish existing homes to be at least level C of the EPC standards.

Solid wall houses

In all cases roofs/lofts should receive a minimum of 250mm of insulation, with pipes and cold water tanks fully lagged. External walls should be insulated to the highest standard that is technically feasible. In the case of ~130mm solid wall construction, where possible this should receive overcladding with at least 100mm of insulation if using mineral fibre or 75mm using phenolic foam finished with a waterproof render. Cavity wall homes from the late 1920s should receive either overcladding with 75mm phenolic foam or dry lining insulation such as proprietary aerogel on backing as well as cavity insulation.

All windows should be replaced with the equivalent of triple glazing preferably in timber frames with a U-value of at least $0.8W/m^2K$. Buildings in conservation areas pose a special problem. Here secondary glazing is often the only option. In all cases external doors should be to current building regulation thermal standards.

One of the most abundant house types where fuel poverty is implicated is 19th-century terraced houses (Figures 9.3 and 9.4). These houses are usually narrow fronted and deep plan, with an L-shaped rear plan. The walls are 9 inch (22.5cm) brick with the front elevation finished in facing bricks and the rear in common bricks.

One strategy that has been suggested is to overclad the rear of these houses – which comprises the majority wall area – and dry-line the front walls with insulation. This operation involves modifications to eave details and soil and rainwater pipes, although not necessarily the ground connections. Other problems may occur at window reveals and corners.

A major source of heat loss is due to the ground floor construction. With solid floors the only option is to lay 25mm of rigid insulation over the existing floor. Doors, skirtings, etc. then need to be modified. Where there are suspended timber floors, the best strategy is to replace them with concrete floors topped with rigid insulation. The alternative is to fill between joists with insulation, which will involve raising the floorboards. If there is sufficient underfloor space to allow access, insulation can be installed without excessive disruption.

It has been claimed that up to 40 per cent of heat lost in older properties is due to leakage. Open fire places are a rapid exit route for heat when not in use. To keep the option of a flame fire, the only solution is a closed wood-burning stove with a flue lining. Draught exclusion is an important part of the thermal efficiency programme. The standard method of measurement of air tightness is to assess the rate of air change per hour through leakage when the building is pressurised to 50 Pascals. A typical new house could have a rate of change of 15 air changes per house (15ACH50P),[2] so we can assume that older dwellings will be significantly worse. To put this into perspective, for new homes it is recommended that the rate is 2ACH50P. In all cases where there are significant improvements in air tightness, it is vital to incorporate mechanical or passive stack ventilation that achieves at least one air change per hour. A reasonable compromise leakage rate for older properties should be 5–6ACH50P.

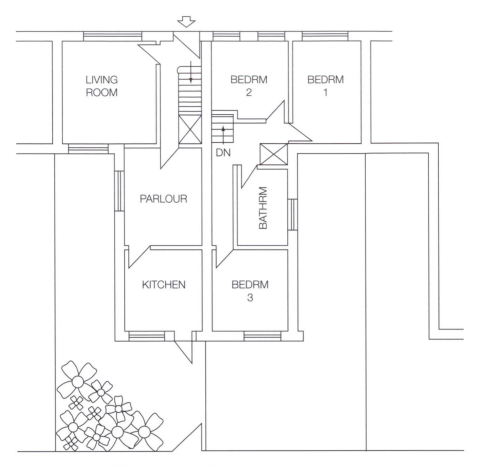

Figure 9.3 Layout of typical 19th-century terraced houses

Figure 9.4 Ubiquitous Victorian semi-detached houses, Sheffield, UK

Extract ventilation over cookers is vital. Consideration should be given to air extraction that is automatically activated by the presence of carbon monoxide/nitrogen dioxide even where there are electric cookers, since these may be converted to gas at a later stage. As a general rule, mains connected smoke alarms should be fitted, but not in kitchens where heat detectors are more appropriate.

For space heating, in wet systems condensing boilers should be suitably sized for the thermal efficiency of the dwelling. All radiators should have thermostatic valves to enable them to be individually set in conjunction with appropriate central controls. Controls and thermostats should be simple to understand and operate.

The domestic item that, in most cases, is responsible for the greatest consumption of electricity is the fridge-freezer. Including an ultra-low energy (Scandinavian) unit in the package would have a significant impact on electricity bills. (For more information see Smith, 2004.)

Case study: Victorian solid wall property

Number 17 St Augustine Road was effectively derelict when Camden Council decided it should be refurbished and let as social housing (Figure 9.5). Its specification includes:

- all windows fitted with high specification wood frame argon-filled double glazing;
- external cladding with Kingspan insulation giving a U-value of $0.19W/m^2K$;
- floor and internal insulation;
- roof insulation with a U-value of $0.15W/m^2K$;
- an air tightness standard of $6.7m^3/m^2/hr$ at 50pa. Note: this is a UK standard; elsewhere the EU and US the measure is: air changes from the total volume per hour at 50pa. There is no way of truly comparing them.

This has been an expensive operation, and Camden Council could not remotely afford to upgrade all its solid wall housing stock to this standard. So, not only is it a demonstration of

best practice refurbishment, it also demonstrates that government support will be essential if the housing problem is to be addressed.

Multi-storey refurbishment

Of the multi-storey housing that remains, much of it is still under local authority or housing association control. This has enabled a widespread programme of refurbishment to be undertaken supported by government subsidies. Sheffield has a typical stock of high rise apartments that are currently undergoing refurbishment (Figure 9.6).

The verdict on completed examples is that there was a small reduction in energy consumption but a big improvement in comfort and health. There was a significant reduction in

Source: Camden Borough Council

Figure 9.5 17 Augustine Road, Camden, London

Figure 9.6 Cemetery Road flats, Sheffield, UK, 2009

associated CO_2 emissions. On the negative side, there was much disquiet at the increase in rent to cover the cost of the improvements.

Case study: Hawkridge House, hall of residence, University College, London

A multi-storey refurbishment that sets the standard for existing high rise buildings has been undertaken by a UK university. According to Tony

Source: Photograph courtesy of Cole Thompson Anders

Figure 9.7 Hawkridge House, London University, after refurbishment

Nuttall of Cole Thompson Anders, Architects for the project: 'Hawkridge House refurbishment was completed this year [2008] with 100mm Stotherm expanded polystyrene external overcladding installed over the existing Reema Precast Concrete Panel construction – mineral wool wasn't suitable due to wind loading. A U-value of 0.28 was achieved.' (Figure 9.7.)

Notes

1   There is a problem with the algorithm underpinning the EPC in that it is derived from RD SAP 05 (Standard Assessment Procedure), considered by some to be flawed.
2   This is the EU/US method of measurement rather than the UK system.

10

Non-domestic Buildings

Across the European Union, buildings account for about half of all CO_2 emissions. In the UK, housing is responsible for about 27 per cent leaving all other buildings responsible for 23 per cent. The 'other buildings' contains: public buildings – government offices, both local and national, hospitals, schools and universities – commercial offices and industrial premises.

The UK government has set targets for CO_2 reductions in its own buildings, and, in almost all cases, has fallen well short, even in the case of some of the most recently constructed buildings. The target is a 12.5 per cent reduction by 2010–2011. Overall there has been a 4 per cent reduction but this is mainly due to savings in the Ministry of Defence (MOD) estate. If this is excluded there is actually an increase of 22 per cent. Even the MOD reductions are distorted by the delegating of some of its role to the private company QuinetiQ. If this is taken into account, the overall reduction across the Crown Estates falls to 0.7 per cent (Sustainable Development Commission, 2007).

The dichotomy between architectural aesthetic quality and energy efficiency is illustrated in the extreme in the Imperial War Museum North. Its architect, Daniel Libeskind, was probably not given an energy efficiency brief, so he cannot be blamed for the fact that his iconic building comes bottom on the Energy Performance Certificate scale, A–G. Some of the sharpest criticism has been levelled against the flagship development of Portcullis House, a recent extension to the Palace of Westminster. In answer to a parliamentary question, it was shown to be consuming about 400kWh/m^2, which is over four times more than envisaged. In part this may be due to the way the building has been used, especially in the exponential growth of information technology (IT) activity. This also confounded the designers of the ground-breaking Zicer Building at the University of East Anglia and it highlights a fundamental problem faced across the non-domestic sector.

A report by the Worldwatch Institute suggests that the growing reliance on the Internet is implicated in the rapid increase in related CO_2 emissions from offices. The prediction is that the energy required to meet the needs of Internet use and data storage can be expected to double by 2020 according to data analysts McKinsey and company (Manyika et al, 2008). Much of this increase is due to rapid growth in Internet use in China and India, where electricity is mostly generated by coal fired plants. In 2007 China accounted for 23 per cent of global carbon emissions related to IT (Block, 2008).

This makes it all the more important that new buildings across the non-domestic sector maximize their energy efficiency. The US Department of Energy (DoE) has launched a Zero-Net Energy Commercial Buildings Initiative (CBI). Advanced green building technology plus onsite renewable electricity generation will aim to achieve the net zeroC goal by 2025. The programme will be driven by the collaboration of five national laboratories on the scientific resources. They will promote the 'transformation of the built environment, lower our carbon footprint in buildings and accelerate commercial deployment of clean, efficiency building technologies' (David Rogers, US Deputy Assistant Secretary for Energy Efficiency, May 2007.)

The Energy Independence and Security Act of 2007 authorizes the Department of Energy to collaborate with the private sector, the DoE's National Laboratories, other federal agencies and non-government organizations to advance high performance green buildings.

The DoE's programme is worth quoting since it has implications for all developed and developing countries. It will promote:

- research and development on technology;
- sponsorship of pilot and demonstration projects across multiple climate zones;
- provision of technical assistance to encourage widespread technology adoption;
- the development of training materials and programmes for builders;
- public education on the need for efficiency in new and existing buildings;
- the work of code-setting bodies to ensure technologies are properly deployed;
- the analysis of incentives for builders, landlords and tenants to ensure cost-effective investments are made on a life-cycle basis;
- the development of a method to measure and verify energy savings.

Zero carbon for offices (defined in Chapter 5) will become mandatory in the UK during the second decade of this century. The scale of the challenge is clear from Figures 10.1 and 10.2 since the standard air conditioned office is still the preferred option in the speculative office sector.

According to services engineers Faber Maunsell, over 50 per cent of CO_2 emissions derive from non-building related equipment. The fastest growing energy demand is from IT equipment. In their prescription for the low carbon office, Faber Maunsell recommend minimizing heating, cooling and lighting demand by means of:

- low energy appliances;
- good air tightness;
- shading;
- solar protection;
- natural light;
- mixed mode ventilation.

This, in turn, requires the efficiency optimization of systems to reduce CO_2:

- heat recovery;
- natural ventilation;
- variable speed drives on pumps and fans (including soft start motors);
- natural ventilation;
- lighting control systems;
- combined heat and power;
- tri-generation where appropriate; e.g. biomass thermal engine producing electricity, direct heat and secondary heat from the exhaust.

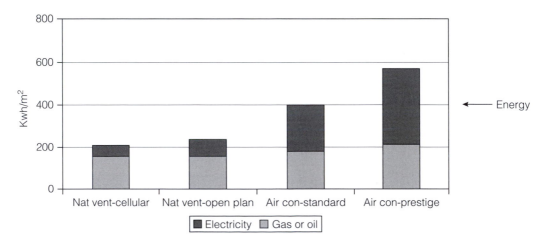

Source: ECON 19 and Faber Maunsell

Figure 10.1 Energy use according to office type

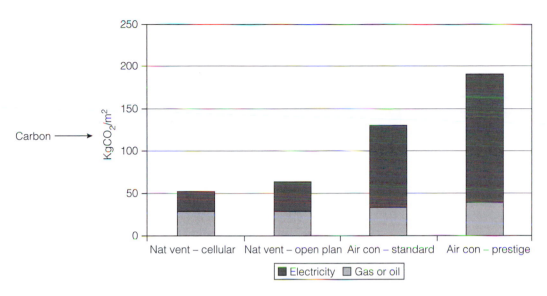

Source: ECON 19 and Faber Maunsell

Figure 10.2 CO_2 emissions according to office type

The UK's building regulations are catching up with the problem of overheating in offices and teaching spaces. Part L2A requires that the risk of overheating must be assessed for rooms without additional cooling. The temperature limit for offices and teaching spaces is 25–26°C.

The overheating criterion for commercial offices is that the temperature should not exceed 28°C for more than 1 per cent of the occupied time. Assessment should be made using the Chartered Institution of Building Services Engineers (CIBSE) Design Summer Year (DSY) guide. The normal range of design temperatures for all main teaching, office and recreational spaces should be 21–26°C.

In Manchester, planners require:

- at least 25 per cent reduction in CO_2 as against Part L2;
- at least 20 per cent of total site energy demand to be met by onsite renewables;
- BREEAM 'Very Good' rating as a minimum.

Case studies

The Innovate Green Office, Thorpe Trading Estate, Leeds

The architects for this development were Rio Architects and the environmental engineers King Shaw Associates.

Speculative offices have, on the whole, been the last to go beyond building regulations in terms of their environmental specification. The Innovate Green Office (Figure 10.3) is an exception, having received the highest ever BREEAM rating at 87.55 per cent. An important contributor to this rating is the high thermal mass of the structural hollowcore concrete used. It emits 80 per cent less CO_2 than a conventional air conditioned office at $22kgCO_2/m^2$. It does this without any contribution from renewable sources of power, making it an outstanding example of passive design based on first principles: orientation, thermal mass, maximization of natural light and

Source: Photograph: Jon Littlewood, TermoDeck

Figure 10.3 Innovate Green Office, Thorpe Trading Estate, Leeds

high levels of insulation (Figure 10.4). It achieves this by means of:

- concrete exposed internally to reduce extremes of temperature by thermal mass;
- use of recycled materials for concrete and reinforcement;
- floor and roof members are planks by TermoDeck with their cross-connected hollow cores to provide supply air. (The TermoDeck system works in conjunction with controlled mechanical ventilation to exploit the heat exchange between the structure and the internal environment. It acts as a thermal labyrinth, emitting air through perforations in the slab. The building's fabric stores solar gain, releasing it overnight);
- a high level of insulation means that internal gains provide the majority of useful heat;

- mechanical ventilation with heat recovery means that heat gains from people, and increasingly from computers, enables an air handling unit (AHU) to collect heat gain and store it within the TermoDeck for later reuse;
- summer cooling is provided by a combination of passive night purging and active cooling from a chiller using TermoDeck as a thermal (cool) store;
- a vacuum drainage system harvests rainwater to be used to flush toilets;
- permeable paving and a natural wetland area reduce the risk of flash flooding.

The result of these measures is a building that is claimed to be 80 per cent more energy efficient than a typical comparable air conditioned office. The proportion of energy needed for space heating is 12 per cent compared with 44 per cent

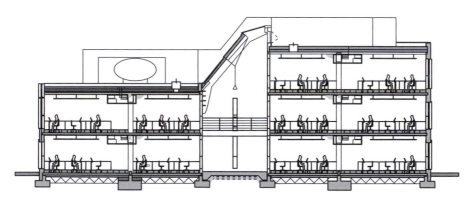

Figure 10.4 Innovate Green Office section

for a conventional office, thanks to ventilation being by means of heat recovery.

The Natural Trust HQ Heelis Building, Swindon

The Heelis building (Figure 10.5) was inspired by the previous occupant of the Swindon site, which was Brunel's railway engineering works. The design was also driven by the requirement that the four disparate arms of the National Trust should be accommodated in a single, open plan building.

The architects, Feilden Clegg Bradley, concluded that the answer was a deep plan, low rise building covering the whole site (Figures 10.6 and 10.7).

The southern part of the building contains the public areas and is naturally lit with full height glazing and roof lights. A colonnade

Source: Courtesy of Feilden Clegg Bradley, Architects

Figure 10.5 Heelis building southeast elevation

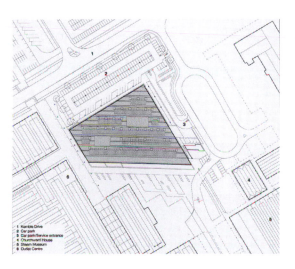

Source: Courtesy Feilden Clegg Bradley

Figure 10.6 Heelis building site layout

Source: Couttesy Feilden Clegg Bradley

Figure 10.7 Heelis aerial view

provides shading as well as an open air extension to the public area. The dominant aspect of the design is the 21st century interpretation of the northlight trusses of the Brunel building. The client, architects and services engineer, Max Fordham, are all strongly committed to sustainability principles in design and so it was inevitable that this would be an iconic example of bioclimatic architecture.

Initially there was a debate regarding the choice of structure between timber and steel. Timber would seem to be the obvious ecological choice. However, if much of the steel was from recycled sources the difference became negligible, especially as the steel could be recycled again more efficiently than timber. Consequently steel was selected, resulting in an unobtrusive internal grid of slender cylindrical columns.

The irregularity of the site inspired the roof geometry that, in turn, provided opportunities to create a variety of internal spaces including two courtyards and an atrium. The accommodation is on two storeys with work stations distributed between ground and mezzanine floors. The northlight trusses are orientated north/south to maximize natural light. The design brief included a requirement to provide as much

electricity as possible from renewable sources. The high ratio of roof to wall made PVs the obvious choice. In deciding on the appropriate PV cells, desk top studies indicated that polycrystalline silicon cells would offer the highest yield. The south facing slopes of the trusses provide a 1400m² platform for photovoltaic cells at a 30° pitch. Accordingly, 1554 PV panels were installed, estimated to meet about 40 per cent of electricity demand. The PVs extend beyond the ridges to provide shading and weather protection.

However, uncertainty surrounds the energy demand from equipment, notably computers. Office equipment has overtaken lighting as the main cause of CO_2 emissions in most recently designed offices and the estimate is that the gap will widen. There is still the problem that the payback period for PVs is well in excess of the expected lifetime of the cells. For the National Trust this problem was resolved by a grant from the Department of Trade and Industry.

The striking features of the trusses are the roof vents or 'snouts' that regulate the building's passive, natural ventilation system. In winter there is the problem that natural ventilation systems can create cold draughts. Consequently a low level mechanical ventilation system has been introduced to recover heat from the exhaust air to warm ventilation air that is then distributed through raised floor plenums. It was expected that this system would reduce the overall heat requirement from 49 to 13kWh/ m²/year. Some opening windows are controlled by the building management system (BMS) whilst others can be operated manually in pursuit of cooling (Figure 10.8).

In a mainly naturally ventilated, low energy building, it is impossible to maintain a consistent internal climate. However, the passive ventilation system was designed to provide a working environment in which the temperature is less than 25°C for 95 per cent of working hours and less than 28°C for 99 per cent of working hours.

One of the most important features of the building is its high thermal mass, the benefits of which will become more apparent as climate change accelerates. The concrete roof and floor slabs are cooled overnight by the BMS-controlled natural ventilation system, which works on the buoyancy principle to expel heat through the snouts. At the same time the system draws fresh air through motorized windows and inlet vents. Additional thermal mass is provided by the external walls of Staffordshire blue engineering bricks bedded in lime mortar to facilitate recycling. Both the roof and windows are made of aluminium, which has high embodied energy but which is countered by the availability of recycled stock.

The timber used throughout the building has been harvested from sustainable woodland, with much of it from National Trust estates. Carpet tiles were manufactured with wool from Herdwick sheep grazed on National Trust farmland. To give the tiles the wearing capacity for office use, the wool was mixed with small quantities of nylon and carbon. In line with current guidelines, the use of volatile organic compounds (VOCs) was kept to a minimum.

The land surrounding the building has been landscaped using indigenous species such as groups of silver birch. These provide shade to the exposed area to the south. Hornbeam and oak define the northern boundary whilst lavender and alliums enrich the colonnade.

One of the reasons for choosing this site was its proximity to the main line railway station, enabling the number of car spaces to be reduced to one for every three members of staff – well below the permitted number under the planning rules. The car park serves another purpose. According to the Environment Agency, the site is at risk of flooding, therefore a underground bunded tank lined with clay intercepts water prior to its discharge into the drainage system.

Post Occupancy Evaluation (POE)

In its first year Heelis performed well. During the hottest period in July, outside temperatures exceeded 30°C on four days but the internal temperatures only once peaked above 28°C and were less than 25°C for over half of the month. The POE has identified areas for improvement and many of these concern the way in which the building is used. The National Trust has implemented staff training to reduce energy use and environmental impact. Despite these inevitable feedback aspects, this building must be close to realizing its design ambition to be the lowest energy consumption office building in the country. (Latham and Swenarton, 2007)

Centre for Energy Efficiency in Building, Tsinghua University, Beijing

It was considered appropriate to include one of the most environmentally advanced buildings in China in this brief overview of the state of the art in 2009. China has much to lose as climate change gathers pace and it is adapting rapidly to changing circumstances.

Completed in March 2005 the Centre for Energy Efficiency in Building is the first demonstration project for ultra-low energy building in China. It accommodates almost 100 energy efficiency technologies including seven different systems in two facades with changeable elements (Figure 10.9).

The 'smart' envelope is designed to cope with the changing climate with ten alternative technologies. Glazed elements have a U-value of

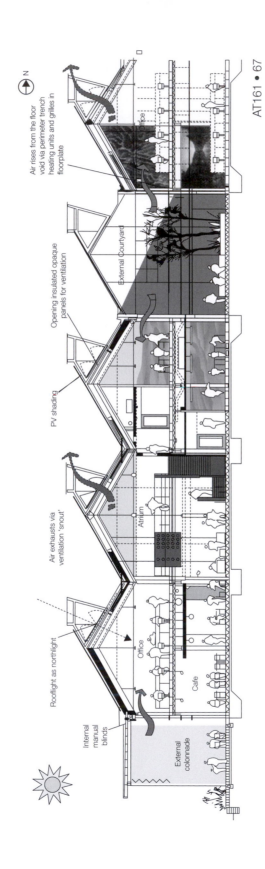

Air rises from the floor void via perimeter trench heating units and grilles in floorplate

N

Office

External Courtyard

Opening insulated opaque panels for ventilation

PV shading

Air exhausts via ventilation 'snout'

Atrium

Rooflight as northlight

Office

Cafe

Internal manual blinds

External colonnade

AT161 • 67

Source: Courtesy Feilden Clegg Bradley

Figure 10.8 Heelis Building: sections showing principles of the ventilation system

Figure 10.9 Centre for Energy Efficiency in Building, Tsinghua University, Beijing

<1.0W/m²K; the insulated walls and roof are <0.3W/m²K. The average heating load in winter is 0.7W/m² with 2.3W/m² in the coldest month. Altogether the heating and cooling load is 10 per cent of conventional offices. Three versions of double skin curtain wall on the east elevation are designed to test thermal performance.

In the first version, the naturally ventilated plenum is 600mm wide (Figure 10.10). The fixed inner pane is double-glazed with low-e glass. The outer skin is single glazed 6mm glass. Motorized inlet and outlet vents help to control the internal temperature. Two light shelves of stainless steel mirrors direct sunlight to the interior. Within the plenum a bottom-fixed blind can be raised just far enough to admit daylight from the upper part of the window. Motorized external blinds in the curtain wall respond to the seasonal solar angle.

On the south elevation, three configurations are demonstrated with different veriations of plenum and ventilation. The west and north facades employ lightweight construction comprising an aluminium rain screen, 50mm of polyurethane insulation, 150mm of fibre insulation and an internal leaf of 80mm gympum blocks. The latter are made of by-products from the desulfurization of power plants. The polyurethane insulation is produced from recycled plastic bottles.

There are two versions of roof. The first is a green roof with nine variations of plant to explore the most suitable types and maintenance regimes. The second is a glazed 'eco-cabin' to house experiments to test the CO_2 fixing capacity of different plants. The floor is raised 1.2m to accommodate service ducts. Phase change materials embodied in the floor plate facilitate thermal storage and even out temperature fluctuations.

The climate of Beijing allows for natural ventilation during spring and autumn. Wind driven ventilation combined with thermal buoyancy aided by a glass chimney enhance the natural ventilation. Air circulates via corridors and three shafts in the staircases. Thermal comfort in the offices is aided by displacement ventilation and radiative/chilled ceilings.

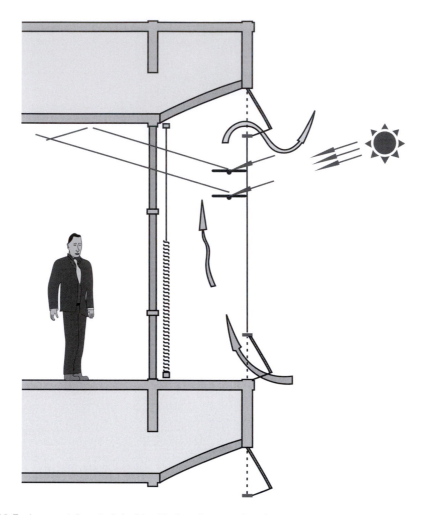

Figure 10.10 Environmental control double skin facade, east elevation

Daylight is directed to the basement by a light duct or sun pipe. The light is captured by a group of parabolic solar discs on the roof that can reflect light 200m with an efficiency of 30 per cent.

Energy systems

Combined heat and power is the principal energy system delivered by a natural gas fired turbine. It meets the electricity demands of the buildings. Any excess is exported to the university grid. In winter the system serves the heating system directly achieving 95 per cent

efficiency by capturing exhaust heat. In summer the low grade exhaust heat is used to regenerate the humidifier liquid to meet the latent heat load. The high grade heat is used to drive a heat pump for cooling. A ground source heat pump exploits the constant ground temperature of 15°C to provide cooling water at 16–18°C. Evaporative cooling supplements the system. The maximum cooling load is 120kW.

An array of 30m^2 of monocrystalline PVs with a peak power of 5kW provides garden lighting with LEDs. The electricity is stored in batteries to provide lighting at night and on dull days. There is also a solar air system with a peak thermal output of 140kW. In summer the warm air is used to regenerate the dehumidifier. In winter it feeds directly into the air conditioning system.

A BMS optimizes services within the building, including heating and cooling water management, natural ventilation and air conditioning. It also meters electricity, gas consumption and heat generated as well as electricity and heat produced by the CHP and solar power. In addition, it logs meteorological data and monitors the thermal performance of the building envelope to the level of room temperatures together with humidity, CO_2 concentration and light levels. In total over 1000 sensors provide information for research and teaching. Figure 10.11 provides a comprehensive key to the environmental and energy efficiency features of the building.

Pujiang Intelligence Valley (PIV)

This is an ambitious development near Shanghai that indicates China's ambition to demonstrate its commitment to the environmental agenda. The complex will feature buildings amounting to roughly 730,000m² in area. Phase one of the development has a site area of 200,000m² and the gross floor area of 240,000m². Six 'business' buildings occupy the centre of the site (Figure 10.12).

Four research and development buildings are located to the west and fourteen administrative buildings to the east of the site. Extensive landscaping centres around lakes amount to 13,000m² (Figure 10.13).

The aim of PIV is to:

- stimulate software research and development (R&D), including animation R&D;
- provide data and design centres;
- create a design and training centre;
- offer multimedia facilities.

It will provide training facilities across a range of subjects. The environmental specification includes:

- high levels of wall insulation;
- low emissivity double glazing U-value 1.5W/m²K;
- 100 per cent natural ventilation, supplying 20m³ per hour for every 15m² with humidity 30–70 per cent;
- low energy lighting;
- external sun shading with solar refracting blinds;
- heating and cooling pipes contained within floors;
- ground source heat pumps;
- photovoltaic cells;
- solar thermal panels;
- rainwater collection and purification system;
- extensive roof gardens;
- landscaping with trees, shrubs and grasslands not just as an amenity for workers but also to attract wildlife.

The 106,000m² buildings already constructed will save 8220 tonnes of CO_2 per year by avoiding coal fired power generation. This is a bold attempt to provide an ambitious development that creates comfortable internal conditions and is set in an extensive natural environment designed to attract wildlife as well as provide recreational space for the workers.

Case study summary

As a conclusion to this first section of the chapter, for the future, offices should follow the example of the few and have highly insulated double skin facades with integral flexible solar shading. The space can act as a plenum or accommodate vertical ducts to carry supply and extract air. The exhaust air will pass through a heat exchanger, perhaps boosted by ground source heat pumps. Natural ventilation via an air handling unit (AHU) must be the norm, if necessary mechanically assisted by low power fans. Air is ducted through floors, for example, by using the TermoDeck system (Figure 10.14).

Flash floods will be an increasing feature of climate change. Swales or depressions to channel water to bunded tanks under landscaping and car

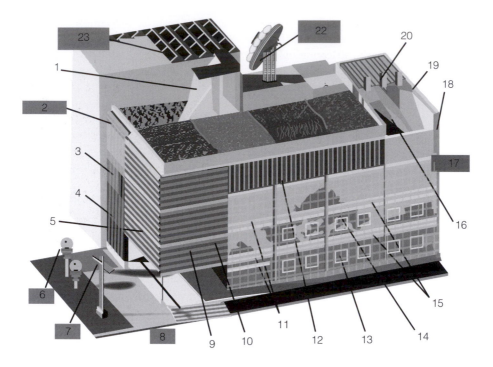

1 Natural ventilation and light shaft
2 PV glass
3 Double skin facade with external ventilation and narrower air gap (prefabricated)
4 Double skin facade with internal ventilation and narrower air gap (prefabricated)
5 Vacuum double facade
6 Solar lighting for basement
7 Solar lighting for night
8 Artificial wetland
9 Curtain wall
10 Motored horizontal shading
11 Motored openable window
12 Motored vertical shading
13 Window with anti-bridge aluminium frame
14 Double skin facade with external ventilation and wider air gap
15 Elevated floor with phase-change material
16 Self-cleaning glass
17 Eco-cabin
18 Insulated window
19 Lightweight insulated wall
20 Chimney for natural ventilation
21 Green roof
22 Solar disc
23 Solar air collector
Source: Derived from the exhibition board in Building Energy Research Centre
Photograph: Ruyan Sun

Figure 10.11 Energy Efficiency Centre environmental agenda

Figure 10.12 Pujiang Intelligence Valley, Business Centre, Shanghai, China

Figure 10.13 Intelligence Valley Phase One

parks will be needed in areas increasingly at risk of flooding. Conversely, severe droughts are also in the frame, and therefore water conservation must take on a new dimension of importance with recycling and purification high on the agenda. The implications for foundations in clay soils must also be taken into account.

Not only because of climate change, but also because of security of supply, energy will increasingly become a matter of concern. The building envelope should aim to be carbon neutral – even carbon negative – with the use of carbon sequestering materials. Its design should provide maximum opportunity for the installation of photovoltaic and solar thermal panels, especially with the prospect of much improved installed cost/kW of PVs in near future. Some sites will favour small scale wind power – bearing in mind that the load factor/COP of wind technology now has little room for improvement. On the

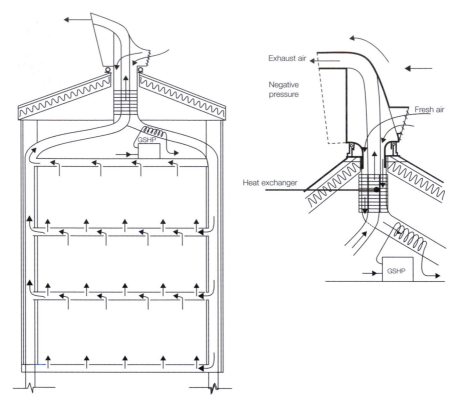

Figure 10.14 Diagrammatic office section with plenum facade and air handling unit (AHU) detail

other hand, there are claims that the COP of ground source heat pumps still has some way to go. Pile foundations coupled with GSHP loops are an economical option.

Whilst the energy requirement of the building envelope may continue to fall, uncertainty surrounds the future electricity demands of IT, which currently can account for 50 per cent of the total for the building. According to Max Fordham 'in a low energy office building [IT equipment] will remain the largest source of carbon dioxide emissions (Fordham, 2007, p131). This is one reason why there should be an adequate margin in the supply of renewable energy, which probably cannot all be obtained onsite.

The harsh reality is that the bulk of offices and institutional/administrative buildings will never achieve zero carbon status even when the contribution from onsite renewables is taken into account. It has already been suggested that

zero carbon can be achieved by purchasing carbon credits under the European Emissions Trading Scheme. The extreme view of this device has been expressed by James Lovelock:

> *Carbon trading, with its huge government subsidies, is just what finance and industry wanted. It's not going to do a damn thing about climate change , but it'll make a lot of money for a lot of people and postpone the moment of reckoning.*
>
> (Lovelock, 2009)

After the debacle of world economics since 2008 there are many who are sceptical about using the market mechanism to counter climate change. There is an alternative: a clean energy levy. In the case of most offices, there is not sufficient surface area to accommodate an adequate capacity of, say, PVs to qualify as zero carbon. The answer is for the calculated annual energy excess over zero to be met by an equivalent contribution to utility scale renewable energy. For example, new offices in London could offer a lifeline to offshore wind power in terms of the cost of the Thames Array. In addition, where there is a significant risk of flooding from a storm surge, as in the Docklands development and Thames Gateway, there should be a special levy, as suggested in Chapter 5, contributing to an estuary barrage. Since this would also generate considerable power, the two levies could be amalgamated with an appropriate overall reduction in the levy.

As an example, current good practice suggests that the consumption for offices should be around 150kWh/m²/year. Taking a modest size office of 10,000m², if it can already be credited with 50kWh/m²/year from onsite renewables, this leaves a levy liability of 100kWh/m²/year. This adds up to 1000MWh/year. Taking the capacity (or load) factor into account, this liability could be fulfilled by meeting the cost of a 500kW wind turbine, or one third the cost of an industry standard 1.5MW machine. This would be a much more accurate method of subsidy than relying on the vagaries of the market. In the face of the twin crises that are looming – climate change and depleting energy reserves – such a levy system is the most appropriate.

Appendix

Standards of performance for offices of the future in the UK

Heating load target	20kWh/m²/year
Electrical load target	25kWh/m²/year
Air tightness	<3m³/hr/m²
Daylighting	100% to BS 8206 Pt2
Artificial lighting controls	Luminance and person detection Dimming controls with building management system override
Heating/cooling	Dual action ground source heat pumps Active chilled thermal mass
Additional cooling	Ground source water cooling for rooms with high internal heat gains Evaporative cooling where viable Solar thermal circuits below car parks for seasonal heat storage In areas prone to flooding, surface water storage tanks below car parks, terraces, etc. Alternatively, permeable surfaces to all hard areas
Insulation	U-values: W/m²K
Walls	0.10
Average for windows	0.8 (triple-glazed)
Roof	0.10
Ground floor	0.10
Plan	Narrow floor plate to maximize daylight and cross ventilation. Where possible include an atrium Ideal orientation: north–south

Appendix

Standards of performance for offices of the future in the UK (*cont'd*)

Structure	Design for wind load of 150mph storm Design for 50°C peak summer temperature re expansion joints and materials stability
Floors	Hollow concrete planks with fairface soffit with cavities facilitating flow and return of ventilation/warm/cool air, for example the Termodeck system
Facade	Double skin facades with integral flexible solar shading, the cavity acting as a plenum for heat retention in winter and cooling in summer. The exhaust air will pass through a heat exchanger, ideally boosted by reversible ground source heat pumps. Natural ventilation via an air handling unit (AHU) (Figure 10.14), if necessary boosted by low power fans
Roofs	Green roofs where possible with Monodraught ventilation units Alternatively, 30° south facing pitch is ideal for PVs and solar thermal. Thin film PVs are promising for the future
Materials	Insulation materials No petro-chemical-based insulants. Insulants from renewable sources, e.g. sheep's wool, cellulose, cork
Structure	Low carbon concrete via pulverised ash aggregate (example: Persistence Works, Sheffield by Feilden Clegg Bradley) Design for dismantling and reuse of elements
Recycling	Maximize prefabrication to minimize waste and facilitate recycling bricks bonded with lime mortar for ease of recycling
Steel	Better recycling potential than concrete
Timber	Should be from certified renewable forests Onsite composting of vegetable matter and paper
Building management systems	User-friendly BMS design with intelligible instructions All-staff training in optimization of BMS performance
Biodiversity	Tree planting with appropriate species offering solar shading Wide range of plant species around buildings Pools for wildlife and evaporative cooling Green facades where possible

11

Community Buildings

Some of the most environmentally advanced buildings are to be found in various buildings designed for community use. One of the leaders in the field is Jubilee Wharf, Penryn quayside, Cornwall (Figure 11.1).

The genetic code of Bill Dunster and the Zedfactory is clearly evident in Jubilee Wharf, Penryn, Cornwall, UK. Its shapes are unconventional, yet architectural critic Jonathan Glancey considers 'It fits, in an appropriately ramshackle way, into the higgledy-piggledy fabric of Penryn ... somehow it all fits together' (*Guardian*, 11 January 2007) (Figure 11.1).

This is a mixed development beside the river in Penryn consisting of two buildings. One comprises 12 studio workshops with six maisonettes above. The other accommodates a Sure Start nursery, the ZedShed public hall offering community facilities and a café that already has a renowned reputation. The two buildings enclose a courtyard establishing a public walkway along the quayside that has already proved a successful social space. It is already a 'lively and bustling space' which, in due course, should accommodate a farmers' market. The design of the waterfront block roof ensures that the brisk winds on the harbour are deflected over the courtyard.

It has been described as a 'state-of-the-art example of green architecture' (Buchanan, 2006). The environmental features of the building are encapsulated in a characteristic architectural/services drawing, Figure 11.2.

The Jubilee Wharf maisonettes are super-insulated and airtight with glazed sun spaces. The floors are concrete, adding to the thermal mass. Natural ventilation is by means of wind-orientating cowls designed to cope with the often extreme wind loads. The workshops have low grade underfloor heating, as do the maisonettes and community spaces. However, the combination of high insulation and solar orientation plus solar thermal panels on the higher roof means that it is hardly ever needed. A wood pellet biomass boiler ensures comfortable conditions in winter. Local labour and materials were used, most notably western red cedar and larch from the vicinity. All wood used in the construction was from sustainable sources and therefore accredited by the Forest Stewardship Council.

Four wind turbines are located on the quayside, and are able to rotate to exploit any wind direction. There are plans to mount photovoltaic cells, which should enable the complex to be a net contributor to the grid.

Jubilee Wharf is a milestone in green design and sets a new example for how small towns can develop, intelligently and economically.
(Peter Buchanan, 2006)

Health

The primary cancer health care and treatment centre at the Churchill Hospital in Oxford is the first major hospital in the UK to be entirely heated and cooled by ground source heat pumps (GSHPs). As such it is deemed to be an exemplar

Source: Courtesy of Zedfactory

Figure 11.1 Jubilee Wharf, Penryn, Cornwall, UK

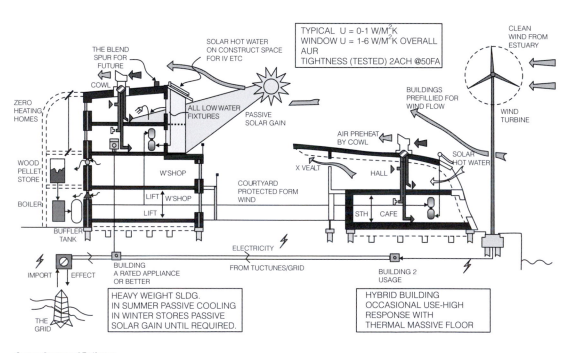

Source: Courtesy of Zedfactory

Figure 11.2 Jubilee Wharf, environmental credentials

for future hospital design. The National Health Service (NHS) operates Europe's largest property portfolio and, as such, has recognized the importance of its estate's environmental impact. It has set itself a target of reducing primary energy consumption by 15 per cent by March 2010. Ground energy is a reliable source of heat, day and night, winter and summer.

The Oxford Radcliffe Hospitals NHS Trust decided from the outset that the new Churchill facilities were to be exemplars of energy efficient, low carbon hospital design. Services engineers Haden Young engaged EarthEnergy as technical advisors on this project to review and audit the ground loop heat exchanger design. It also undertook in situ thermal conductivity testing of the installed boreholes and used computer modelling of the ground loop to assess its thermal performance over its design life. It is an all-closed loop ground source heating and cooling system. This consists of 8×500kW heat pumps delivering around 2.5MW of heating. Because it is a hospital, redundancy had to be designed into the system. There are no alternative heating or cooling backup systems for the hospital (Figure 11.3).

This is the first major public building to rely on GSHP technology for its heating and cooling and demonstrates that this technology should have an important role to play in the future in a low energy environment, even for large building complexes.

Source: Photograph courtesy of EarthEnergy Ltd

Figure 11.3 Ground source heat pumps plant room, Churchill Hospital, Oxford

Education

Because the school environment shapes malleable minds, a building that responds to the environmental challenges of the age should leave a lasting impression. Environmental determinism has taken on a new meaning, equipping students to play a leading role in the difficult times ahead. In 2006 the UK government produced a consultative document on sustainable schools. It states: 'By 2020 the DCSF [Department for Children Schools and Families] would like all schools to become models of energy efficiency and renewable energy, showcasing wind, solar and biofuel sources in their communities.' Part L2 of the 2006 Building Regulations requires that a school's energy demand must be reduced by 25 per cent as against the 2002 Regulations. In 2007 the Department for Communities and Local Government (DCLG) stipulated that all new schools should achieve at least 'very good' under the BREEAM Schools (Building Research Establishment Environmental Assessment Method for Schools). This would involve:

- energy;
- water use;
- materials;
- pollution;
- ecology;
- management and health.

However, a pacemaker building that predates the environment and energy crises is St George's School in Wallasey, Cheshire. It was the first truly passive solar educational building designed by Charles Emslie Morgan of Cheshire County Architects Department and completed in 1961. It features a passive solar wall extending across the whole south elevation. It has an innovative natural light and ventilation system, with insulation standards well ahead of its time. This resulted in a dramatically reduced heating load compared with the norm of the day. Due to falling rolls it is now a school catering for special needs – a function for which it was not designed.

St Francis of Assisi, Liverpool

Under the Building Schools for the Future (BSF) scheme, the UK government aims to renew or rebuild every secondary school in England within 15 years. Under this BFS standard, schools must achieve a 'very good' rating under the BREEAM Schools assessment scheme.

One of the schools to set the pace for current environmental standards is the Academy of St Francis of Assisi in Liverpool, designed by Capita Architecture and completed in March 2006. The Anglican Bishop of Liverpool was chairman of the governors of the predecessor building. He formulated the brief for a new building on the basis that it would be an outstanding example of sustainable design and therefore a whole-building teaching aid about the environment. The Catholic Archbishop of Liverpool became a partner in the project, a symbol of the amicable relationship that marked a radical change from Liverpool's past (Figure 11.4).

The restricted site presented a challenge to meet the accommodation requirements without destroying the views of neighbouring properties. The answer was to locate the school hall underground, resulting in a five-storey building. However, most accommodation is in the two-storey elements above ground (Figure 11.5). The services engineers were Buro Happold.

The detailed brief included these requirements:

- the building should be naturally ventilated with heat recovery – this system is 50 per cent efficient;
- there should be occupant control rather than automated services;
- all classrooms and corridors to feature glass rotating louvres;

Source: Photograph courtesy of CABE

Figure 11.4 St Francis of Assisi school: interior with translucent ethylene tetrafluoroethylene roof

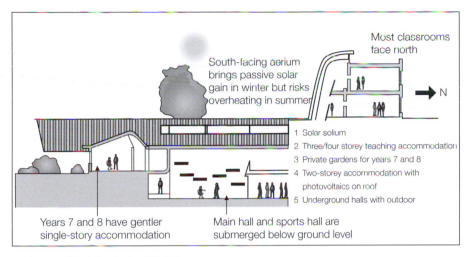

Source: Design of Sustainable Schools Case Studies, DfES 2006

Figure 11.5 North–south section of St Francis of Assisi school

- to maintain air quality, craft and science rooms and underground areas like the dining room to be mechanically ventilated;
- in the two information and communications rooms and cyber café there is to be central mechanical cooling;
- a variable refrigerant flow system can operate in either heating or cooling modes.

Renewable energy

The roof of the two-storey above-ground element supports 187.3m² of PVs with a peak capacity of 24kW and an estimated output of 19.440kW/year. It was sized to meet 10 per cent of the school's electricity demand. However, based on the first 6 months of operation it only met 3.5 per cent of the demand, which has saved only approximately 2 per cent of CO_2 emissions. A 5m² array of evacuated tube solar thermal panels with an output of 2,600kWh/year pre-heats the domestic hot water.

The school was completed before the BREEAM Schools standard was implemented. However, it achieved a provisional rating of 'excellent'.

Howe Dell Primary School, Hatfield, Hertfordshire

A leading example of an eco-school is Howe Dell Primary (see Figure 11.6), opened in 2007 as the first phase of an educational campus. Located on an unusual brownfield site – the former Hatfield Aerodrome – the school was conceived as a pathfinder project for 'integrated wrap-around care and sustainable building design' (DCSF, 2008).

As part of the government's eco-schools strategy, Howe Dell, designed by Capita Architecture, was a beacon project for Hertfordshire County Council. As such it was awarded the ECO Green Flag Accreditation – the highest award in the eco-schools programme. The super-insulated building includes:

- solar thermal panels to heat water for the school kitchens;
- a grid-connected photovoltaic array;
- natural ventilation coupled with TermoDeck fan-assisted heating and cooling, exploiting the thermal mass of the building to help stabilize the temperature;

Figure 11.6 Howe Dell Primary School, southern elevation

- natural lighting from high performance solar protecting windows, coupled with roof lights in deep plan areas; light wells admit natural light to ground floor corridors; low energy artificial lighting is used throughout;
- sedum green roofs help with insulation whilst managing water runoff;
- the toilets are supplied with rainwater harvested from the main roof, and the excess used to irrigate the wetland biodiversity area within the school grounds.

In addition, a 50kW wind turbine is planned, which will export excess electricity to the grid. The outstanding and unique sustainability feature of the school is its system of interseasonal heat transfer (IHT) installed by ICAX. Solar energy is captured by a network of pipes beneath the surface of the playground that are filled with water and anti-freeze – called the 'collector'. The tarmac of the playground can often reach 15°C above ambient temperature (Figure 11.7).

Source: DCSF, 2008

Figure 11.7 Pipe network beneath the school playground

Heat energy is stored in computer-controlled 'thermal banks' beneath the school (Figure 11.8). When it is needed to heat the building, it is delivered to a heat pump and a series of heat exchangers. These are connected to both the underfloor heating system and the TermoDeck ventilation system that can deliver either warm or cool air, using the thermal mass of the building to moderate extremes of temperature. This is claimed to be the first system of its type in the UK and possibly even the world. It saves 50 per cent of the CO_2 emissions attributable to conventional boilers.

A further advantage of the thermal banks is that they can store heat from the solar thermal panels during the summer holidays when normal services are suspended. Otherwise the panels would suffer damage.

The school curriculum is underpinned by sustainability principles and an important element in the design of the building is that a user-friendly school-wide software interface allows pupils to monitor the various environmental systems, in particular the renewable energy. It indicates how much energy is stored as heat and how much electricity is exported to the grid. Real-time data are also displayed on screens within the school entrance area.

Fulcrum Consulting played a central role in developing the sustainable features of the school, particularly the IHT heating/cooling system. They consider this to be 'a demonstration project assisting in placing ideas in the public domain'.

Sharrow Combined Infant and Junior School, Sheffield

It is worth recording that local authorities can not only commission schools but they can still also design them, as in the case of Sharrow School in Sheffield (Figure 11.9).

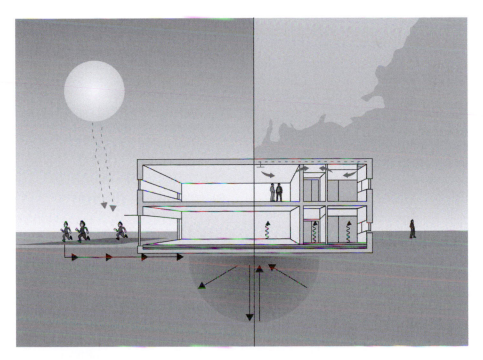

Source: Courtesy of Mark Hughes, ICAX

Figure 11.8 Thermal banks beneath the school

Figure 11.9 Sharrow Combined Infant and Junior School, Sheffield

The Sharrow School resulted from a decision by the Sheffield City Council to amalgamate junior and infant provision on the same site to replace a nearby Victorian building. The aim of the Council's architect, Cath Baslio, was to produce the greenest school in Sheffield. A lengthy consultation process involving staff, governors, parents and council staff led to an open plan design with no corridors. A green roof not only controls rainwater runoff but also replicates a meadow, making it a valuable teaching resource. It is designed to attract a range of wildlife, especially birds. The school is linked to a substantial open green space that is primarily for the use of pupils but is also available to the community after school hours. The landscape designer was Helen Mitchell.

However, what makes the school special is the fact that hot water for all purposes comes from ground source heat pumps linked to 21 boreholes. These supply low grade heat to underfloor circuits of 20mm high density polyethylene piping over three floors that can provide space heating at a lower temperature than radiators. In total 11km of pipe was used. There is 'token' backup from an immersion heater to cover extra-heavy demand.

The school is designed to facilitate group working by teachers and pupils from different year groups to learn from each other. Altogether the school is a valuable community resource at the heart of one of the more deprived areas of Sheffield.

Summary of indicators for sustainable design

To accommodate the potential future changes in climate, as far as possible, sustainable community buildings should be designed to:

- reduce to zero, or compensate for, the use of fossil-based energy in terms of the energy embodied in the materials, transport and the construction process and the energy used during the lifetime of the building;
- provide, at the same time, sufficient thermal mass to enable the building to moderate

extremes of external temperature, with night cooling;

- use recycled and recyclable materials where available and obtain natural materials from accredited sustainable sources;
- ensure that the proposed development will be designed to facilitate dismantling and recycling in the future;
- avoid the use of materials containing volatile organic compounds;
- design to make maximum use of natural light whilst also mitigating solar glare;
- exploit the potential for natural ventilation in the context of an overall climate control strategy that minimizes energy use to achieve a climate within the range of comfort conditions;
- make the best use of passive solar energy whilst employing heating/cooling systems that are fine-tuned to the needs of the occupants, avoiding air conditioning except in special circumstances;
- ensure that building management systems are user-friendly and not over-complex and that the system has an explanatory manual that can be understood by the building's occupants as well as services managers;
- exploit to the full opportunities to generate integrated or onsite renewable electricity;
- identify the potential for exploiting the constant ground temperature to even out the peaks and troughs of summer and winter temperatures by means of GSHPs or direct underground or flowing water cooling;
- minimize the use of water; harvesting rainwater and grey water and purifying for use other than human consumption;
- minimize rainwater runoff by limiting the extent of hard external landscape and, if possible, create runoff underground storage and subsequent drainage in the event of flash flooding;

- create an external environmental that is both a visual amenity and also offers environmental benefits such as summer shading from deciduous trees and evaporative cooling from water features;
- whilst taking account of these key indicators, ensure that designs meet the highest standards of technical proficiency in combination with aesthetic excellence.

Chapters 10 and 11 have illustrated that there are leading edge non-domestic buildings already approaching the optimum in terms of carbon savings, climate control and the ecological approach to materials in terms of toxicity and sourcing. The purpose here is to suggest that an increasingly aggressive climate will involve a recalibration of some design standards. For example, for structures, wind loading calculations may have to assume storms in excess of 140mph with considerable turbulence. For relatively long life buildings like schools, universities, government offices, etc., cooling and ventilation systems should be designed to cope with 45°C extended summer days and 35°C nights. Buildings will need to have a significant thermal mass and there may also be a requirement for mechanical intervention to moderate temperatures and realize night cooling.

Finally, almost all the buildings featured in Chapters 10 and 11 are bespoke, that is, designed for a specific user. Most offices are built speculatively with the future occupier bearing the energy costs. The only way that the construction and environmental standards discussed here will be achieved is by building regulations requiring them. At the same time there must be enforced standards for building control during construction together with rigorous post occupancy checks. Local authorities will claim they need additional funding for such measures, and they will be right.

12

Conventional Energy

Demand versus reserves versus global warming

Ultimately the prospect of a survivable future hinges on energy and how rapidly societies shift from fossil fuel dependence to near carbon neutral energy. The case for renewable energy is being strengthened by increasing anxiety over the alleged gap between new discoveries of reserves of fossil fuels and rising demand, especially from China and India. Rapid economic growth in the developing world means that predicted energy demand under the high emissions CO_2 scenario is outpacing gains in energy efficiency and could reach over three times the current level of primary energy demand by the end of the century (Figures 12.1 and 12.2).

To be precise, energy consumption in 1980 was equivalent to 7,223 million tonnes of oil equivalent (mtoe). By 2030 it is expected to reach 17,014 mtoe, due mainly to economic growth in India and China.

A schizoid tendency is evident here since both the World Energy Council (WEC) graph and the International Energy Agency (IEA) histogram seem to deny the existence of another graph known as the Hubbert Peak. The bell curve shown in Figure 12.3 was conceived in 1956 by Marion King Hubbert, and subsequently named after him, to describe the path of the relationship between reserves of oil and increasing demand.

There is considerable uncertainty regarding levels of reserves of oil especially by Organization of Oil Exporting Countries (OPEC). The Association for the Study of Peak

Oil (ASPO) considers that 'peak oil' was reached in 2006 with peak gas expected about a decade later. The consequence will be prices volatility and ultimately conflict. 'Climate change and soaring energy demand are combining to create a "perfect storm" during the next half century' (Alan Greenspan, former chairman of the US Federal Reserve) (Figures 12.4 and 12.5).

The reason for the uncertainty surrounding the matter of reserves of oil is that, in 1986, OPEC decreed that its members should only export oil in a fixed proportion of their reserves. Within weeks many countries revised their reserves upwards, for example Saudi Arabia added 100 billion barrels to their reserves. Altogether the total suddenly rose from 353 billion to 643 billion barrels of oil, yet there had been no significant discoveries of new reserves. It is virtually certain that reserves are still being exaggerated (Coleman, 2007, p53).

Interviewed for the *Guardian*, the chief economist of the International Energy Agency, renowned for its caution, concludes that 'In terms of non-Opec, we are expecting that in three to four years time, the production of conventional oil will come to a plateau and start to decline… In terms of the global picture, assuming that Opec will invest in a timely manner, global conventional oil … will come around 2020 to a plateau as well' (interview for the *Guardian*, 14 April 2009).

A report by Robert Hirsch for the US Department of Energy estimates that, to avoid economic collapse, it will be necessary to initiate 'a mitigation crash programme 20 years before peaking'. He adds: 'Without timely mitigation the economic, social and political costs will be

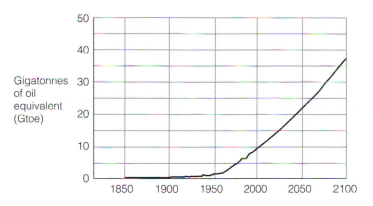

Figure 12.1 World Energy Council worst case Business as Usual scenario

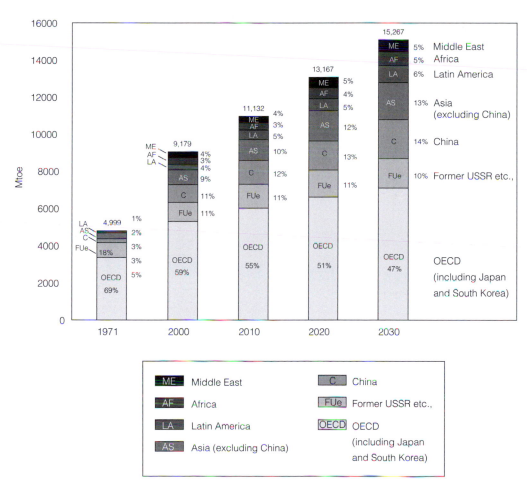

Source: International Energy Agency/World Energy

Figure 12.2 World Energy Outlook

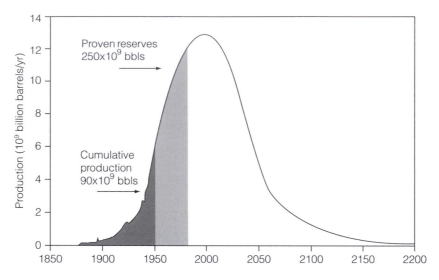

Source: Association for the Study of Peak Oil

Figure 12.3 The Hubbert peak

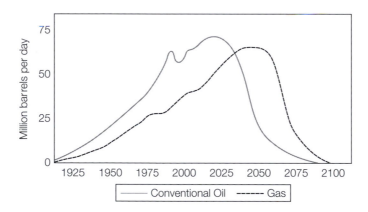

Figure 12.4 Peak oil and gas: after ASPO

unprecedented.' There are no signs of a crash programme, which should already be well under way.

It is no wonder that John Hutton, as UK Secretary of State for Business and Enterprise, has warned: 'The subject of energy security is likely to be one of the most important political and economic challenges we face as a country' (speech at a UK Trade and Investment conference, December 2007).

Alongside concerns about climate change, it is therefore imperative that nations rapidly install technologies that are an alternative to fossil fuels. For the UK the urgency is even greater as over 30 per cent of its generating capacity will become obsolete within the next decade and a half. And confusion reigns over the prospects for next generation of nuclear power when even the problem of medium and high level waste disposal from existing plants has not been

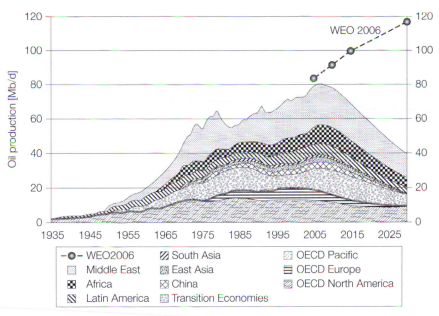

Source: Energywatch

Figure 12.5 Peak oil, breakdown by nation

resolved. There is also the deadly legacy of plutonium waste from the weapons programme.

Conflict over oil reserves will increase. Alan Greenspan has described Iraq as the first of the major oil wars. These could become more widespread as the reserves-to-demand ratio moves down the bell curve (Figure 12.6).

In addition, peak gas and peak coal reserves are expected around 2025 as will be discussed in Chapter 13.

The UK's chief scientist, Professor John Beddington, predicted that energy, food and water shortages by 2030 would create a 'perfect storm' echoing the verdict of Alan Greenspan (address to the government's Sustainable Development UK conference, London, 20 March 2009).

As anxieties about the status of reserves of oil and gas gather pace, the fall-back position of resorting to coal is becoming increasingly

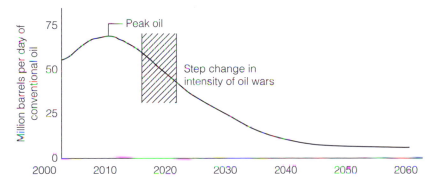

Figure 12.6 Potential for oil wars

attractive to governments. For rapidly expanding economies like China and India, exploiting their reserves of coal is irresistibly tempting. China is commissioning new coal fired plants at a rate of about 50 per year. Even the UK is planning a new generation of coal fired plants. All this is despite the fact that the technical and cost problems surrounding carbon capture and storage (CCS) are far from having been resolved. Possibly hundreds of new plants will be in operation before CCS is viable, and most of them will not be amenable to CCS retrofit. This will be discussed in the next chapter.

Therapy for an ailing planet: the Tyndall remedy

The only answer according to the Tyndall Centre is for fossil-based energy to be abandoned *long before reserves are exhausted* if the world is to avoid catastrophic climate change. The Centre spells out why: 'The only scenario that avoids dangerous climate change over the long term is the minimum emissions scenario, which allows for only about one quarter of known fossil fuels to be used' (about 1000Gt Carbon equivalent, out of a total of 4–5000GtC). In other words three-quarters of it must stay in the ground (Figure 12.7).

For the UK the Tyndall Centre has specific recommendations. Because the UK has high per capita carbon emissions at 9.6 tonnes per head, the instruction is that we should achieve 'deep cuts in the use of fossil fuels. This translates to a 90 per cent cut in greenhouse gas emissions by 2050 if there is to be any chance of avoiding irreversible climate change (Lenton et al, 2006). To achieve this target, emissions of CO_2 must be stabilized by 2012. Beyond 2010 there should be a 9 per cent annual cut for 20 years leading to a 70 per cent reduction by 2030 and 90 per cent by 2050 (Figure 12.8).

This is substantially greater than UK government commitment under the Climate Change Bill and the reason for this is that it fails to take account of emissions associated with air transport and shipping. It has huge implications for clean energy (Figure 12.9).

So, could some relief be found from a new generation of nuclear generating plants?

The nuclear option

There are 440 existing plants with a further 168 planned so far. With the prospect of a proliferation of nuclear power generation, any decision about proceeding with a new generation of nuclear plants should first consider a number of popular myths:

1   *Nuclear is carbon neutral.* This ignores the CO_2 component in the:
    - construction of power plants;
    - mining, milling and enrichment of uranium;

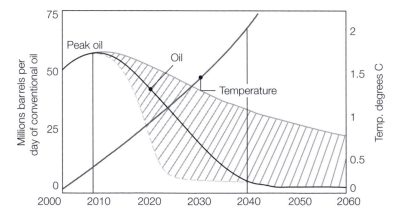

Figure 12.7 Fossil fuels to be avoided, mostly coal (hatched)

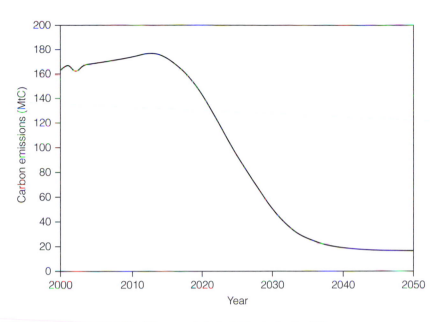

Figure 12.8 Tyndall recommended CO_2 90 per cent abatement rate for the UK

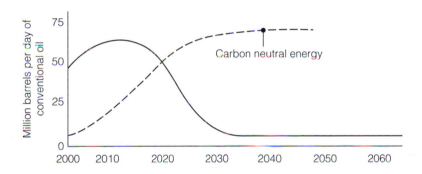

Figure 12.9 Implication for carbon neutral energy for the UK

- transport of fuels and waste;
- disposal of waste in long-term security;
- decommissioning of plants and safe disposal of remains;
- development of new mines and rehabilitation when exhausted.

2   *Nuclear is cheap*. A fourth generation nuclear plant would cost up to £1.7 million per MW. With an installed capacity of ~1300MW this amounts to £22.1 million. In addition there is the cost of mining uranium ore, waste disposal and decommissioning. By comparison, a combined cycle gas generation plant costs £350.000/MW.

3   *There will be no taxpayer subsidy*. 'The government will not provide subsidies, directly or indirectly to encourage Britain's energy companies to invest in new nuclear power stations' (Malcolm Wicks as Energy Minister October 2006). This includes the £70 billion estimate for waste disposal. The answer is to give the contract to the French company EDF, which *will*, by definition, qualify for a subsidy.

For politicians, the fundamental question of the limitation of reserves of high grade uranium is resolved by the prospect of reprocessing spent nuclear fuel to create plutonium that can be reused several times over. This is despite the embarrassment of the Thorpe reprocessing enterprise.

The main concern here is that separated plutonium is only mildly radioactive. This means that a small amount could easily be handled illicitly and a only a few kilograms would be needed to make a nuclear weapon. This danger came to light after the US shared reprocessing technology with India who then used the separated plutonium to make an atomic bomb. In 1998, the Royal Society warned that the plutonium stockpile from reprocessing spent fuel 'might, at some stage, be accessed for illicit weapons production'. In 2007 a second report repeated that 'the status quo of continuing to stockpile a very dangerous material is not an acceptable long term option' (von Hippel, 2008, p70).

Worldwide, 440 nuclear power plants account for 14 per cent of global energy use at the time of writing. As the international energy situation becomes increasingly fraught, politicians are reconsidering their position regarding nuclear energy. For example, India is planning to install 470GW of nuclear capacity by 2050. China is planning for 80GW by 2020. The UK could stand proxy for the nuclear Organisation for Economic Co-operation and Development (OECD) countries in this respect. The note of alarm is reaching an ever higher pitch among UK politicians as they realize that the country really does face an energy crisis during the next decade. This is because of the inevitability that the output from nuclear power stations will fall from around 23 per cent of the total to about 7 per cent by 2020 as old plants are decommissioned. In fact it will be nearer 5 per cent if predictions about the growth in energy demand are correct. The question is, what will bridge the gap?

In the Energy White Paper of 2002 there was confidence that renewables would go a long way to meeting the shortfall. Most of the bets were placed on wind power. A decision on nuclear power was placed on hold. There would be a concentration on wind power up to 2020. However, since then it has become increasingly obvious that a focus on wind alone will guarantee that the vacuum will *not* be filled, especially if we consider that energy demand will have risen on the basis of a net 1 per cent per year growth from 9.87EJ in 2002 to 11.8EJ in 2020.

One option would be to resort to fossil fuels. An increase in gas generation would be an obvious stratagem, but this commodity is not only becoming more expensive, it would also blow a hole in the government's commitment to reduce CO_2 emissions by 10 per cent by 2010 with a target of 20 per cent by 2020. At the time of writing both goals seem to be receding. There could be a resurrection of coal generation but this would be difficult as large scale generating plants like Drax in Yorkshire are in terminal decline. And again, the climate change commitment would be undermined.

For these reasons amongst others, more and more politicians are becoming reconciled to the fact that a new generation of nuclear plants is the only way to fill the generating gap without reneging on CO_2 abatement commitments. But this opens a new Pandora's box of problems. First there are the logistics of initiating a programme of new stations. There is a general acceptance that the critical mass of stations to make a programme viable in terms of economy of scale is ten, which would certainly fill the energy void left by the demise of all present generation plants. Is this feasible?

According to Professor Tom Burke of Imperial College, a former adviser to the one-time Department of Energy, even if work were started immediately (June 2005), a plant would not be operational before 2015. It would take an optimist to believe that three plants would be operational by 2025. In fact, when account is taken of the licensing and planning process and the business of putting together a financial package, the timescale is considerably extended. Then there is the construction phase, which can be up to 10 years. Next there is the question of cost. Gone is the optimism that once stated that 'nuclear electricity would be too cheap to meter'. Now the estimate is that a plant would cost between £1.3 million and £1.7 million per Megawatt installed capacity. The capacity of each plant would be between 1200 and 1500MW. Gas plants, by comparison, cost around £350,000 per MW capacity.

The government will have a hard job persuading the market to invest in capital intensive projects carrying a number of risks within a liberalized and therefore uncertain energy market. The risks include:

- open-ended lead-in time including licensing and planning consents;
- public opposition; there is still a hard core of committed opponents who will galvanize public opposition;
- security risks in an environment of increasingly sophisticated terrorist operations;
- the chance of fissile material falling into the hands of rogue states;
- safe long-term waste disposal including the waste from existing generation plants;
- the reluctance of lending institutions to provide capital for high risk, long-life, capital intensive projects;
- the track record of the nuclear industry in its concealment of accidents;
- insecurity regarding return on capital unless the government guarantees a 40 year feed-in tariff, which is against the principles of a liberalized EU market.

On the last point one banking adviser has stated: 'You need some kind of government or regulatory commitment to force people to contract to buy nuclear power. You would have to be careful to make it apply to all suppliers so none are disadvantaged and all share the same risk' (*Observer*, 'Business Focus: the Energy Debate', 8 May 2005, p3). The verdict on this by Tom Burke is: 'The argument that the government makes people sign a forty year contract to take nuclear power and then agrees to take back the liabilities and uses public money to do it is ludicrous' (*Observer*, ibid).

An additional problem relates to the skills base necessary to create a new generation of nuclear plants. Currently there are shortages at all levels: scientists, engineers, technicians, craftspeople and manual workers. Graduates do not perceive the industry as a good career choice. Nor are there people with the skills necessary to administer regulatory and licensing procedures. This is highlighted by the fact that the Health and Safety Executive's present capacity to examine new technologies is one-tenth of a person per year according to the Institute of Physics.

Emissions and waste

Nuclear plants do not emit CO_2, SO_2 or NO_x gases. Radioactive discharges are claimed to be negligible and not significantly above background levels of natural radiation. The problem of high and intermediate level waste disposal has still not been solved. The stumbling block appears to be the requirement that it should be recoverable for reprocessing. This would seem to be an impossible condition that ultimately must be abandoned. When that happens a promising solution that has been researched at Sheffield University Institute of Mines should be considered.

Up to the time of writing there have been numerous problems arising from attempts to bury high and intermediate level waste, not least the ill-fated attempts by Nirex to bury the waste near Sellafield. Fergus G. F. Gibb and Philip G. Attrill have conducted a series of high pressure, high temperature experiments to address these problems. They have demonstrated that deep boreholes in the continental granite crust could provide the answer. High level waste in special containers is placed at the base of 4–5km deep boreholes, sunk into the granite. Radioactive decay gradually heats up the waste to a temperature sufficient to cause the granite to melt. As the heat dissipates the granite cools and recrystallizes, sealing the waste in solid granite. Any fissures in the surrounding rocks are sealed by annealing and low temperature hydration mineralization. The timescale suggests the melting and recrystallizing can be realized in a matter of years rather than decades. This system has the potential to satisfy the safety requirements under the 100,000 year rule.

If nuclear power is to be politically viable, it is this kind of technology that provides some degree of assurance, provided that every other carbon neutral source of energy is fully exploited. If there is to be a new generations of nuclear power plants, it is essential that it does not divert funds from optimizing renewables.

Health issues

In June 2005 the Committee on Medical Aspects of Radiation in the Environment (Comare) published a report that was the outcome of a study begun in 1993. The committee considered 21 sites comprising 13 power stations and 15 other nuclear installations. It confirmed earlier reports that there were clusters of excess leukaemias and non-Hodgkins lymphomas near the reprocessing plants of Sellafield and Dounreay and the atomic weapons facility at Burghfield. There was also a slight increase above the norm of childhood cancers around Aldermaston, Burghfield and Harwell.

However, the committee could not be certain as to the cause. There were high numbers of leukaemias around Sellafield according to the Black report of 1984. These could have been linked to the high number of radioactive discharges from the site in the 1960s and 1970s, which were 200,000 times greater than Aldeburgh and Burghfield combined. On the other hand the clusters could have been the result of the influx of a migrant workforce and the transfer of new viruses involved in the development of cancer.

On balance the committee concluded that nuclear power stations were not responsible for childhood cancers in Britain. However, the report will not necessarily allay the fears of the anti-nuclear lobby, fears that may have been reinforced by a report by the International Agency for Research on Cancer – an arm of the World Health Organization. In June 2005 it reported on a study of 400,000 nuclear power workers, which concluded that the long-term low doses of radiation they received increased their risk of cancer. The current standards for assessing the risks from radiation are based on studies of survivors of the atomic bombs on Nagasaki and Hiroshima in 1945, victims who were subjected to a sudden high level exposure to radiation. This report is the first to comment on the risk associated with long-term exposure to low level radiation. However, the report does make the point that the risk is reduced, although not eliminated, for present day operatives in nuclear installations.

Advocates

In a UK TV documentary, James Lovelock, originator of the Gaia theory, asserted that 'it would be fine if we had another 50 to 100 years, but we don't have time. And the only energy that I know of that is immediately, or nearly immediately available and could provide large amounts of energy quickly without doing anything to the greenhouse is nuclear.' He then admitted that accidents will happen but 'people have got to realize that [they] will be trivial compared with the dangers of the global greenhouse' (Channel Four, 8 January 2004). Lovelock cannot be dismissed lightly.

The Nuclear Industry Association (NIA), which represents about 200 companies, claims that nuclear can be an attractive proposition for private investment *provided* that risk can be appropriately managed. That must mean involving a third party.

Technology

The international energy uncertainty is fuelling interest in third generation (IIIG+) nuclear plants. These will be of modular design, reducing the construction time. They will produce much less waste than present day reactors and will incorporate passive safety systems. They are likely to use new materials and possibly contain sealed-for-life elements. They will be much cheaper and more rapidly constructed, using many factory built components.

The only IIIG+ nuclear plant presently under construction in the EU is the Olkilouto 1.6MW plant in Finland. This is a European Pressurised Reactor also called an Evolutionary Power Reactor (EPR). Pressurized water in the primary system is used to slow down the neutrons, allowing a nuclear reaction to take place in the core. It has four steam generators or heat exchangers to transfer the heat generated during the reaction to power turbines (Figure 12.10).

The shell of the building is designed to be proof against aircraft impact; one of several new safety features. The EPR system was selected on the grounds of its specification, economic cost and estimated 60-year service life. It should have a lower environmental impact than existing plants, first because it uses 15 per cent less uranium than its predecessors and, second, because of the lower level of waste produced. The project, managed by the French group Areva, has been subject to a number of setbacks resulting in a delay of three years. The latest completion date is 2010.

Energy companies EDF and E.ON have selected the EPR system for the UK's nuclear programme, should it materialize. To accelerate the planning process, wherever possible new plants will be built on the site of previous reactors, making use of existing infrastructure.

A second major contender for the IIIG+ market is the Westinghouse Advanced Passive Series, which includes the AP1000 advanced reactor. This is a development from current technologies. Around 50 per cent of the 440 nuclear reactors in the world are based on Westinghouse technology. The AP1000 is a pressurized water reactor (PWR) with a capacity of 1154MW. Its modular construction will allow many construction activities to take place in parallel. The estimated construction time is 36 months. The design has been greatly simplified compared with the Magnox and AGR plants, which are in the process of being decommissioned. Waste production would be greatly reduced. It is claimed that a 40-year programme of replacing the existing UK nuclear output with the AP1000 would only add 10 per cent to the existing waste accumulation. Decommissioning would be simpler and cheaper, involving less irradiated material than with existing plants (Figure 12.11).

Developing nations

It is widely recognized that the developing world will experience rapid growth in energy demand, once the current recession is over. This has led

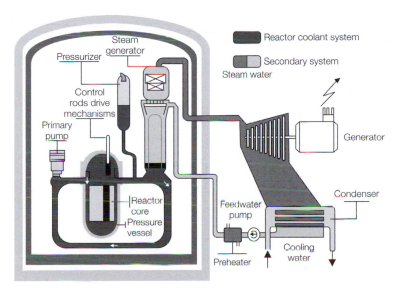

Source: Courtesy of Areva

Figure 12.10 Diagram of the EPR reactor building

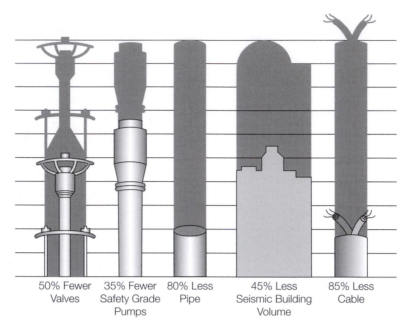

Source: Westinghouse

Figure 12.11 Efficiency savings in the Westinghouse AP1000

the Global Nuclear Energy Partnership (GNEP) to identify as a priority the development and demonstration of small to medium sized reactors (SMRs) that can be globally deployed without adding to the risk of nuclear proliferation. Lead-cooled systems are the favourite technology.

In 2004 the US Department of Energy began the development of a 'small, sealed transportable, autonomous reactor' (SSTAR). In this device the nuclear fuel, liquid lead coolant and steam generator are sealed within a secure casing. Steam pipes would be connected to a turbine generator. Security was the major concern and monitors will shut down the reactor if faults occur or tampering is detected. A warning will be sent via secure radio channels to the monitoring agency. The reactor would be expected to generate power for 30 years, after which it would be returned to the supplier to be disposed of or recharged. An advantage of this system is that it is modular and can provide power in increments from 10 to 700MW. In addition, its size allows the unit to be located

close to areas of demand. A 100MW version would be 15m tall and 3m in diameter and would weigh around 500 tonnes. The smaller version would weigh about 200 tonnes. This is the US Generation IV lead-cooled fast reactor system, and it looks capable of reaching places where other reactors are not viable.

Uranium

Nuclear power is widely perceived as being potentially limitless. Its primary fuel is uranium. An estimate by the World Energy Council in 1993 gave uranium reserves a lifetime of 41 years. From 2009 that is until about 2035–40. However, renewed interest in nuclear generation, especially from major nations like China, India and Russia, may put even this date in doubt. The reprocessing of spent fuel is the only long-term hope, although, to repeat, efforts in this direction in the UK have, so far, been a failure. Consider these two cautionary quotes: 'There are almost certainly no major new discoveries [of uranium] ahead' (Council of German Industry UK) and 'As uranium hoarding begins, a major shortage could arise sooner than 2013' (Michael Meacher, former UK environment minister). Two thousand scientists in India are working on a system to combine plutonium waste with thorium to breed stockpiles of uranium (*Guardian*, 30 September 2009, p22).

Finally, one of the problems with nuclear power is that it is inflexible. Modifying output to match short-term demand is not an option. However, as the prospect of the hydrogen economy looms larger, the power output during demand troughs could be directed to the electrolysis production of this gas. This could be an increasingly valuable income stream as transport embraces fuel cell technology. Electricity storage in Vanadium Flow Batteries may also come into prominence.

Nuclear fusion

Nuclear fusion is a process whereby a massive quality of energy is released. The world first experienced uncontrolled fusion with the hydrogen bomb developed at the end of the Second World War. Since then the aim has been to achieve controlled fusion for the production of electricity.

The principle is that all nuclei have a positive charge due to their protons. Identical (or like) charges repel and the aim of fusion is to overcome this electromagnetic repulsion and allow the two nuclei to get close enough for the attractive nuclear force to be sufficiently strong to achieve fusion. The fusion of lighter nuclei creates a single heavier nucleus plus a free neutron, releasing more energy than is needed to effect the fusion. This can be achieved by accelerating the nuclei to extremely high speeds in a tokamak-type (doughnut shaped) reactor and heating them to thermonuclear temperatures in the process.

The attraction of nuclear fusion is that, theoretically, it delivers ten times more fusion energy than the heat energy needed to force the nuclei to fuse together: an exothermic process that can produce a self-sustaining reaction. Break-even, or self-sustaining, controlled fusion reactions have been achieved briefly in a few tokamak-type reactors around the world.

Some of the most advanced fusion research is being conducted at the UK Rutherford Appleton Laboratories at Didcot near Oxford, known as the HiPER project. This European High Power Laser Energy Research facility is designed to demonstrate the feasibility of laser-driven fusion. It will use seawater as its principle source of fuel and will not produce any long-life radioactive waste. Demonstration of proof of the principle is expected between 2010 and 2012 as part of a continuous international programme. Then it will be a matter of moving from the scientific proof of principle to a commercial reactor (Figure 12.12).

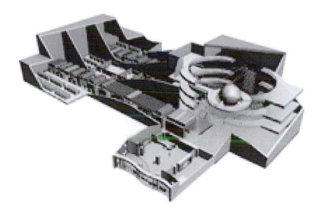

Source: Courtesy of Rutherford Appleton Laboratory

Figure 12.12 Graphic of the HiPER facility at the Rutherford Appleton Laboratory.

Fusion used to be 50 years away. Perhaps that can now be reduced to 30 years, just in time to replace third generation nuclear fission reactors. Whether any country apart from the richest industrialized nations will be able to afford it is an open question.

Whatever the ultimate decisions concerning next generation nuclear plants, the responsibility for supplying the bulk of energy needs in the latter half of the 21st century will fall on renewables. The energy resource waiting to be more widely exploited is the sun, which radiates an average of about 288 Watts per square metre onto the Earth's surface. The challenge lies in capturing as much as possible of that energy to keep the wheels turning and eliminate poverty.

The dilemma of sustainable development

This brings us to another conflict of aspirations. The aim of the UK government is for economic growth of 2–3 per cent per year, but under the cloak of 'sustainable development'. This would mean that the economy of the UK would double in strength in 23 years. 'Each successive doubling period consumes as much resource as all the previous doubling periods combined' (Professor Rod Smith of Imperial College in an address to the Royal Academy of Engineering, May 2007). Clearly 'sustainable development' is a phrase capable of a range of interpretations, so it is time for a definition that acknowledges the real world of climate change and fossil fuel depletion.

The only way that sustainable development will be viable in the present context is if it includes a radical reduction in the demand for primary energy to a level that can be provided by near carbon neutral energy technologies.

Sustainable economic development is possible by virtue of the immense opportunities inherent in the transition to a post fossil fuel economy. The challenge for science and industry is to create conditions that will enable the UK to remain economically secure, even if all around are falling apart. 'Sustainable development' involves being decoupled from the raw pursuit

of wealth (which is now stigmatized in any case) and directed to the task of keeping the lights on, wheels turning and food on the shelves in a world where all old certainties will have crumbled. The relentless pursuit of wealth could have even more cataclysmic consequences.

Threats from space

In previous books (Smith, 2005, 2007), I have discussed the merits of distributed electricity generation by means of mini-grids, which, in government parlance, is called 'islanding'. One of the benefits of such a grid system is that it would be much better at accommodating small-scale renewable technologies in the kilowatt range rather than the national grid dedicated to megawatt-scale generation. At the same time it would protect against catastrophic collapse in the event of a local failure of one of the components of a national grid. Now another argument has come to light supporting the case for changing to distributed generation via mini-grids that can either be networked or act independently. It is contained in a report issued by the US National Academy of Science (NAS).

The central theme of the report is that the world is getting perilously close to possible disaster, but this time from outer space. The reason for this verdict is that Western society has become increasingly reliant on technology for its smooth running, and, as such, it has 'sown the seeds of its own destruction', according to the report. Is this an extravagant claim? The answer lies in space.

The Aurora Borealis is a renowned spectacle seen mainly in northern latitudes, but it has a sinister side that can be lethal. This can be apparent when the sun ejects plasma-charged particles carried by solar winds that contain billion-tonne fireballs of plasma called a 'coronal mass ejection'. This penetration of plasma into our atmosphere clashes with the Earth's magnetic field causing it to undergo change. Why this matters is because the rapid economic growth in the West and now in the East has caused a significant increase in the demand for electricity that, in turn, has caused the grids to handle higher voltages over ever larger distances. For example, China is installing a 1000 kilovolt grid – twice the voltage of the US'. These high-power grids act as antennae, or channels for a massive transfer of direct current (DC) from space into electricity grids not designed either for DC or the sudden increase in load.

The result is that an enormous DC is transmitted to local power transformers that are designed to convert power from its transport voltage to domestic level voltage. As a consequence the copper wires in the transformers soon melt, producing a cascade of power failures. The steady global rise in the demand for electricity is increasing the potential for such failures. The Chair of the NAS committee that produced this report has stated: 'We're moving closer and closer to the edge of a possible disaster'; According to John Kallenham,[1] an adviser to NAS, the scale could be global: 'A really large storm could be a planetary disaster'.

The NAS report warns that a 'severe weather event' could induce ground currents that would disable 300 key transformers in the US in less than two minutes. As a result, 130 million people would be without power. The knock-on effect would be a crash of almost all life-support systems including health care, water supplies, fuel and food distribution, heating and cooling. NAS estimates that it would take between four and ten years to recover from such an event.

A dedicated satellite can provide, at best, a 15 minute warning of incoming geomagnetic storms. However, a coronal mass ejection arrives faster that the time it takes for a satellite message to reach the Earth. The only guaranteed safeguard is a massive reconfiguration of electricity distribution by means of local, semi-independent grids that can support small-scale and intermittent generation and which can have fail-safe connections with the wider grid network, automatically severing the link as soon as an anomaly in the current is detected (data from Brooks, 2009).

This is another case of a win–win situation for the green lobby, except that, in this case, it is 'win–win–win'. Small scale generation to a system of mini-grids offers the following three benefits:

- distributed generation accommodating the range of renewables technologies is the route to drastic CO_2 emissions abatement;
- energy security in the face of declining fossil fuel reserves;
- protection against apocalyptic plasma invasions.

To restate the Nicholas Stern injunction, in this time of need it is more urgent than ever to take rapid precautionary action. After the event, the cost of remediation, according to the NAS, could be as much as $125 billion, and that is just for the US.

Considering the big picture, we have probably already lost Round One in the war against climate change. Round Two must be focused on immediate action to buy time in the hope that science will ultimately rise to the challenge of changing the Earth/atmosphere CO_2 balance in favour of humanity. This means that massive resources should be directed to:

- adapting to the inevitabilities and uncertainties of an increasingly turbulent climate, especially in terms of critical infrastructures and the built environment;
- addressing the urgent problem of installing ultra-low carbon energy systems as distributed generation for climate reasons, and to replace the diminishing reserves of fossil fuels, and to protect against geomagnetic storms.

We are probably already committed to irreversible climate change. Adaptation to an ultimate extremely hostile environment is a matter of highest priority and must begin *now*.

Note

1   John Kallenham is an analyst with the Metatech Corporation, California.

13

Coal: Black Gold or Black Hole?

In 2006 it was estimated that global recoverable reserves of coal amounted to 905 billion tonnes (gigatonnes) according to the US Energy Information Administration 2008. The World Coal Institute estimates that this will last 147 years at current rates of consumption. According the Hermann Scheer, environmentalist member of the German Bundestag, when coal is substituted for gas and oil, reserves will be exhausted well before 2100 (Scheer, 2002, p100). Since he wrote his book, estimates of reserves have increased, but so also have the expectations for synthetic fuels. The organization World Energy Outlook has compiled a graph of coal reserves by region up to 2100. It suggests that peak coal will be reached by 2025. This may prove optimistic (Figure 13.1).

Coal accounts for 41 per cent of the world's power supply. Of this total, 250 billion tonnes is located in the US. Consequently, nearly 50 per cent of its power comes from coal. At the same time India and China are forging ahead with coal fired generation. China has massive reserves that are powering its economic development which continues at 8 per cent per year despite, the world economic downturn. Until recently it was said to be constructing the equivalent of two 500MW coal-fired plants per week, each of which would produce 3 million tons (US) of CO_2 per year. Coal emits twice as much CO_2 as natural gas and globally at the time of writing it accounts for 37 per cent of all CO_2 emissions. According to the International Energy Agency, this is set rise to 43 per cent by 2030, thanks mainly to expanding power generation in India and China.

New coal fired power stations are being constructed in the developed and developing world in the expectation that technology will render them environmentally benign. Governments are claiming that the future lies in clean technology and that future power stations will be 'capture-ready'.

The UK Secretary of State for climate change, Ed Miliband, asserted in March 2009 that nuclear and coal-fired plants were central to the energy strategy. 'Coal will remain part of the energy mix in this country certainly for some years to come but it needs to be clean coal' (reported in the *Guardian*, 6 March 2009).

Will it be possible to have 'clean coal' or is it just a cynical oxymoron? There are two main methods of converting coal to energy without, allegedly, harming the planet. The first involves the use of conventional coal fired steam turbines but includes carbon capture and storage (CCS). In the second case, coal is converted to liquid fuels.

In the first category there are three principle types of CCS:

- *Pre-combustion capture*. Pulverized coal particles are mixed with steam, which produces hydrogen and CO_2. The hydrogen is burnt to generate electricity and the CO_2 buried. This system has to be incorporated into the design of power plants and is therefore not suitable for CCS retrofitting.
- *Post-combustion capture*. Coal is burnt in the normal way and the CO_2 produced is captured and buried. It involves scrubbing the exhaust gases from the flue. The appeal

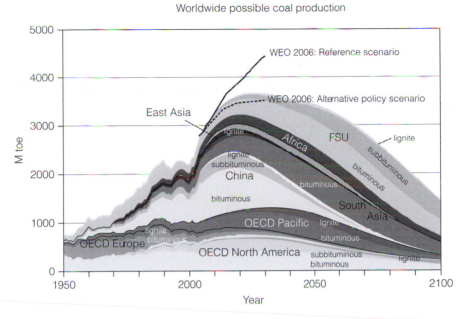

Worldwide possible coal production

Note: The International Energy Agency (IEA) has created a mathematical construct, the World Energy Model, which is designed to replicate how energy markets function. It is the basis of World Energy Outlook's annual assessments. WEO 2009 was published in November.
Source: World Energy Outlook.

Figure 13.1 World coal reserves to 2100

of this technology, which is advocated by the UK government, is that it can be retrofitted.

- *Oxy-fuel combustion.* Coal is burnt in pure oxygen. This produces a high temperature reaction resulting in few polluting by-products. This is probably the most expensive option.

Carbon capture and deep storage have been practised for a decade by the Norwegians. An exhausted gas field below the Sleipner East platform in the North Sea has received a million tonnes of CO_2 each year. Engineers have studied the fate of the gas and have concluded that there is no leakage; it remains trapped in the interstices of the subterranean sandstone. The longest running carbon storage experiment has been deemed a success by scientists, opening the way to a much wider exploitation of this storage option.

The world's first demonstration coal fired plant with CCS went into production in the autumn of 2008. It was built next to the 1600MW Schwarze Pumpe in north Germany. Its capacity is about 12MW of electricity and 30MW of thermal power. The design claims to capture 100,000 tonnes of CO_2 per year by first compressing it and then burying it 3000m below ground in the depleted Altmark gas field. This is located about 200km from the plant. This pilot plant uses an oxy-fuel boiler burning coal in an atmosphere of pure oxygen. The outcome is almost pure CO_2, which can then be buried.

All the components of CCS have been tried and tested; as yet they have not been combined to create a commercial full-cycle CCS plant. Developing this final stage is likely to be very expensive. In the UK, Tim Laidlaw, the chief executive of energy company Centrica, has stated that full-blown CCS is unlikely to be ready to make a significant impact on CO_2 emissions before 2030 (Tim Webb in the *Guardian*, 26 Feb 2009). His reasons are that the geology of the country is not suited to the technology and that the technology is costly.

The UK government favours post-combustion technology since it can be retrofitted to existing power stations. On the other hand, Centrica has been developing pre-combustion technology, only suitable for new plants. The company considers that there is a risk that post-combustion CCS will never be fitted to the next generation of coal fired power stations, like the planned Kingsnorth plant, for technical reasons and also because, in many cases, of the distance to North Sea aquifers for storage, which will be another addition to the costs.

There are some vehement critics of this technology. The most prominent is James Hansen who asserts: 'coal is the single greatest threat to civilisation and all life on our planet... The dirtiest trick that governments play on their citizens is the pretence that they are working on "green coal"' (Hansen, 2009).

The head of science at the British Geological Survey believes that 'coal is going to be available as a source of energy for at least another century and countries like China, India and Russia have particularly rich resources' (Hansen, 2009).

As oil and gas reserves become exhausted, coal will be the fuel of last resort and there is no guarantee that nations will be willing to bear the extra cost of retrofitting CCS once it becomes viable. Since the technology is still under development, it will take decades before it is widely available, by which time many new power stations will have been built. Consequently billions of tonnes of CO_2 will have been emitted from this source alone, even assuming that widescale retrofit CCS is adopted.

The attitude of the UK is that new coal-fired plants will be designed to be CCS-ready in the hope that it will ultimately be both technically efficient and cost-effective. In contradiction of this pledge, it is only funding research into post-combustion CCS technology. Retrofit is what matters. Alternatively it is leaving it to the US to perfect pre-combustion CCS. Nevertheless, this creates the impression that the potential energy crisis over fossil fuel reserves means that coal will be vital to keep existing plants operational whatever the outcome of CCS.

Liquefaction

The second potential destiny for coal is in the provision of liquid fuels via coal to liquids (CTL) technology. There are two basic approaches to liquefaction: direct and indirect.

Direct liquefaction

One method of direct liquefaction is the Bergius process, which involves breaking down the coal in a solvent at high pressure and temperature. There is then an interaction with hydrogen and a catalyst, which produces a synthetic fuel.

A second direct route to liquefaction was developed in the 1920s by Lewis Karrick by the process of low temperature carbonization. Coal is converted to coke at temperatures between 450 and 700°C. The result is the production of coal tars that can be processed into fuels.

Indirect liquefaction

The indirect route was developed in 1923 by Franz Fischer and Hans Tropsch. Their synthetic fuel was used extensively by Germany and Japan in the Second World War. It is said to be cheaper than oil. Production first involves the gasification of coal to make a syngas that is a balanced, purified mixture of carbon monoxide and hydrogen. Then Fischer–Tropsch catalysts are used to convert the syngas into light hydrocarbons that can be further processed into petrol or diesel fuel. In addition, syngas can be converted into methanol, which can be used as a fuel or a fuel additive.

CTL and CO_2

Both of these liquefaction processes are far from carbon neutral. In fact the conversion process releases more CO_2 than is released in the refinement of oil to petroleum. If petrol and diesel were to be replaced by coal-based synthetic fuels the result would be a considerable increase in CO_2 emissions. Sequestration would impose a significant cost penalty. At the same time it is claimed that, when burnt, this form of synthetic fuel produces twice as much CO_2 as petrol (Figure 13.2).

Coal gas

As stated in the Fischer–Tropsch process, generating syngas is a stage in the production of liquid fuel. It is a fuel that dates from the 19th century when it was a by-product of the coking process. Then it was usually called 'town gas'. In the Second World War vehicles were equipped with huge balloons on their roofs containing gas for fuel. Coal gas is mainly a mixture of the calorific gases, hydrogen, carbon monoxide, methane and volatile hydrocarbons. It also contains small amounts of carbon dioxide and nitrogen.

Integrated gasification combined cycle (IGCC)

Another developing technology is called 'integrated gasification combined cycle' (IGCC). In the plant coal is converted to syngas. The

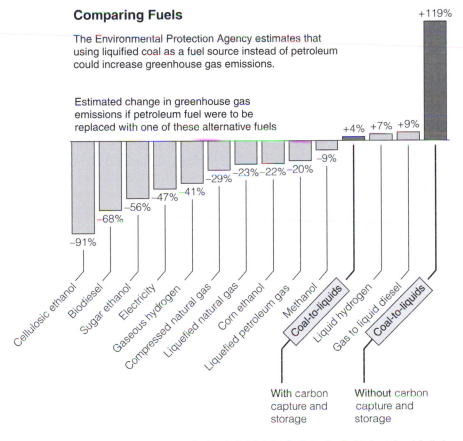

Comparing Fuels

The Environmental Protection Agency estimates that using liquified coal as a fuel source instead of petroleum could increase greenhouse gas emissions.

Estimated change in greenhouse gas emissions if petroleum fuel were to be replaced with one of these alternative fuels

+119%

+4% +7% +9%

−9%

−29% −23% −22% −20%

−47% −41%

−56%

−68%

−91%

Cellulosic ethanol
Biodiesel
Sugar ethanol
Electricity
Gaseous hydrogen
Compressed natural gas
Liquefied natural gas
Corn ethanol
Liquefied petroleum gas
Methanol
Coal-to-liquids
Liquid hydrogen
Gas to liquid diesel
Coal-to-liquids

With carbon capture and storage

Without carbon capture and storage

Note: The estimates include emissions from all parts of the process of making the fuels including fossil extraction, feedstock growth and distribution as well as averaging for the different methods of producing the fuels.

Source: US Environment Protection Agency

Figure 13.2 Estimated increase in greenhouse gases with coal to liquids (CTL)

carbon is then removed for sequestration, leaving the remainder as a fuel to power turbines. This is an expensive technology adding up to 65 per cent to the cost of electricity. Nevertheless, there are at least 50 IGCC plants at the planning stage worldwide.

Underground gasification of coal (UGC)

UGC is a process invented in the Soviet Union in the 1930s, but obviously without carbon capture. In the UGC process the coal remains in the ground where it is converted to syngas and extracted through a well. The volume of the coal is thereby reduced, allowing the captured carbon to be pumped into the ground. The process involves drilling two shafts into a seam of coal. The coal is ignited in one shaft aided by pumping in air or pure oxygen. The amount of air/oxygen is controlled so that only a part of the coal is burnt, producing combustible gases. The syngas is removed from the second shaft in a relatively raw state. If all the carbon is removed, the residue is pure hydrogen. However, the process is expensive. A more cost-effective option is to remove half the carbon leaving a fuel that is reasonably cheap and cleaner than natural gas. Since the technology avoids both the cost of mining and transporting the coal and the disposal of the CO_2, it is significantly cheaper than above ground gasification and sequestration.

The verdict

Liquefaction in all its versions will probably do nothing to stem the Gadarene rush to 4°C. As for CCS, there is perhaps a potential revenue opportunity in forming partnerships with farmers and market gardeners to enhance crop growth. Power companies could be linked to polytunnel fields containing captured CO_2 offering a second income stream. There could also be an opportunity to boost the growth of algae for the production of biodiesel. It will be some time before CCS is technically and commercially viable. Meanwhile coal fired generation continues to expand.

14

Filling the Gap: Utility-scale Renewables

To get things into perspective, it will be useful to start with a breakdown of the renewables' share of global final energy consumption in 2006 compared with fossil fuels and nuclear, as shown in Table 14.1.

This highlights the fact that there is still much to do to scale up the contribution from renewables. Nevertheless, over the last decade, electricity derived from renewables has almost doubled (International Energy Agency (IEA). In 2006 they accounted for 433 terawatt–hours (TWh) or 2.3 per cent of the 19,014TWhs of electricity generated worldwide. Theoretically renewables could meet global needs several times over at 310,600TWh. The breakdown of the technical potential of systems in TWh/year is:

Geothermal	138,000
Wind	106,000
Solar	43,600
Biomass	23,000

Source: New Scientist, 11 October 2008, p33.

Figures for wave and tidal power are not available, but in certain countries like the UK and Canada they could be considerable.

Technically it would be possible to meet 100 per cent of world electricity needs from renewables. However, if the UK's total energy needs to be met by renewables, which excludes nuclear and coal with CCS, huge areas of land and sea would be consumed by any one of the main technologies. For example, take biomass: even if 75 per cent of the country were to be covered with energy crops, this would still not be nearly enough to meet the energy needs of the nation. Meeting electricity demand from photovoltaics would require PV farms covering an area the size of Wales. However, this assumes a steady state in terms of energy demand. According to the IEA, by 2030 world demand will increase by six times the capacity of Saudi Arabia.

Table 14.1 Global energy consumption by source

Fuel	Share of global energy consumption (%)
Fossil fuels	79
Nuclear	3
Renewables	
Traditional biomass	13
Large hydropower	3
Hot water/heating	1.3
Power generation	0.8
Biofuels	0.3
Total	18.4

Source: Renewable Energy Policy Network for the 21st Century (2008), Renewables 2007 Global Status Report

Scenarios for renewable energy resources

In 2005 world energy use came to 477 exajoules (10^{18}). The IEA has estimated the growth in energy demand according to the different technologies, including renewables. One of the problems in making comparisons between projections is the variety of units employed. The IEA uses tonnes of oil equivalent (toe). To put this into perspective, 5000Mtoe is equivalent to 210 exajoules (Figures 14.1 and 14.2).

Buildings use about 40 per cent of global energy and are responsible for approximately the same percentage of CO_2 emissions. Roughly half of their demand is for direct space heating and hot water and the remainder is associated with the production of electricity for lighting, space cooling, appliances and office equipment

(Worldwatch Institute, 2009). The theoretical potential of renewable energy is ~3000 exajoules, according to the UN Development Programme (Chapman and Gross, 2001) (Figure 14.3).

According to the IEA, funded by the energy companies, the share of the world's primary energy drawn from renewables will be around 13 per cent by 2030. However if some of the national policies that are currently proposed are implemented, this could rise to 17 per cent with 29 per cent of electricity derived from renewables.

Rethinking the grid

The UK government is planning for at least 33GW of wind power, mostly offshore. According to wind energy expert Hugh Sharman, experience from Denmark and

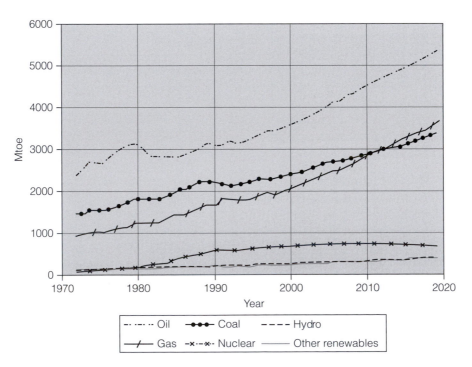

Source: Courtesy of IEA

Figure 14.1 Energy consumption projections to 2020 by fuel

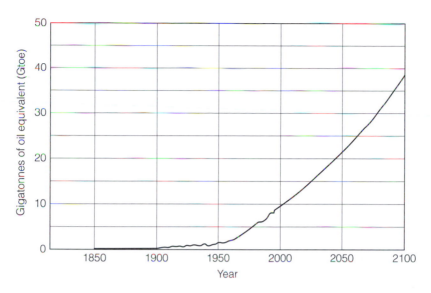

Note: 1 gigatonne of oil equivalent (Gtoe) = 42 exajoules.

Figure 14.2 World Energy Council forecast of global primary energy use to 2100

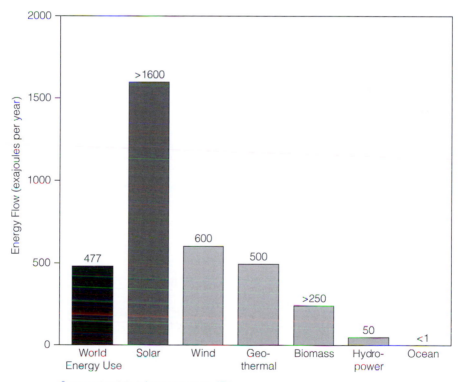

Source: UNDP, Johansson et al., IEA

Source: Courtesy of IEA

Figure 14.3 World energy use in 2005 and annual renewables potential with current technologies

Germany indicates that this country will find it impractical to manage much more than 10GW without major changes to the system. He concludes that 'while wind power should be exploited as fully as possible, it must not be at the expense of renewing firm generating capacity' (Sharman, 2005). So, what can be done, short of completely replacing the grid?

The UK's Royal Commission on Environmental Pollution made this pronouncement back in 2000.

> *The electricity system will have to undergo major changes to cope with ... the expansion of smaller scale, intermittent renewable energy sources. The transition towards a low-emission energy system would be greatly helped by the development of new means of storing energy on a large scale.*
> (Royal Commission on Environmental Pollution, 2000, p169)

Balancing supply and demand in the context of a steep rise in the contribution from renewables is a matter of considerable research interest. One project at the demonstration stage is termed 'dynamic demand management'. This relies on a symbiotic relationship between the electricity grid and appliances. It works, for example, by a fridge having the facility to respond to slight variations in the frequency of the supply. In the UK supply is around 50 hertz (US, 60Hz). If, for example, a large scale wind farm off the Thames Estuary were to experience a flat calm, the rest of the grid generators would have to cope with the deficit. In the process the frequency may drop to about 48.8Hz, which means that some load would have to be shed. At the moment load shedding is under the centralized control of the power companies. However, if appliances like fridges were to be part of the control network, this could obviate the need for load shedding on the grid scale. A control mechanism in the fridge detects the change in frequency and, at the same time, checks the temperature. This enables it to calculate how long it can remain sufficiently chilled without power and automatically switches off for that period. If the system were fitted to enough fridges, this could create enough 'down time' to alleviate the problems caused by intermittent generation. It is estimated that, if the 30 million fridges in the UK were fitted with the system, it would reduce peak demand by ~2GW. The cost of the modification would be around £4 per appliance, which would be a small price to pay for achieving security of supply.

Another approach would be to adopt a smart grid system. This also operates on the basis of two-way communication between an appliance and the electricity company. The difference is that the appliance is the passive partner. The utility predicts the output from, say, wind power, using information from local short-term weather forecasts. It then uses information fed by the appliance to balance demand with supply. It is then able to cause non-essential appliances to switch off when necessary to relieve the load on the grid. For example, an air conditioning system could be switched off for about 15 minutes without causing any discernible rise in indoor temperature. The City of Boulder, Colorado, is the proving ground for the technology to assess the viable maximum operational scope for wind power in the region (Boulder Convention and Visitors Bureau, 'Leading the way in Green – from science to sustainability').

Information technology is now capable of managing the complexities of a system with a large number and variety of distributed inputs to the grid without centralized control. In dealing with the interplay of supply and demand, it can provide hour by hour least-cost outcomes to the benefit of consumers.

Renewables at utility scale

Wind power

In 2007 wind power was the largest source of new generating capacity in Europe and in the US, in 2008, 8.3GW of new capacity was installed. This brings the US total at the time of writing to 25GW.

For the UK the best opportunities for power from wind reside in the seas. Offshore wind is about 50 per cent more productive than onshore alternatives. There are two categories: shallow and deep offshore. Shallow turbines operate in depths under 25m and are roughly twice the cost of onshore equivalents. Deep offshore opportunities are in depths of 25–50m. In 2005 the average load factor for all major wind farms was 28 per cent. The average for all the main onshore farms was 26.4 per cent.

In December 2007 the UK government announced that it would give permits for a capacity of 33GW of offshore wind electricity. Given its load factor, this would deliver an average of 10GW (33 per cent). This would require at least 10,000 3MW machines. The cost, based on the Kentish Flats farm off the Thames Estuary completed in 2005, would be £33 billion. Since then, unit costs for wind power have risen appreciably. An extra £3–4 billion would be needed to supply the 50 or so installation, or 'jack-up' barges. If the costs were to be met by the taxpayer it would now amount to ~£600 per person. There is a view, expressed by a member of the Wind Energy Association, that such a project is 'pie in the sky' (Mackay, 2008, pp60–67).

Recently the view has been aired that the focus should be on shallow offshore wind farms with much lower installation and connection costs. However, this would limit the viable size of machine.

On 21 October 2008, the British government claimed that it had surpassed Denmark in the installation of wind power and that it now had enough capacity to power 300,000 homes. However, on the same day it was announced that the Crown Estates, who are responsible for licensing wind farms within 200 miles of the coast, is offering to enter into partnership with wind energy companies to exploit the huge offshore wind resource enjoyed by the UK. Despite long transmission lines, the advantages are that the wind regime is fairly consistent and more powerful than inshore and onshore sites, and that larger turbines can be employed. To endorse the latter point, a 7.5MW offshore machine is being assembled at Blyth, Northumberland. The view in the industry is that 10MW is the maximum viable size for deep offshore machines.

A drawback with offshore turbines is the high cost of the foundations. A demonstration project underway off the Norwegian coast involves a floating turbine to overcome this problem. The principle is that a flotation chamber provides buoyancy while extended legs anchor the system to the seabed by suction. It is a joint project, with Siemens providing the turbine and Hydro of Norway the foundation technology. The latter will adapt the technology it has employed on floating oil rigs. Completion is planned for 2009.

There has been a pronouncement by the UK government that 20 per cent of its electricity will come from renewables by 2020. About 75 per cent of this, it is said, will be provided by wind power. It remains to be seen if there are pies in the sky.

As a postscript to wind, one factor that has been inhibiting the development of wind power is the interference threat they pose to aircraft radar. This is because current systems are unable to distinguish between aircraft and rotating turbines. A UK engineering firm, Cambridge Consultants, has devised a scanning process that simultaneously scans the whole sky every 4 seconds. This produces a 3D image of the airspace, which its inventors call 'holographic radar'. The increased scanning rate provides the level of resolution necessary to distinguish between planes and turbines. However, this technology may be overtaken by the application of military stealth technology to turbine blades, making them invisible to radar.

The Achilles heel of wind power is its chaotic intermittence. There are several approaches to solving this problem. At present the preferred option is to resort to gas–turbine generation, which is sufficiently flexible to provide balancing power. The power company E.ON has claimed that wind power needs 90 per cent backup from coal and gas plants (*Guardian*, 4 June 2008). However, the post-fossil fuel age will demand other systems. If intermittent systems are to be fully exploited, they must be in association with developments in both the storage of electricity and serious changes to the grid.

Electricity storage

A tried and tested system is pumped storage, which was originally introduced to smooth the peaks and troughs of demand that caused problems for nuclear power stations such as Trawsfynydd in north Wales (Figure 14.4). It was coupled with two lakes, one adjacent to the plant, the other high in the hills into which it pumped water during periods of low demand and therefore energy price. At peak periods it was returned to the lower Lake Trawsfynydd, powering conventional turbines in the process.

Pumped storage is also one of the options being considered in combination with a tidal barrage in the Severn Estuary.

For some years compressed air has been utilized as a storage technology, notably in underground caverns in Alabama, US. A similar plant is under construction at Huntorf, Germany. Studies suggest that compressed air storage would allow wind power to provide base load power. Such a storage system could be a cost-effective way of wind power meeting 80 per cent of the demand for the grid.

Battery storage is also breaking new ground. Lead acid batteries do not have the energy density to store megawatt scale power. However, one alternative is the sodium sulphur battery, which operates at a high temperature. It promises high power and energy densities. However, the sodium has to be above its melting point (98°C), which causes problems of thermal management and corrosion. However, it has the capacity to store tens of megawatts so it must have a future with intermittent technologies. Its main threat is from the advancing development of lithium batteries.

For some time there has been support for the fuel cell as a method of facilitating the storage of electricity. The standard method of producing the necessary hydrogen is either through reforming natural gas, since methane has a high hydrogen content (CH_4), or electrolysis. However, neither is a carbon-free option unless the electrolysis of water is powered from renewable sources.

Here, too, there are promising developments. Electrolysers are, in effect, reverse fuel cells, using electrical current to split water into its constituents of two parts hydrogen to one part oxygen. A Sheffield based company, ITM Power, is claiming a revolution in electrolyser and fuel cell technology. The major cost element of both technologies is the membrane, which is based on

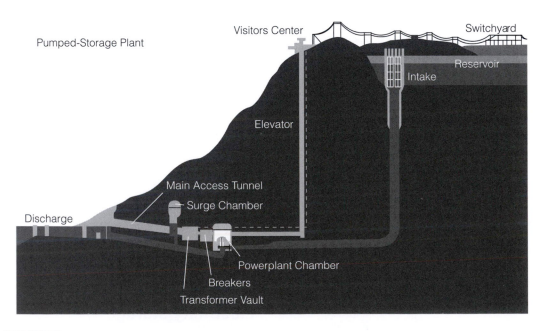

Figure 14.4 Pumped storage using natural contours

platinum. In its place the company has created a unique low-cost polymer that offers an economic option for manufacturing hydrogen. At present there are demonstration programmes to test the technology for both vehicle and domestic application (see Chapter 15).

Flow battery technology

The most promising technology for megawatt scale renewable energy storage is the Vanadium Flow Battery (Figure 14.5). This is not a new technology, but it has only recently been scaled-up to store enough electricity to offer multi-megawatt hours of current. The process comprises two storage tanks filled with electrolyte solution, each with slightly different ionic characteristics. The tanks are separated by a proton exchange membrane that allows ionic interchange to occur. Both tanks are linked to storage tanks and pumps permitting large amounts of electricity to be stored. Under the charging condition, electrodes force a charge from one tank to the other. Ionic change occurs when electrons are moved from the positive tank across the membrane to the negative tank. Current is discharged when the process is reversed.

This technology is highly suitable as a balancing power system because the battery can rapidly discharge current, making it particularly useful for chaotic intermittent renewables like wind power. Its main disadvantage is that it occupies a large area in proportion to the kilowatt hours stored. However, in the case of wind farms or tidal energy, this is a problem that could probably be overcome. The system is currently being installed in a 39MW wind farm in Donegal, Ireland, by VRB Power Systems of Vancouver.

In The Netherlands there are plans to create a man-made island to accommodate pumped storage of water from the North Sea. It is designed as a backup to wind power and to generate peak-time power. Water will be pumped when supply exceeds demand. It will have a capacity of 1.5GW and should provide power to two million homes. If it is successful, other smaller islands could be constructed to provide power to other countries, notably the UK, which looks like being excessively reliant on wind power.

Massive dykes would be built to keep back the sea. The centre of the island would be excavated to 40m below sea level. Pipes in the dykes would allow water to pour into the cavity, generating power in the process. It would be pumped out when full to capacity. The electricity needed to pump out the store would at least be matched by the electricity generated in the charging stage. The prime purpose of the facility would be to ensure continuity of supply from wind turbines with between 30 and 40 per cent capacity factor.

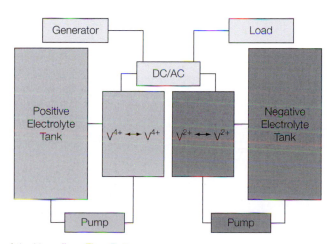

Figure 14.5 Principle of the Vanadium Flow Battery

Solar electricity

Areas with a high rate of sunshine and high level of solar intensity, such as southern Spain and north Africa enjoy considerable potential for converting that energy into electricity. Two technologies are available: concentrated solar power and photovoltaics (PV). Both can produce power in the multi-megawatt range.

Concentrated solar power (CSP)

According to *Renewable Energy World.com* (2 September 2008) 'concentrated solar thermal power is emerging behind wind as a significant source of renewable wholesale generation capacity'. In mid-2008 the total CSP installed capacity was 431MW, mostly in Spain, with an estimated 7000MW due by 2012. Of this, 44 per cent will be in the US, 41 per cent in Spain and 10 per cent in the Middle East.

Southern Spain receives over 3000 hours of sunshine per year. In 2004 Spain pioneered the idea of a feed-in tariff for renewables. It was set at 27 eurocents/kWh for CSP plants up to 50MW. It will last for 25 years increasing with inflation minus 1 per cent. The outcome is that southern Spain is the test bed for two approaches to solar thermal electricity. One is the 'power tower'. In the first of the genre in Europe, north of Saville, 600 flat mirrors or heliostats, each 120m², track the sun to focus on a boiler to generate steam at the tower's apex 115m above ground. It generates 11MW of electricity, which, it is claimed, will power 6000 homes (Figures 14.6 to 14.8). The second system is the

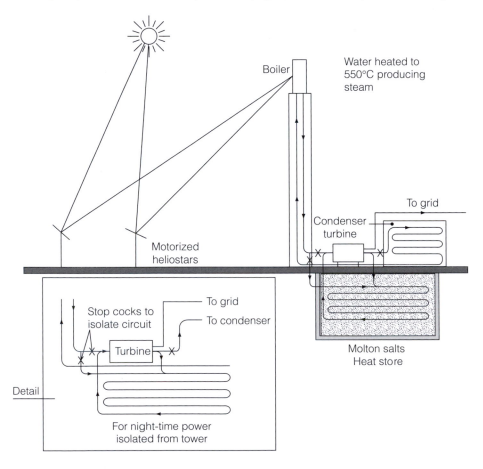

Figure 14.6 Concentrated solar power principle

Source: Wikipedia

Figure 14.7 PS10 Solar Power Tower, Sanlúcar la Mayor, near Seville

Source: Wikipedia

Figure 14.8 Heliostats for solar thermal electricity, California

ground-based linear reflector focusing on a heat pipe that generates steam.

Solar power is obviously intermittent, so the storage of thermal energy is a valuable facility. In this case, heat is stored in tanks as pressurized steam at 50 bar and 285°C. The steam condenses and flashes back to steam for generating when the pressure is lowered. It only provides one hour of storage. However, molten salts as a storage medium will duly replace this system. Extended storage not only increases the generating time but also allows solar to provide power when the energy price is at its peak. In parallel, electricity could also be stored in a Vanadium Flow Battery, as discussed above.

The PS10 is the first of a series of towers scheduled for the site, which will raise the capacity to 300MW by 2013. The second tower, PS20, is nearing completion. On the same site is Sevilla PV, which is the largest ground concentration of PVs in Europe.

Horizontal CSP generation

The alternative to the power tower is a linear parabolic trough generator. The sun is directed by parabolic mirrors onto an absorber pipe containing a heat transfer fluid, usually oil. The heated fluid is pumped to a heat exchanger that creates steam to drive a turbine. The US and southern Spain are the key sites for this technology (Figure 14.9). The troughs are mostly aligned along a north–south axis and rotated to follow the angle of the sun throughout the day.

A variation on the horizontal approach is being trialled in Almeria, southern Spain, using Fresnel lens technology. It has been designed in association with the Fraunhofer Institute for Solar Energy Systems (ISE) and uses flat mirrors that can be angled to echo the profile of the parabola. They are about 15 per cent less efficient than parabolic mirrors but the cost savings more than compensate for the difference. The State of Nevada is planning to invest $50 billion in Fresnel solar power plants, which is an indication of two things; anxieties over security of supply and the potential of the technology (Figure 14.10).

Source: Wikipedia

Figure 14.9 Parabolic reflectors in the Mojave Desert, US

Source: Wikipedia

Figure 14.10 Fresnel solar thermal electricity, southern Spain

However, it is north Africa that could be the jewel in the crown of solar electricity. Solar intensity in the region is twice that of southern Spain and is rarely impeded by clouds. Horizontal concentrated solar thermal energy in conjunction with coastal wind farms 'could supply Europe with all the energy it needs'. Only a fraction of the Sahara, about the size of a small country, would be sufficient (Dr Anthony Patt of the Institute for Applied Systems Analysis in Africa, at the Copenhagen climate change conference, March 2009).

'The largest technically accessible source of power on the planet is to be found in the deserts around the equatorial regions of the earth' (Trans-Mediterranean Renewable Energy Cooperation (TREC) website homepage in October 2008). TREC was formed in 2003 and has since developed the Desertec concept with a view to establishing a super-grid connecting Europe with north Africa. It would transmit high voltage direct current (HVDC) to Europe with relatively low transmission losses. TREC has high ambitions as signified by its '*Forum Solar 10,000GW*' at the 2008 Hanover Fair.

One of the advantages of solar thermal systems is that they can work with conventional turbines using the generators that operate in fossil fuel power stations. Or, they can operate as hybrid systems. Exploiting existing technology could be crucial in recommending the technology to developing countries.

Gigawatt-scale photovoltaics

Until relatively recently PV technology has been confined to relatively small projects, often integrated with buildings. Until recently Germany had been setting the pace with projects like the 15MW+ PV farm at Arnstein, Bavaria. The PV industry owes its success in Germany to a feed-in tariff. However, it is being dwarfed by burgeoning activity in the US. Here, uncertainties about the security of fossil-based energy have led to a massive expansion of utility-scale PV farms. The most ambitious project to date is the dual agreement between the Pacific Gas and Electric Company (PG&EC) and Topaz Solar Farms for 550MW thin film PVs and High Plains Ranch II for a 250MW PV farm. Both are located in San Luis Obispo, California. The total of 800MW should deliver 1.65 billion kilowatt hours of renewable electricity a year. The project is expected to be online in 2010 and fully operational in 2012.

The ultimate destiny for PVs would seem to be 'very large-scale photovoltaic systems' (VLS-PV) in the multi-megawatt range. These would be located in desert regions, for example, north Africa, the Gobi Desert and the Australian interior. One third of the Earth's surface is barren desert. Covering a small fraction of this area with PVs could meet current global primary energy demand. As much of this area is located within the least developed and energy deprived countries, such projects could ultimately transform the lives of millions of people by the export of power to Europe.

A one gigawatt farm consisting of standard single-sun modules would typically cover an area of 7km². However, this area could be reduced by the use of multilayer concentrated solar PVs. There would also be the benefit of economies of scale that could make it cost-competitive with solar thermal electricity.

Electricity by inflation

'Cool Earth Solar' has recently patented a low cost concentrated solar PV system. It consists of a thin plastic film inflated balloon lined with reflective material concentrating the sun's rays onto a PV cell (Figure 14.11). An automated

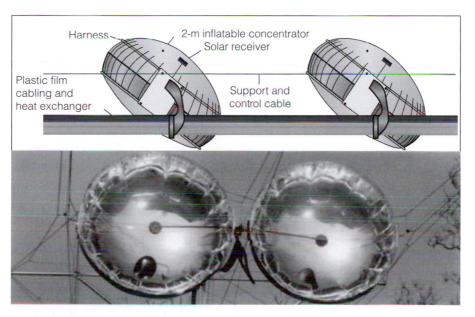

Source: Courtesy of Cool Earth Solar Inc

Figure 14.11 Inflatable solar PV concentrator

flow of water ensures that the balloon's pressure is kept constant. At the same time a closed loop circulation of water at one gallon per minute ensures that the device is kept cool.

The first demonstration project is a 1.5MW array covering ~12 acres near Tracy, California. Its installed cost is $1.0 per watt and it is due to be grid-connected in mid-2009. It is designed as a utility-scale technology.

The future of PV

Finally, where is PV heading? The US National Renewable Energy Laboratory (NREL) has achieved a conversion efficiency of 40.8 per cent. This is close to the record and was achieved with a wafer thin, solar tracking, triple junction, solar concentrated cell. The solar concentration was 326 suns. Its chemical composition splits the solar spectrum into three equal parts to be absorbed by the three junctions.

Prime opportunities for the UK

For the UK, the seas, in terms of currents and tidal elevation, will be its salvation. Since the 1920s the Severn has been a candidate for a tidal barrage. It has been consistently opposed by groups such as the Royal Society for the

Protection of Birds (RSPB). The latest proposal is for a prefabricated system on the lines of the Mulberry Harbour in the Second World War (Figure 14.12). Being a modular system, it could conceivably generate power from tidal currents as each module is installed until the barrage is complete and it achieves its design capacity.

There is another overwhelmingly urgent case for an estuary barrage that was highlighted in a forecast by the Met Office concerning the storm surge risk in northwast Europe. In Chapter 2 the Thames was identified as having the highest risk of all and a solution was offered in the shape of an estuary barrage. A conventional barrage in the Severn Estuary, as shown in Figure 14.12, would generate 14.8GWp producing 25TWH per year (DECC, 2008b).

Non-barrage options

A high energy density system has been conceived by Blue Energy Canada consisting of 3m diameter vertical rotors that can generate power on both ebb and flow tides. It could be an option for the Severn and could pacify the RSPB. It would be prefabricated and considerably cheaper to install than a hard barrage (Figure 14.13).

Figure 14.12 Prefabricated barrage proposal for the Severn Estuary

One advantage of the energy bridge concept is that it would be constructed on a modular basis. As the Worldwatch Institute points out, a 1000MW generating plant takes 10 years to build, only operating from year 11. A modular design such as the tidal fence would comprise 10MW modules, each taking about 12 months to install. This would be generating electricity after year one producing 8.8MWh in that year, with each subsequent module generating as soon as it comes online. By the end of year 11 it will have produced five times as much as the large unit in that year. As there will a return on capital after the first year, growing incrementally to year 10, this makes it a much more attractive investment option than the conventional barrage.

An alternative version of the tidal fence under consideration for the Severn from Minehead to Aberthaw also features in the Department of Energy and Climate Change (DECC) Feasibility Study. Its peak capacity is 1.3GW and its output, 3.5TWh per year. It consists of horizontal axis rotors within a bridge structure. It is proposed by engineers Pulse Tidal. A variation on the theme of vertical rotors is the helical or 'Gorlov' underwater rotor (Figure 14.14).

Alexander Gorlov was inspired by the Darrieus vertical axis rotor patented in 1931. Gorlov modified the concept by twisting the blades into a helical form. The blades are modelled on the aerofoil profile of the wing of a Boeing 727. Tests conducted by the US Marine Hydrodynamics Laboratory demonstrated that the rotor would start spinning in water moving at as little as 2 knots and could capture about 36 per cent of the kinetic energy of the current.

In 2002 the Korean government began tests of the rotor in the rapid tidal current of the Uldolmok Strait. Their success led to the installation of a demonstration project in which a 15 foot diameter turbine produced 1MW of power. The Korean government is now considering an array of Gorlov turbines in the Strait, sufficient to deliver 3.6GW of electricity.

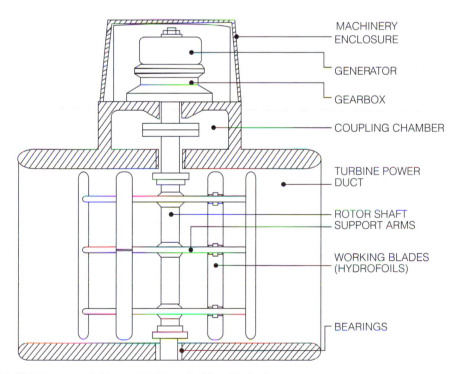

Figure 14.13 Tidal energy bridge or 'tidal fence' with vertical rotors

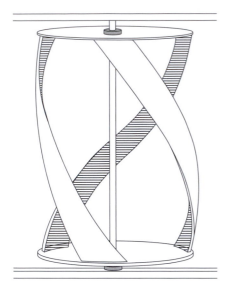

Figure 14.14 The Gorlov helical rotor

Tidal impoundment

Another variation on the barrage theme has been proposed in the 'Ecostar Scoping Model' devised by Stuart H Anderson. This approach is known as coastal impoundment, comprised of D-shaped pounds connected to the coast, which therefore differ from offshore tidal lagoons. Together these sites could offer gigawatts of electricity. The areas most suitable are Liverpool Bay and the north Wales coast. The impoundments largely follow the 10m underwater contour and would be extensions of the coastline. For access to Liverpool, the barrage would have to incorporate an ocean lock. Smaller locks would be needed elsewhere for leisure boating (Figure 14.15).

The coasts of Britain also offer huge opportunities for tidal stream power. The

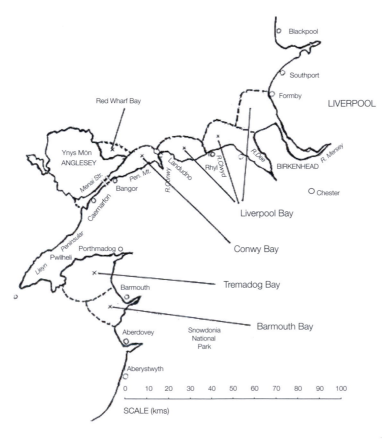

Source: Courtesy of Ecostar

Figure 14.15 Northwest coastal impoundment proposal UK

government estimate is that there are over 40 sites around the UK suitable for tidal stream energy and significantly more if the Channel Islands are included. Marine Current Turbines have an underwater tidal mill under test in Northern Ireland. It echoes a wind turbine in its technology but offers more reliable power at a higher energy density.

An innovative system currently under test has been developed by OpenHydro. It consists of giant fans with blades connected to a rotor that spins inside the structure as water flows through. Electricity is generated as the rotor turns past a magnet generator on the outer rim of the structure (Figures 14.16 and 14.17).

An OpenHydro scheme is being evaluated by the Channel Island of Alderney, which has a tidal race between the island and France of up to 12 knots. The generating potential is estimated to be up to 3 gigawatts.

Vortex induced vibrations for aquatic clean energy (VIVACE)

'Vortex Induced Vibrations for Aquatic Clean Energy' or VIVACE is a technology designed to harness energy from slow moving ocean and river currents (Figure 14.18). It has been proposed by a team led by Professor Bernitsas of the University of Michigan and works by producing vortex-induced vibrations, which are undulations that a circular or cylinder shaped object creates in a flow of fluid. The cylinder creates alternating vortices to form above and below the cylinder, pushing it up and down on springs creating mechanical energy. This energy then powers an electrical generator. Such vortices have a destructive track record in the form of wind, for example, destroying cooling towers at the Ferrybridge Power Station in the UK in 1965 (Figure 14.19). VIVACE is designed to operate in currents moving slower than 2 knots or ~2.5mph. This means that it has huge potential as a method of harnessing energy from the massive currents that circumnavigate the Earth as well as currents in rivers and estuaries or around land masses.

Figure 14.16 OpenHydro on test

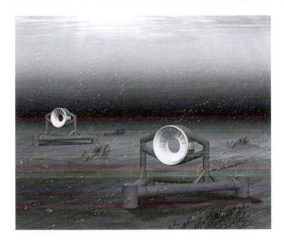

Source: OpenHydro Ltd

Figure 14.17 OpenHydro in operation on the seabed

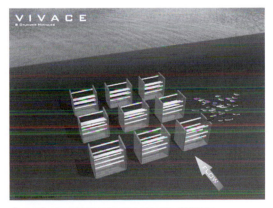

Source: Courtesy of Michael Bernitsas, University of Michigan

Figure 14.18 A VIVACE layout

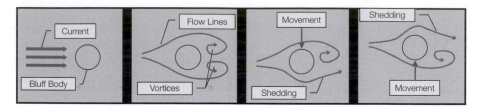

Source: Wikipedia

Figure 14.19 Vivace: induced opposing vibrations producing oscillation

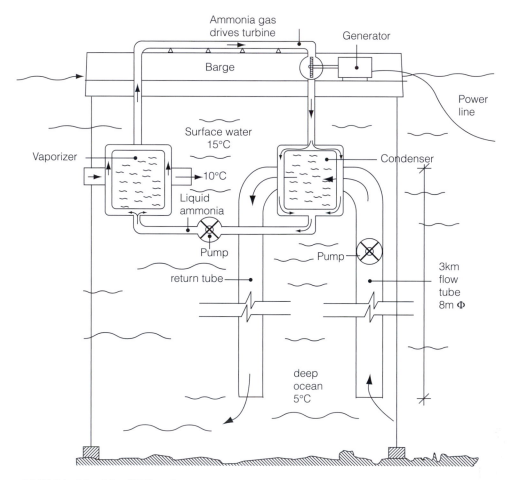

Figure 14.20 Principle of the OTEC system

Ocean Thermal Energy Conversion (OTEC)

Ocean thermal energy conversion technology, as its name suggests, exploits the difference in temperature between water near the surface of the ocean and water deeper down (Figure 14.20). The surface water heats a fluid with a low boiling point. Ammonia is an obvious choice. At boiling point it turns into a gas with enough pressure to drive a turbine. The gas is then cooled to a liquid by passing it through cold water pumped from the deep ocean. To give an idea of the scale of the operation, for an output of 100MW the cooling tubes are about 3000m long and about 8m in diameter. As the price of fossil fuels rises, companies from Japan to Hawaii are in a race to build OTEC machines. The US is investigating the feasibility of 500MW OTEC plants on offshore platforms sending power to an onshore grid. The first, much smaller, plant is due to be operational by 2011, sited off the island of Diego Garcia in the Indian Ocean to serve a US military base. There are also plans to build a 100MW OTEC plant off the coast of Indonesia. Its electricity will be used to produce hydrogen to power vehicles.

Conclusion

This chapter has focused mainly on technologies that could achieve multi-gigawatt capacity and be extremely attractive to utility companies. However, talk of meeting the world's demand for energy at its current level from renewables is unrealistic. Renewables can rescue the world from energy starvation. But quality of life will only be sustained with massive cuts in the demand for energy.

The UK has special problems. While much of its present generating capacity will have been decommissioned in the next 15–20 years, by 2020 15 per cent of its energy will have to be carbon free according to EU rules. This translates to saying that roughly 35 per cent of its electricity will have to come from renewables. As mentioned the Energy Saving Trust has estimated that 40 per cent of electricity could come from, mostly domestic, small scale generation. This is an improbable target unless homeowners and small to medium-sized enterprises (SMEs) are given some incentive, such as a significant feed-in tariff, comparable to that offered in Germany. The stark reality is that the UK will have to be ahead of the pack in reducing the demand for energy if it is to enjoy a sustainable, although possibly stand-still, economy beyond 2030.

Inevitably, the UK faces a revolution in the supply of energy, first in terms of its availability but, secondly, in the reform of the supply system. There must be a rapid transition to a binary system, that is, local, community networks connecting micro- and mini-renewables like household PVs. For balancing power they could be connected to a slimmed-down national grid supplied by gigawatt scale renewables like tidal power and offshore wind, meeting perhaps 35 per cent of current capacity.

The conclusion by Mackay (2008, pp113–114) is that 'To sustain Britain's lifestyle on its renewables alone would be very difficult. A renewable-based energy solution will necessarily be large and intrusive.' His conclusion, like Lovelock, is that Britain needs nuclear power.

15

The Age Beyond Oil

The predicted demise of reserves of oil and gas has fuelled speculation that hydrogen will be the answer to an impending energy black hole. If it works for the sun, why not for us? Harnessing this most abundant gas is the challenge of the century, for its applications from fusion to fuel cells.

To be precise, hydrogen is not a fuel but an energy carrier. It is bound up with other chemicals and so, first, has to be released. It can be burnt directly as a fuel or used to generate electricity via a fuel cell.

Production of hydrogen

Hydrogen can be produced by four methods:

- electrolysis, which splits water into its constituents of hydrogen and oxygen, ideally using renewable electricity;
- a thermochemical reaction that releases hydrogen from water or biomass;
- a thermo-dissociation of hydrogen-rich compounds, again ideally using renewable electricity, for example, reforming of natural gas (methane);
- microbial activity that releases hydrogen from organic compounds like biomass waste.

Currently the most popular method of obtaining hydrogen is by reforming natural gas by heating it with steam in the presence of a catalyst. At this stage in the spread and efficiency of renewables, this is a far from zero carbon process, especially as it produces CO_2 as a by-product. It is often claimed that PVs can ensure that fuel cells are carbon-neutral. In the domestic sector this is highly unlikely. For example an average house in the UK with roof-mounted PVs would generate about 3000kWh/year of electricity via a fuel cell. This is about one-eighth the requirement of an average house.

The second best production method is splitting water into its constituents of oxygen and hydrogen by electrolysis. Electrolysers are effectively reverse fuel cells, and, as with fuel cells, require platinum electrodes. Passing electricity through water produces hydrogen at one electrode and oxygen at the other. This is where the main installation cost penalty is incurred. There are only five platinum mines in the world. The platinum in a fuel cell currently costs around $3000 for 100 grams. In the auto-industry there is confidence that a car fuel cell will only need 20 grams by 2015. If true, that cost advantage will also benefit the domestic energy market.

The fuel cell

There are numerous industrial uses for hydrogen but its true destiny lies in generating electricity from fuel cells. A fuel cell is an electro-chemical device that generates direct current (DC). It consists of two electrodes, an anode and a cathode, separated by an electrolyte, which might be a solid membrane. Unlike a battery, it requires a continual supply of a hydrogen-rich fuel that enters at one electrode and oxygen at the other. Essentially it is a reactor that combines hydrogen and oxygen, via catalysts, to produce electricity, water and heat as by-products (Figure 15.1).

This is described as a redox reaction, propelling electrons around an external circuit, and it is an electrochemical equivalent of combustion. It is a robust technology with no moving parts and an efficiency of up to 60 per cent.[1]

The commodity price of platinum is the main obstacle to the widespread adoption of fuel cells. There needs to be an alternative method of catalysis for electrolysers and fuel cells avoiding platinum and ITM Power claims to have found it. Most fuel cells at present are the PEM type. This means that the fuel cell is acidic and therefore needs the platinum catalyst. The ITM Power solution is to install an alkaline membrane, with nickel replacing platinum. The company has developed a solid but flexible polymer gel that is three times as conductive as a platinum based PEM. In mass production the cost of the membrane would be $5/m^2$ as compared to $500 for existing PEMs. The result

is that an electrolyser would cost $164 per kilowatt of capacity as against the current average of $2000/kW.

The ITM manufacturing facility in Sheffield is at present concentrating on home electrolysers. It is the size of a large refrigerator, would be connected to mains water and driven, in part, by renewable energy. The hydrogen produced could be used as a direct fuel, as it was for cooking in the Fraunhofer Institute's experimental zero carbon house (page 31). As hydrogen is odourless, appliances have to be fitted with sensors to immediately identify leaks. Car firm BMW uses compressed hydrogen to fuel its demonstration piston engine hydrogen car. Even more ambitious are the hydrogen powered shuttle buses in Vancouver. They used hydrogen, which is the waste stream from the production of chlorine. The buses retain their conventional piston engines but ran on compressed hydrogen gas.

In a home hydrogen could be used to produce electricity, either by driving a turbine/generator or

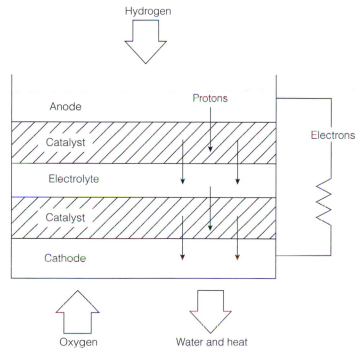

Figure 15.1 Basic Proton Exchange Membrane (PEM) fuel cell

a fuel cell. The chief executive officer (CEO) of ITM Power is confident that mass production will bring the cost of the home electrolyser down to less that £10,000 per unit. This is just one factor that raises concerns about the cost of converting to hydrogen. David Strahan (2008) cites an example. A large house able to accommodate 60m² of photovoltaics on its roof would generate 10,000kWh/y and cost in the region of £50,000. If used to power a 60 per cent efficient fuel cell, the effective yield would be 6000kWh/y. This is only 25 per cent of the energy (heat and power) used by an average house in the UK. Used to power a small car by means of a fuel cell, this would provide for about 7200km in a year, which is half the average annual mileage of a British car.

ITM Power admit that the figures are not attractive at this stage, but its CEO states: 'that's how every technology starts. There are early adopters and then mass production brings down costs hugely'. However, Strahan points out that, whilst ITM may have solved a major problem of the cost of fuel cells and electrolysers, 'nobody has solved a more fundamental problem: the inefficiency of the whole hydrogen fuel chain' (Strahan, 2008).

As described in Chapter 7, there may be an answer for the domestic market, thanks to Ceres Power, which has developed a solid oxide micro-fuel cell (SOFC) for the home (Figure 15.2).

The Ceres Power SOFC can operate on natural gas, methane or propane and delivers a maximum electrical output of just over 1kW. Its dimensions are 205mm × 305mm × 305mm. Weighing 25kg means it can be wall-mounted. For most households its capacity to reform

natural gas is the key to its future promise and is the reason why the company has been able to secure a major distribution agreement with British Gas. The fuel cell was bench tested during the first quarter of 2009 and thereafter tested in selected homes. It is expected to be market-ready by 2011.

Hydrogen storage

This is another area where there may be a high energy, and therefore, high cost involvement. Hydrogen gas has a high energy density by weight but poor energy density by volume compared with hydrocarbons. Therefore it needs a larger storage vessel for a given amount of energy compared with petrol, diesel or compressed natural gas. Pressurizing the gas improves its energy density, but this carries an energy penalty together with a requirement for increased container strength.

The Space Programme has led to higher volumetric energy density being developed through liquefying the hydrogen. Storage requires the gas to be cooled to −252.882°C (−423.188°F) involving a large energy deficit. Highly insulated tanks must ensure that this temperature is maintained. A quite small temperature rise could cause boil-off of the gas. Even under these conditions, liquid hydrogen has only one-quarter the energy density by volume of hydrocarbon fuels.

Considerable research effort is being directed at alternative methods of storage, notably metal hydrides. Solid hydride storage is a favourite medium for mobile use. However, a hydride storage tank is about three times larger and four times heavier than a petrol or diesel tank containing the equivalent energy. There are still safety as well as efficiency issues to be overcome with this technology. At the same time, the hydrogen must be of high purity. Contaminants can undermine absorption.

The Universities of Birmingham, Loughborough and Nottingham are members of a Midlands consortium devoted to fuel cell research including hydrogen storage. As stated, conventional methods like compressed or

Figure 15.2 Ceres Power 1kW SOFC unit

liquefied hydrogen consume process energy and require high strength storage tanks. In the case of liquefied hydrogen, they must also be heavily insulated. The alternative is to use materials that absorb or adsorb large amounts of hydrogen at lower pressures and better volumetric storage densities. According to scientists at the University of Nottingham Technologies Research Institute 'Compact solid state storage of hydrogen is crucial if we are to meet the long term targets for hydrogen systems' (Walker, 2008). These include high capacity light–metal hydrides and complex hydrides such as magnesium and borohydrides (Figure 15.3). The aim is to improve the binding strength of the hydrogen molecules in porous framework materials such as zeolites. This enables the gas to be stored at, or near, room temperature.

Carbon nanotubes initially offered the promise of a 50 per cent by weight storage capability. This storage route still attracts considerable research attention.

Ammonia is another candidate as a storage medium, with its relatively high hydrogen content (NH_3). The hydrogen is released in a catalytic reformer and can offer high storage density as a liquid with only moderate pressurization and cooling. It can be stored at room temperature and atmospheric pressure when mixed with water. It is the second most commonly produced chemical enjoying a large infrastructure for production and transportation. When reformed to hydrogen there are no waste products.

In September 2005 scientists at the Technical University of Denmark devised a method of storing hydrogen in the form of ammonia saturated in salt. They claim it will be a safe and inexpensive method of storage. Time will tell.

Towards zero carbon transport

Hydrogen is considered by many to be the holy grail for transport. To appreciate the scale of the challenge, in 2007, 71 million cars were produced worldwide. Not only is this sector a major carbon contributor, it is closely related to buildings and

Figure 15.3 Metal hydride storage containers in the Protium Project

where they are located. It accounts for roughly 25 per cent of primary energy consumption in OECD countries and that equates to approximately the same CO_2 emissions. It is also highly sensitive to oil shocks and the prospect of depleted reserves of oil. As with the built environment, it is high time that the related sectors responded to the urgent need to reduce their reliance on oil, with the simultaneous effect of slashing their carbon emissions.

Considerable progress is being made in improving the efficiency of petrol and diesel engines, especially with the emergence of various kinds of hybrid technology. The consumption target of 100 miles per gallon (mpg) is already being achieved and will become commonplace within the next decade. The most promising technology is that employed in the GM Volt. This is a battery powered vehicle with a small petrol/diesel engine employed to charge batteries on demand. It is estimated that the car will travel 40 miles before needing to be charged. This is likely to be the first medium sized family car to breach the 100mpg barrier.

There are still those who put their faith in biofuels as the cure for the addiction to oil. Taking the year 2003 as the benchmark for a developed country, in that year the transport sector in the UK consumed about 50 billion tonnes of oil. To suggest that biofuels could substitute for this scale of consumption is impractical, principally on the basis of the area of land that would be committed to energy crops at the expense of food production. However, there may be a source of biofuel that does not prejudice food production: microalgae.

The UK Carbon Trust is embarking on a multimillion pound initiative to promote this biofuel, which can be cultivated and manipulated to produce high yields of oil. It can be used as a feedstock for refining into transport oil. Since it does not require arable land, fresh water and does not compete with food crops, it promises to represent 'a disruptive technological breakthrough' (Carbon Trust). The challenge is to make it commercially viable. The Carbon Trust Algae Biofuels Challenge (ABC) will channel funds into R&D with the aim of moving to large scale production of algae oil.

Nevertheless, there are good grounds for believing that the long-term means of propulsion for land transport is via electricity. This implies two energy sources: batteries and hydrogen. Meanwhile, hybrid technology will offer significant carbon reductions in the short to medium term. In this case a relatively modest fossil fuel engine works symbiotically with a powerful battery. The Toyoto Prius was the commercial innovator of this technology. The latest versions use plug-in technology, which allows batteries to be recharged at home overnight, or in the day whilst in the company car park. In 2008, Toyota revealed the prototype of its plug-in Prius. There is a claim that it can achieve 100mpg (2.4L/100km) if the batteries are recharged when the car is not in use. The secret of its success is the additional nickel-hydride battery pack that increases range and speed.

The hydrogen path

To repeat, hydrogen gas can either be used as a direct fuel for a conventional piston engine, or as feedstock for a fuel cell. It is more efficient than an internal combustion engine (ICE), but, for the present, more costly per kilometre. As a direct fuel (as in the prototype BMW) it is around 8 per cent more efficient than a petrol engine, whereas a fuel cell is at least twice as efficient. At present it is the high cost of fuel cells at about $5500/kW that is the main barrier to progress, although this may be about to change as indicated below. The other problem is that fuel cells for vehicles would need hydrogen with a purity as high as 99.999 per cent.

For these reasons, the widespread adoption of fuel cell technology is some way off. One kilogram of hydrogen has the energy equivalent of one gallon of petrol. On the US market this makes hydrogen about four times more expensive than petroleum-based fuel. However, since a fuel cell vehicle should be twice as efficient as an ICE equivalent, the fuels will break-even when hydrogen drops to twice the price of petrol. But if the hydrogen were to be carbon-free during production as well as use, and the avoided external costs were to be factored-in, then hydrogen would already be cost-effective.

However, several factors are coalescing to make the fuel cell vehicle more attractive to the market than its ICE counterpart:

- the inexorable rise in oil price, $75 a barrel at the time of writing;
- rising uncertainty over secure supplies through a combination of resource depletion and an increasingly destabilized Middle East;
- present generation ICE vehicles are nearing the peak of their efficiency, which the industry regards as 30 per cent. With international research being directed towards fuel cell technology, it is very possible that their efficiency will rise from 50 per cent now to at least 60 per cent.

For some years Honda has been investigating the potential of fuel cell technology, and the fruit of this work is the Honda FCX Clarity. This is not an adaptation of an ICE model but a pure-bred innovative vehicle and the first of the genre to be released on the market, albeit on a leasehold basis (Figure 15.4).

The practical availability of the FCX Clarity is presently limited to greater Los Angeles, Orange County, where there are five hydrogen filling stations. It has a range of 270 miles and, in terms of running costs, it is claimed to be the equivalent of 81 imperial mpg. In terms of its performance, it can achieve 100mph and manage 0–60mph in 10 seconds.

Honda began research into fuel cell propulsion for cars in 1986, so the FCX is the fruit of a long period of research and development. Now that Honda has withdrawn from Formula One racing, much more investment should be available for a technology that will shape the future of automotive engineering.

However, enthusiasm for the Honda should not blind us to the problems that will have to be

Source: Courtesy of Honda UK

Figure 15.4 Honda FCX Clarity

addressed, especially if hydrogen is not derived from green technologies. According to energy consultant Hugh Sharman, to supply the UK transport sector with the hydrogen/fuel cell option would need 2150PJ/year, which equals 864.000GWh/year at 2003 transport density. This equates to an installed capacity of 98.6GW. If the electricity were to be obtained exclusively from wind power at a 30 per cent load factor this rises to 329GW and would need 110,000 3MW turbines. Spaced at 500m (the norm) they would occupy 27,000km², which is rather more than the area of Wales (Sharman, 2005). These figures are conservative because the energy consumed by transport in 2007 was 2511PJ.

At the same time, if the 71 million cars worldwide were converted to hydrogen it would require 1420 tonnes of platinum, which is six times the present rate of production. Reserves would be exhausted in 70 years (Strahan, 2008). It remains to be proved whether the ITM Power breakthrough in terms of catalyst costs involved in the transition to hydrogen can be upscaled to cater for the entire transport sector.

Using hydrogen as a direct fuel, it has been calculated that, from electrolysis to compression for storage as a fuel, only 24 per cent of the energy involved does useful work. Battery powered cars and plug-in hybrids use 69 per cent of the original energy. According to Gary Kendall of WWF 'Cars running on hydrogen would need three times the energy of those running directly on electricity... The developed world needs to completely decarbonise electricity generation by 2050, so we can't afford to throw way three-quarters of primary energy turning it into hydrogen' (Kendall, 2008).

The battery option

The consultancy E4Tech states in a report to the UK Department for Transport (DfT) that if the UK were to switch to battery power for transport, the charging load would add 16 per cent to electricity demand. The hydrogen/fuel cell alternative would increase demand by more than 32 per cent. Using hydrogen as a direct fuel for piston engines, of the energy needed for

electrolysis and compression, only 24 per cent would end up at the wheels.

The Pacific Northwest National Laboratory for the US Department of Energy has indicated that much of the electricity generated at night remains unused. This coincides with the time battery vehicles will need to be recharged. A 2006 study by the Laboratory found that the surplus off-peak capacity of the US grid would be sufficient to recharge 84 per cent of all vehicles in the US, assuming all vehicles were battery powered.

Despite these difficulties, all major manufacturers are developing variations on the theme of electric propulsion with a view to launching models within the next five years. If the Honda Clarity is the signpost to the future for fuel cell cars, the GM Chevrolet Volt E-REV (extended range electric vehicle) is carrying the banner for battery power. It is sometimes referred to as a hybrid vehicle; this is inaccurate. In scale it is a medium-size family saloon about the size of a Vauxhall Astra. Propulsion is solely from a powerful electric motor. An on-board petrol engine recharges the battery when output is depleted (Figure 15.5). Along the central axis is a T-shaped 16kWh lithium-ion battery; at the front right is a 1.4 litre petrol engine for charging the battery; at the front left is the 360 volt electric motor producing 150bhp. When the car is moving on overrun, the electric motor becomes a generator for the battery.

GM now has its sights on the European market with its Opel/Vauxhall Ampera (Figure 15.6). It was launched at the Geneva

Source: Courtesy of GM

Figure 15.5 GM Volt concept model

Motor Show in March 2009. It employs the GM Voltec system first revealed in the GM Volt. According to the GM Europe chief marketing officer: 'With the Ampera, Opel will be the first European automobile manufacturer to provide customers several hundred kilometres of non-stop electric driving.' It is claimed to have a 60km range on just its lithium-ion battery, charged from a 230 volt socket. For longer distances it will continue under battery power, but, like the Volt, this will be continually charged by a small petrol engine. The Ampera received the 2009 *What Car?* Green Technology Award.

GM rival Chrysler is also developing a range of electric vehicles, with three plug-in electric cars due in 2010. It aims to use some form of electric propulsion for all its vehicles. Instead of designing all-new cars, this company plans to adapt its existing models using a technology similar to the GM Volt. It has one all-electric sports car that only has a lithium ion battery offering a range of 150 miles. Ford is pinning its

hopes on its plug-in Escape Hybrid that features lithium-ion batteries. The company claims it will have a fuel economy of 120mpg (2L/100km). In the US, the market for all-electric cars is boosted by the availability of a tax credit up to $7,500.

German car companies Mercedes and VW-Audi will soon be offering variations on the plug-in hybrid theme by around 2011. BMW has also entered the electric car arena with the Mini E. It has a 150kW electric motor powered by a lithium-ion battery capable of a top speed of 95mph and a range of 150 miles. The battery occupies the space formerly taken up by the rear seats. The firm will produce an initial 500 vehicles that will go on urban trials in the US and Europe.

Generally, it still appears that most family all-electric cars will be limited to a range of 40–50 miles that, for most, only makes them viable as a second vehicle, unless there is a breakthrough in battery technology. Perhaps the ZENN car (see p162) is the shape of things to come.

Source: Courtesy of GM Europe

Figure 15.6 Opel/Vauxhall Ampera

Advances in battery technology

There are two main contenders for the future battery market:

- the UltraBattery;
- Supercapacitator Battery.

The UltraBattery

The UltraBattery exploits the virtues of both lead acid battery technology and the Supercapacitator, which offers rapid charging and long life. The advantages of this system are said to be:

- life cycle four times longer than conventional batteries;
- 50 per cent more power than equivalent lead acid batteries;
- about 70 per cent cheaper than current hybrid vehicle systems;
- faster charge and discharge rates than conventional batteries.

Its manufacturers claim it will not only revolutionize battery-powered transport but will also play an important role in providing electricity storage and balancing power for intermittent renewable energy technologies. According to its specification (see 'UltraBattery: no ordinary battery' at www.csiro.au/science/ UltraBattery.html) it 'can be integrated into wind power systems to smooth intermittency and potentially "time-shift" energy production better to match demand'. This is a polite way of saying that, with grid connection, it can maximize price opportunities.

The Supercapacitator Battery

Developed by EEStors, this technology could represent a breakthrough in electrical storage technology. Unlike conventional batteries, no chemical reactions are involved in the process. A capacitor stores energy by means of two plates in parallel. A negative charge applied to one of the plates will repel electrons from its opposite. This charge difference will be maintained as long as the two plates remain electrically isolated and can be employed to provide an electric current. A characteristic of capacitors is that they can rapidly store a charge, in contrast to the long charging time needed by chemical batteries. The fact that there is no chemical reaction means that the battery has an indefinite lifespan. It is a solid state device so it has the ability to store a considerable amount of power in a very compact footprint.

The key to the breakthrough with supercapacitors lies in the composition of the insulation separating the two plates. According to its patent application, it relies on barium titanate ($BaTiO_3$) to provide the insulation capable of supporting a high charge of up to 52kWh, which is over ten times the power density of a standard lead-acid battery.

A manufacturer of lightweight electric cars, ZENN Motor Company, which produces the cityZENN car, is adopting this battery as the sole source of power. It is estimated to have a 250 mile range between charges and a top speed up to 80mph. It is not sensitive to cold or heat and so is suitable for all climates. According to ZENN, 'this vehicle specifically will meet the driving needs of probably 90 per cent of people in North America, and even more outside North America in terms of driving habits'.

Finally, to cap its virtues, it uses a raw material, barite, which has massive reserves – over 2 billion tonnes. Lithium, on the other hand, has more limited reserves and a global switch to lithium batteries for propulsion could exploit them to exhaustion.

In the short to medium term, supercapacitator batteries could outrun fuel cells in the propulsion race. In the longer term, hydrogen is effectively limitless and so there is little doubt that it will be the ultimate source of energy for the world.

For vehicles 'hydrogen, with its higher energy density and thus superior range, will eventually win ... it really could happen in the middle of the next decade' (Thiesen, 2008, p41). (Peter Thiesen is director of hydrogen strategy for GM.)

Water-based transport

The UK House of Commons, Environmental Audit Committee produced a report in 2006 called *Reducing Carbon Emissions from Transport*. It concluded:

> There are clear advantages in terms of carbon emissions of shifting freight from road to water, and the Department for Transport needs to do more to actively encourage this shift ... We urge the Government to lead the international community in drawing attention to carbon emissions from international shipping, and to make sure they are brought under an effective reduction regime in the post-Kyoto phase.
>
> (House of Commons, 2006, p14)

Rivers and canals

In 2008 a report *The Future of Transport – a network for 2030* was published by the Department for Transport. It states:

> A key aspect to the harmonisation of freight transport will undoubtedly be the re-emergence of inland water systems... [Giving rise to the need] to fully explore the estimated 5.100km of navigable waterways in England and Wales.

With congestion on the roads and the price of fuel, the canals are slowly returning to favour as a much more energy efficient means of transporting goods in bulk than by road. In 2005–2006 freight carried on inland waterways increased by 10 per cent.

Some years ago the concept of a contour canal was broached, following a single contour down the centre of England. As such it would be free of locks and could be designed to permit high speed travel for broad beam barges – about 10 knots. It could begin at Leeds with branches to Sheffield, Derby, Nottingham, Leicester, Northampton and Bedford and linking into the Thames.

Hybrid technology is ideally suited to canal transport. Battery/petrol or diesel hybrid engines could be recharged or refuelled at quaysides or locks. As with car projects like the GM Volt, the petrol engine would only be used to maintain the charge in the batteries. Unlike cars, the weight of lithium-ion batteries would not be a problem for barges. Barges would be well suited to electric propulsion, either by battery or fuel cells. The EEStors battery system would seem to be appropriate. Rapid recharging could occur *en route* as necessary. The charging points could be served by PV cells.

The fuel cell barge has already arrived in the shape of the 'Ross Barlow' (Figure 15.7). As part of the Protium Project, Birmingham University Fuel Cell researchers have converted a canal narrow boat donated by British Waterways to fuel cell propulsion. In place of the diesel engine there is a proton exchange membrane fuel cell with its hydrogen stored in metal hydride cylinders at room temperature and 10 bar pressure. The metal hydride powder weighs 130kgs and the hydrogen is released by decreasing the pressure. This system enables the PEM fuel cell to receive ultra-pure hydrogen – essential for extending the life of the fuel cell.

Congestion is beginning to encourage passenger transport to expand along the tidal Thames. It could be massively increased, offering reductions in journey times, for example, from Teddington via Westminster to the City, Tate Modern or Docklands. If the 200,000 homes materialize in the Thames Gateway, that is another potentially lucrative commuter opportunity.

Shipping

Carbon emissions from shipping do not come within the Kyoto agreement. Nor is there a

Source: Courtesy of the University of Birmingham

Figure 15.7 The 'Ross Barlow' fuel cell powered narrow boat

proposal from the European Commission to introduce legislation to rectify the situation. Yet various studies show that maritime carbon dioxide emissions are not only higher than earlier thought, but could rise by as much as 75 per cent in the next 15–20 years if world trade picks itself up from the recession and growth accelerates on the rebound. At the end of 2007 carbon emissions from shipping were double those of aviation. There is every reason to believe that, from 2010, the rate of increase will be restored.

Whilst the focus has been on aviation, shipping has quietly been transporting 90 per cent of world trade; double the percentage of the 1980s. According to the Tyndall Centre for Climate Change Research: 'The proportion of [greenhouse gas] emissions from international shipping continues to receive scant regard within government. Shipping has been missed off the climate change agenda.' The Tyndall Centre is currently undertaking research into shipping emissions (report in the *Guardian*, 3 March 2007).

The air industry

It is likely that the major victim of the demise of fossil fuels will be the aircraft industry. It has been said that for an aircraft to be able to cross the Atlantic fuelled by hydrogen would mean that the entire fuselage would have to be a hydrogen store. Biofuels are probably the only hope for a much slimmed-down industry. Maybe helium-filled airships will return to favour.

Hydrogen will be the ultimate engine of the world economy. Advances in battery technology may delay its advance, but its final triumph is inevitable. The challenge will be to make it an accessible source of power to the least developed nations as well as the economies of the West.

What can be done?

If transport were to face the real costs of the energy it uses, this would concentrate minds to look for alternatives. Ultimately solid oxide fuel cells may be the answer since the requirement is for mainly steady power output, with the bonus of usable heat. Alternatively, shipping could be the main beneficiary of the bulk production of biodiesel from microalgae, since land transport will have access to electricity in a variety modes.

An emerging technology that might avoid the cost-effectiveness trap is under development by 'Skysail', a company established in Germany in 2001. It seems counter-intuitive for the massive freighters that populate oceans. However, Skysail has developed a computerized system that controls the launch and recovery of a massive wing-like sail the size of a soccer pitch. Launch and recovery takes 10 to 20 minutes. The computer controls its flight path and altitude, which are calculated to maximize wind strength. It operates not only downwind but also up to 50 degrees variation to the direction of the wind. In addition, the shape of the sail was engineered to ensure the ship remains on an even keel. Based on the 2007 oil price, Skysail claims that the payback time is 3–5 years. Perhaps the world is on the verge of a new age of sail!

For all renewable technologies the yardstick of cost-effectiveness will continue to undermine their uptake until costs factor-in the global value of avoided carbon emissions and the rising price of oil and gas as reserves decline. The problem is that having left the uptake of new technologies to market forces will mean that we have left things too late.

Note

1   A general description of fuel cells is given in Smith (2007, ch. 7).

16

The Thread of Hope

If it seems that the climate countermeasures recommended in this book are based on a highly pessimistic view of the likely progress of global warming, then the Copenhagen conference of climate scientists held in March 2009 should act as a corrective. The 4°C average global temperature rise, which was the precautionary outcome underlying the book, was, at the start of writing, a possible but unlikely scenario. Now it has graduated from the possible to the probable. Speaking at the Copenhagen conference, Nicholas Stern admitted that his 2006 report was too conservative and that policymakers should be thinking about the likely impact of severe temperature rises of 6°C or more. Stern stated: 'Do the politicians understand … just how devastating 4, 5, 6 degrees centigrade would be? I think not yet' (Adam, 2009).

Both Stern, and Professor Bob Watson chief scientist at Defra, warned that governments, at the very least, need to prepare for a 4°C rise by 2100. The conference heard that a 4°C rise would lead to the loss of 85 per cent of the Amazon rainforest and place up to 300 million people at risk of coastal flooding each year. This echoes the concern expressed in February 2009 by Dr Chris Field co-chair of the IPCC that, if tropical forests 'dry out just a little, the result can be very large and destructive wildfires. It is increasingly clear that, as you produce a warmer world, lots of forest areas that had been acting as carbon sinks could be converted to carbon sources'. The result could lead to runaway warming (reported in the *Guardian*, 16 February 2009). Chris Field will oversee the next IPCC report in 2014. How flammable forests can be

was demonstrated in 2008–2009 in the bush fires in southwest Australia.

So, is the writing already on the wall or can human ingenuity devise adequate geo-engineering solutions? In Chapter 1, James Hansen of NASA was quoted as expressing the view that the challenge is not merely to stabilize the concentration of CO_2 in the atmosphere but significantly reduce the concentration. How can this be done?

A paper by Professor Tim Lenton and Nem Vaughan of the University of East Anglia (UEA) making a comparative assessment of the climate cooling potential of various geo-engineering schemes was published on 28 January 2009. Among the schemes considered were nutrient fertilization of the oceans by seeding with iron filings; sunshades in space, stratospheric aerosol injections and ocean pipes. According to Lenton, 'The realisation that existing efforts to mitigate the effects of human induced climate change are proving wholly ineffectual has fuelled a resurgence in geo-engineering… This paper provides the first extensive evaluation of their relative merits in terms of their climate cooling potential and should help inform the prioritisation of future research' (Lenton and Vaughan, 2009). The key findings are:

- It would be possible for carbon sinks to reduce CO_2 to pre-industrial levels by 2100, but only if combined with strong mitigation of CO_2 emissions.
- Stratospheric aerosols and sunshades in space have the potential to cool the climate by 2050, but also carry the greatest risks, not

least of how to arrest the process at the right level of greenhouse gas concentration and avoid runaway cooling.

- Injections into the atmosphere of sulphate or other manufactured particles have the most potential to return the climate to its pre-industrial temperatures by 2050, but it would have to be continually replenished, otherwise warming would rapidly return.
- Adding phosphorous to the ocean may have the greater long-term cooling potential than adding iron or nitrogen.
- There has recently been a suggestion that roofs and facades of buildings should be painted white to increase the albedo effect and compensate for shrinking snow and ice. The authors consider that this might have some impact on the heat island effect but the global effect would be minimal.
- Stimulating biologically driven increases in cloud reflectivity is considered to be ineffective, as are ocean pipes.

The most promising remedies are:

- reforestation on a massive scale;
- the production of charcoal by burning bio-waste at a very low oxygen level to produce bio-char. This is ploughed into the fields where the majority is converted to carbon. Only a small mount of CO_2 is released in the process. A new CHP plant at UEA is exploring this technology.

In conclusion Lenton states: 'We found that some geo-engineering options could usefully complement mitigation, and together they could cool the climate, but geo-engineering alone cannot solve the climate problem (Lenton and Vaughan, 2009).

James Lovelock dismisses the idea that sequestering carbon can stabilize CO_2 emissions at an acceptable level calling it 'a waste of time' although he does endorse the UEA report in one respect: 'There is one way we could save ourselves and that is through the massive burial of charcoal. It would mean farmers turning all their agricultural waste – which carbon that the plants have spent the summer sequestering – into non-biodegradable charcoal [or char] and

burying it in the soil. Then you can start shifting really hefty quantities of carbon out of the system and pull the CO_2 down quite fast.'

From geo-engineering to geopolitics

Writing at a time of world recession unprecedented in its suddenness and scale, the book has to conclude with a consideration of the possible impact on climate change policies. The hope is that investment in green technologies on the demand and supply sides will be the engine of recovery. The immediate threat to economic survival is in danger of displacing the longer term threat that James Lovelock has spelled out. Beyond the Copenhagen conference there is a growing consensus that the global average temperature rise will be around 4°C by 2100. 'Then', said Lovelock in an interview in the *Guardian* newspaper (Lovelock, 2008), 'the biggest challenge will be food'. He predicts that 'about 80%' of the world's population will be wiped out by 2100.

The sub-prime crisis originating in the US has taught us how rapidly stable situations can collapse into chaos. What started in the rarified world of money has now spread to every component of life, embracing the developing as well as the developed countries. The forecast is that it could be the 2030s before there is a return to stability. It will be a very different kind of stability. At first it was thought that the sudden economic instability was an episode of passing turbulence; now it is perceived as a phenomenon of historic magnitude. It seems we have been living on borrowed time as well as money.

The economic slide has demonstrated that globalization has its downside. There is no room for redundancy, that is, reserve capacity. Once global society develops beyond a certain level of complexity it becomes increasingly fragile. 'Eventually it reaches a point at which a minor disturbance can bring everything crashing down' (Bar–Yam, 2008). So, a local hiccup in Wall Street and, in no time, the world is in free fall.

Ecologists are familiar with the problem. It is the nature of cycles in ecosystems to become ever more complex and rigid. Equilibrium is preserved within a normal range of conditions, but is overturned when there is a cataclysmic event like a forest fire, drought or insect infestation. The old ecosystem collapses, to be replaced by a newer, less complex ecosystem.

Part of the reason for the apparent impotence of governments in the face of an international crisis is that globalization has led to the erosion of their power in the face of multinational corporations. These are where the real wealth and, therefore, power resides: transnational corporations like energy companies, Tesco, Microsoft or Tata in India and, until recently, the secretive world of hedge funds. Companies with shareholders demand quick returns on capital, driven by quarterly accounting and performance reviews. Governments are also infected by short-termism with the result that investment in renewable energy and radical demand side measures has been minimal compared with the magnitude of the threat facing society.

In the UK this has had an effect on its transition to renewable energy. Its feeble performance so far is due to the fact that it has focused on wind energy, which, of all the technologies, offers reasonably quick returns on capital due to subsidies and despite an overall load factor of a mere 28 per cent. Higher capital cost but much higher energy density technologies like tidal power remain subjects for discussion rather than action. The reason is that a technology with a long lead time but long life expectancy does not produce the required rapid returns. The sure way to appear justified in avoiding such technology is to make it cost-*in*effective by imposing a high discount rate (Figure 16.1).

Michael Grubb drew attention to this anomaly in 1990, pointing out that the Severn Barrage, 'Assessed at a 2 per cent discount rate would be a bargain; at a market rate, it is hopelessly uneconomic.' He goes on to say that 'the environment is clearly a limited and deteriorating resource ... in environmental terms, our descendants will be considerably poorer than we are today. That being so, we should consider a *negative discount rate* [my italics] at least for valuing endangered environmental assets' (Grubb, 1990).

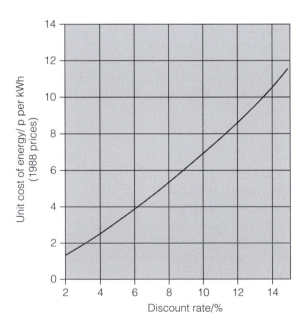

Source: Department of Energy and Boyle (2004)

Figure 16.1 Cost versus discount rate, the Severn Barrage

Since this was written the perceived consequences of climate change have grown by orders of magnitude. Yet, while governments are stubbornly committed to the principle that the markets rule, such technologies with initial high cost but long life, look like having little chance of succeeding.

The global credit crisis reached its climax in 2008–2009. The result has been that climate change issues have slipped down the agenda of priorities. In the long term this may not be wholly unfortunate. It has administered a profound shock, not only to the world of economics, but also to industries affected by reverberations from the crisis. It has fractured long-standing certainties. It may even have undermined the belief that the Earth is infinitely bountiful. Perhaps it is dawning on political leaders that survival will depend on the acceptance that there will have to be retrenchment; that sustainable development *is* compatible with maintaining a steady state regarding the world's natural resources.

One positive result of the 'crunch' is that the slowdown in manufacturing may cause a temporary reduction in CO_2 emissions. However, remembering the time lag between emissions and their climatic consequences, the world may not record the dip in emissions until around 2040. By then the CO_2 concentration will almost certainly be well past the tipping point of 450ppm and the 2°C average temperature rise leading to devastating impacts from climate change.

Gus Speth, former head of the UN Environment Agency, is forthright in his verdict: 'My conclusion is that we're trying to do environmental policy and activism within a system which is simply too powerful. It is today's capitalism with its overwhelming commitment to growth at all costs, devolution of tremendous power into the corporate sector and its blind faith in a market riddled with externalities.' He concludes that the fault lies in 'our pathetic capitulation to consumerism' (Speth, 2008).

The 'credit crunch' has additionally obscured the fact that there is also an evolving crisis in energy, temporarily shielded by a drop in price. As demand for fossil fuels increasingly overtakes the level of reserves, renewables will not be an option but a dire necessity. This global jolt to the system should persuade both the politicians and manufacturers that economic revival should be spearheaded by a global shift into renewable energy. This could reveal a picture of a world that can live within its regenerative capacity, including energy.

The cardinal lesson from the *Stern Report* of 2006 was that the cost of stabilizing the climate will be considerable, but still only a fraction of the cost of inaction. This applies whether it is building a new barrage in the Thames Estuary to protect against rising sea levels and storm surges, or designing buildings to withstand the worst of future climate impacts. To build precautionary measures into structures now will be much more cost-effective than waiting until after the event.

There may be cries of outrage from the construction industry and estate agents, who are both wedded to short-termism. Interestingly, house builders have not been up in arms against the Code for Sustainable Homes. This is doubtless because the levels of insulation and heat recovery erquired under the Code can be achieved relatively cheaply with timber frame and panel construction, the elements of which can be manufactured offsite. House building has become a 'kit-of-parts' operation. Include regulations that demand high levels of thermal mass to make life bearable in torrid summers, and there will be resounding protests if this involves heavyweight construction methods.

This is not mere speculation since house builders have made this kind of protest in the past. Most of the building regulations that set the thermal standards for housing are in Part L. In the 1980s and 1990s, each time Part L was reviewed and upgraded in draft, the Royal Institute of British Architects (RIBA) made strong recommendations for improvements in thermal standards that were often sympathetically received by civil servants. In the event it was most likely the politicians who, bowing to pressure from the industry, caused the recommendations to be watered down.

Climate science elder statesman James Lovelock believes it is already too late to prevent a catastrophic outcome. 'Global warming has passed the tipping point and catastrophe is unstoppable.' He concludes: 'Enjoy life while you can. Because, if you're lucky it's going to be 20 years before it hits the fan' (Lovelock, 2008). As far as the built environment is concerned, therefore, it could be that the die is already cast. If so, nothing we do from now on will prevent massive perturbations of climate. On the balance of probabilities, we should design our buildings and infrastructure accordingly.

We will never know if Lovelock was right, but our grandchildren surely will.

References

Adam, D. (2009) 'Stern attacks politicians over climate devastation', *Guardian* (Friday 13 March 2009)

Katherine Ainger (2008) 'The tactics of these rogue elements must not succeed', *Guardian*, 28 August, p34

Anderson, K. and Bows, A. (2008) 'Reframing the climate change challenge in light of post-2000 emission trends', *Philosophical Transactions A*, Royal Society, 366, pp3863–3882

Association of British Insurers (ABI) (2003) Report, ABI, London

Atelier Ten 'Put to the test: heavyweight vs lightweight construction', *Ecotech* 17, a supplement to *Architecture Today*, p14

Bar-Yam (2008) 'Are we doomed?', *New Scientist*, 5 April, pp33–36

Block, Ben (2008) 'Office-related carbon emissions surge', Worldwatch Institute, 31 October

Boulder Convention and Visitors Bureau 'Leading the way in Green – from science to sustainability', Boulder, CO, online at www.boulder coloradousa. com/docs/Leading%20the%20Way%20in%20Gre en%20Guide.pdf

Boardman, B. (2005) *40% House*, Environmental Change Institute, Oxford, pp100–101

Boyle, Godfrey (ed.) (2004) *Renewable Energy*, Oxford University Press, Oxford

Brooks, Michael (2009) 'Gone in 90 seconds', *New Scientist*, 21 March

Buchanan, Peter (2006) 'A hybrid of buildings and upturned boat, the wind turbines and cowls have a nautical feel', *Architect's Journal*, 14 December

Callcutt Review (2007) *An Overview of the Housebuilding Industry*, Communities and Local Government Publications, Wetherby, p88

Chapman, J. and Gross. R. (2001) *Technical and economic potential of renewable energy generating technologies: potentials and cost reductions to 2020*, Performance and Innovation Unit report for the Energy Review, The Strategy Office, Crown Copyright

Coleman, Vernon (2007) *Oil Apocalypse*, Publishing House, Barnstaple, UK

Daviss, Bennett (2008) 'Our solar future', *New Scientist*, 8 December, p37

DCLG (2008) 'Definition of Zero Carbon Homes and Non-domestic Buildings', December, DCLG, London, p10

DCLG (2009) Policy Planning Statement: Ecotowns, Introduction, DCLG, London

DCSF (2008) 'The Use of Renewable Energy in School Buildings', report by Department for Children, Schools and Families, London

DECC (2008a) 'Renewable Energy Strategy Consultation', Department of Energy and Climate Change, London, June

DECC (2008b) *Severn Estuary Tidal Power Feasibility Study*, Department of Energy and Climate Change, London, December

Department for Environment, Food and Rural Affairs (Defra) (2008a) *Adapting to Climate Change in England: A Framework for Action*, Defra, London

Department for Environment, Food and Rural Affairs (Defra) (2008b) *A Study of Hard to Treat Homes using the English House Condition Survey*, Defra, London

DTI (2004) *Foresight Future Flooding Report*, Department of Trade and Industry, London

Department for Transport (2008) *The Future of Transport: A Network for 2030*, Department of Transport, London

Energy Saving Trust (2006) *England House Condition Survey*, Energy Saving Trust, London

Fordham, Max (2007) *Feilden Clegg Bradley: The environment handbook*, Right Angle Publishing, Melbourne

Green Alliance (2009) 'Climate change: the risks we can't afford to take Part 2, The danger of delaying public investment', report, Green Alliance, March

Groundsure (2008) 'Groundsure Flood Forecast', *Sustain*, vol 9, issue 2, p14

Grubb, Michael (1990) *Energy Policies and the Greenhouse Effect*, vol 1, Dartmouth, RIIA

Gwilliam, J. et al (2006) 'Assessing Risk from Climate Hazards in Urban Areas', *Municipal Engineer*, vol 159, no 4, pp245–255; www.k4cc. org/bkcc/asccue

Hadley Centre (2005) 'Climate Change and the Greenhouse Effect – a briefing from the Hadley Centre', Met Office, p50

Hansen, James, Makiko Sato, Pushker Kharecha, David Beerling, Valerie Masson-Delmotte, Mark Pagani, Maureen Raymo, Dana L. Royer, James C. Zachos (2007) 'Target atmospheric CO_2: where should Humanity aim?', University of East Anglia researchpages.net.

Hansen, James (2009) 'Coal fired power stations are death factories. Close them', *Observer*, 15 February

Helm, D. (2007) report on 'Britain's hidden CO_2 emissions', Oxford University, December

House of Commons Environmental Audit Committee (2006) *Reducing Carbon Emissions from Transport*, The Stationery Office, London

Hurst, W. (2007) 'Design fault threatened exemplar eco-town', *Building Design*, 15 June

Intergovernmental Panel on Climate Change (IPCC) (2000) *First Assessment Report*, IPCC, Geneva

Intergovernmental Panel on Climate Change (IPCC) (2007) *Fourth Assessment Report*, IPCC, Geneva

International Rivers (2007) 'Failed Mechanism: Hundreds of Hydros Expose Serious Flaws in the CDM', report, Berkeley, CA, December, online at www.internationalrivers.org/node/2326

Jenkins, Simon (2008) 'Eco-towns are the greatest try-on in the history of property speculation', *Guardian*, 4 April

Kendall, Gary (2008) 'Plugged-in, the end of the oil age', WWF, Gland

Latham, Ian and Swenarton, Mark (eds) (2007) *Feilden Clegg Bradley: The environment handbook*, Right Angle Publishing, Melbourne

Lee, K. (2009) reported in 'Sea absorbing less CO_2 scientists discover', *Guardian*, 12 January

Lenton, T., Loutre, M.F., Williamson, M., Warren, R., Goodess, C., Swann, M., Cameron, D., Hankin, R., Marsh, R., Shepherd, J. (2006) 'Climate change on the millennial timescale', Tyndall Centre Technical Report 41

Lenton, Timothy M. (2007) *Tipping Points in the Earth System*, University of East Anglia, Norwich, Earth System Modelling Group

Lenton, Tim and Vaughan, Nem (2009) 'Geoengineering could complement mitigation to cool the climate', *Atmospheric Chemistry and Physics Discussions*, 28 January

Lohmann, Larry (ed.) (2006a) 'Carbon Trading; A Critical Conversation on Climate Change, Privatisation and Power', online at www.carbontradewatch.org/index.php?option=com_content&task=view&id=137&Itemid=169

Lohmann, Larry (2006b) 'Carry on Polluting', *New Scientist*, 2 December

Lovelock, James (2008) 'Enjoy life while you can', *Guardian*, interview with Decca Aitkenhead, 1 March

Lovelock, James (2009) 'We're doomed, but it's not all bad', *New Scientist*, interview with Gaia Vince, 24 January

Lynas, M. (2008) 'Climate chaos is inevitable. We can only avert oblivion', *Guardian*, 12 June, based on his book *Six degrees: our future on a hotter planet*, Fourth Estate, London

Mackay, David J. C. (2008) '*Sustainable Energy – without the hot air*', published as a free web book, June, p40

Malone, D. and Tanner, M. (directors) (2008) 'High Anxieties: the Mathematics of Chaos', BBC 4, 14 October

Manyika, James M., Roberts, Roger P. and Sprague, Kara L. (2008) 'Eight business technology trends to watch', *McKinsey Quarterly*, McKinsey & Company, London

Mitchell, John (2008) *New Scientist*, 8 September, p26

Observer (2008a) 'Is this the greenest city in the world?', *Observer Magazine*, 23 March

Observer (2008b) 'So, just how green will the eco-towns be?', *Observer*, 13 July

Olcayto, R. (2007) 'Eco-homes fail final build test', *Building Design*, 9 November

Parliamentary Business and Enterprise Committee (2008) 'Energy policy: future challenges', reported in the *Guardian*, 12 December

Parry, Martin, Palutikof, Jean, Hanson, Clair and Lowe, Jason (2008) 'Squaring up to reality', *Nature Reports – climate change*, pp68–71 (29 May), online at www.nature.com/climate/2008/0806/full/climate.2008.50.html (last accessed 7 August 2009)

Patt, A. (2009) Copenhagen climate change conference, March

Pearce, F. (2008) 'Carbon trading: dirty, sexy money', *New Scientist*, 19 April, p38

Pielke, R., Wigley, T. and Green, C. (2008) 'Dangerous assumptions', *Nature*, 452, pp531–532

Pieper, E. (director) (2008) 'The Jet Stream and Us', BBC 4, 20 February

Pitt, Michael (2008) *Flooding Review – the Pitt Review*, available at The Stationery Office and http://archive.cabinetoffice.gov.uk/pittreview/_/media/assets/www.cabinetoffice.gov.uk/flooding_review/pitt_review_full%20pdf.pdf (last accessed 6 August 2009)

Pope, Vicky et al (2008) 'Met Office's bleak forecast on climate change', *Guardian*, 1 October

Power, Anne and Houghton, John (2007) 'Sprawl plugs', *Guardian*, 14 March

RIBA in association with the University of Westminster (2007) 'Fabric energy storage for low energy cooling of buildings', *RIBA Journal*, February, pp81–84

Rogers, David, (2007) Statement before the Sub-Committee on Energy and Air Quality, Committee on Energy and Commerce, US House of Representatives, May

Royal Commission on Environmental Pollution (2000) *Energy, the Changing Climate*, 22nd report, The Stationery Office, London

Scheer, Hermann (2002) *The Solar Economy*, Earthscan, London

Scheer, Hermann (2008) 'Bring on the solar revolution' in an interview with F. Pearce, *New Scientist*, 24 May, p44

Schmidt, Gavin (2008) *New Scientist*, 6 September, p12

Sharman, Hugh (2005) 'Why UK wind power should not exceed 10GW', *Civil Engineering*, vol 158, Paper 14193, November, pp161–169

Sharples, S., Smith, P.F. and Goodacre, C. (2001) 'Measures to improve the energy efficiency of the housing stock in England and Wales by 2010', School of Architecture, Sheffield

Shaw, Robert (2007) *Adapting to the Inevitability of the 40 degree C city*, London, Town and Country Planning Association

Shaw, Robert, Colley, Michelle and Connell, Richenda (2007) *Climate Change Adaptation by Design: A Guide for Sustainable Communities*, TCPA, London, p18

Smith, Peter F. (1983) 'Saved in the nick of time', *New Scientist*, 24 November

Smith, Peter F. (1998) 'A Programme for the Thermal Upgrading of the Housing Stock in England and Wales to SAP 65 by 2010', in *Renewable Energy 15,* Pergamon, Kidlington, UK, pp451–456

Smith, Peter F. (2001) 'Existing housing: the scope for a remedy', lecture delivered at Royal Institute of Public Health, 26 October

Smith, Peter F. (2004) 'Eco-refurbishment – a guide to saving and producing energy in the home', Architectural Press, London

Smith, Peter F. (2005) *Architecture in a Climate of Change*, 2nd edn, Architectural Press, London

Smith, Peter F. (2007) *Sustainability at the Cutting Edge*, 2nd edn, Architectural Press, Oxford

Speth, Gus (2008) 'Swimming upstream', *New Scientist*, 18 October, pp48–49

Sterl, A., Severijns, C., Dijkstra, H., Hazeleger, W., Jan van Oldenborgh, G., van den Broeke, M., Burgers, G., van den Hurk, B., Jan van Leeuwen, P. and van Velthoven P. (2008) 'When can we expect extremely high surface temperatures?', *Geophysical Research Letters*, vol 35, pL14703

Stern, N. (2006) *The Economics of Climate Change*, HM Treasury and Cabinet Office, Cambridge University Press, Cambridge, UK

Stern, Nicholas (2009) reported in 'Top economist calls for green revolution', *New Scientist*, 21 January, p26

Strahan, David (2008) 'Whatever happened to the hydrogen economy?', *New Scientist*, 29 November, pp40–43

Sustainable Development Commission (2007) *Sustainable Development in Government,* report by the Sustainable Development Commission, Stationery Office, London

TCPA (2007) 'Climate change adaptation by design', Town and Country Planning Association report, London, p2

Thiesen, Peter (2008) *New Scientist* 29 November, p41

Oliver Tickell (2008) *Kyoto2: how to manage the global greenhouse*, Zed Books, London

UK Climate Impacts Programme (UKCIP) (2005) *Beating the Heat: Keeping UK Buildings Cool in a Warming Climate*, UKCIP Briefing Report 2005, UKCIP, Oxford

UK Climate Impacts Programme (UKCIP) (2008) *Building Knowledge for a Changing Climate*, Swindon, Engineering and Physical Science Research Council (EPSRC)

UK-GBC (2008) 'Low Carbon Existing Homes', *Carbon Reduction in Existing Homes project*, UK Green Buildings Council, October

Vince, Gaia (2009) 'Surviving a warmer world', *New Scientist*, 28 February

von Hippel, Frank N. (2008) 'Rethinking nuclear fuel recycling', *Scientific American*, May

Walker, G.S. (ed.) (2008) *Solid State Hydrogen Storage: Materials and Chemistry,* Woodhead Publishing, Cambridge, UK

David Wasdell (2006) 'Climate feedback dynamics: a complex system model', Meridian Programme

Watson, R. (2008) reported in 'Climate change: prepare for global temperature rise of 4C', *Guardian,* 7 August

Welch, D. (2007) 'Enron environmentalism or bridge to the low carbon economy?', *Ethical Consumer*, June, online at www.ethicalconsumer.org/Free Buyers Guides/miscellaneous/carbonoffsetting. aspx

Wheeler, D. and Ummel, K. (2008) 'Desert Power: The economics of solar thermal electricity for Europe, North Africa and the Middle East', Working Paper, Centre for Global Development, Washington DC

Worldwatch Institute (2009), 'State of the World 2009, The Worldwatch Institute at www. worldwatch.org

WWF (2006) *Stormy Europe: The Power Sector and Extreme Weather*, World Wildlife Fund for Nature, Gland, Switzerland

Index